GW00645284

So Many Opportunities

The prize is a fair one, and the hope great.

I thoroughly enjoyed my many years there; few girls can have been given so many opportunities to learn, to think, to reason – even to rebel!

(Elsa Christie, Aylmar 1928–32)

Cricket on the School Field, 1920.

So Many Opportunities

A Historical Portrait of Sherborne School for Girls

1899–1999

Barry Williams

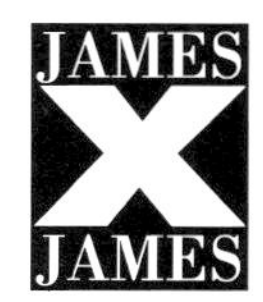

To Ann

Picture Acknowledgements

The majority of illustrations come from the School Archives or from private photographs kindly loaned by OGs or members of staff. For the others the author and publishers are indebted to the following:
for colour plates: Eyecatchers Photography, Yeovil, facing page 120 (top); John Keeling, facing pages 24, 25, 48, 96 (main picture), 97 (bottom), 120 (bottom), 121;
for black and white pictures: *The Architects' Journal* 23; Hanya Chlala 106 (bottom); Oliver Hatch 85; *The Independent* 45, 56; John Keeling 62, 95 (top right); NFWI Library 83; Rendells of Sherborne 52, 110; Rendells of Yeovil 29 (bottom), 116; Sweetman of Tunbridge Wells 21; Virago Press 64; The Wimbledon Lawn Tennis Museum 99 (bottom); *Western Gazette* 32, 133; 3-Star Press Agency, London 38 (right).

First published in 1998

ISBN 0 907383 70 X
Designed by Susannah May
Printed and bound by Butler & Tanner Limited, Frome, Somerset

Published by
James & James (Publishers) Ltd
Gordon House Business Centre
6 Lissenden Gardens
London NW5 1LX

Foreword

by Anne Dixon

Thurstan 1943–49, Head Girl
Aylmar Housemistress 1967–82
at present Senior Trustee, Sherborne Old Girls' Union

The Centenary is a time for celebration. It is also an appropriate moment to reflect upon and take stock of the past – the purpose of this book. It must have been a daunting task to write it. Histories commissioned to commemorate special events so often hover between paeans of uncritical self-congratulation and a sleep-inducing list of facts and figures. I do admire Barry's skill in successfully avoiding these pitfalls. He has written a lively, informative and, where necessary, an affectionately critical account of Sherborne School for Girls' first hundred years. There is something of interest here for everyone and I hope that it will evoke many happy memories.

Institutions are shaped by all those who pass through them and contribute in countless ways to their ethos and growth. Sherborne has been fortunate in having its share of distinguished and far-sighted Governors, Headmistresses, staff and girls who have left their mark on the School. Two things shine through the book. First, most people have got out of Sherborne a sense of enjoyment and achievement in some field or other, whether it be academic, artistic, musical or sporting or from simply belonging to a generally openminded, friendly society. Secondly, there is a deep awareness of the importance of each individual and of the need to make some contribution to the community – not in a pious but in a down-to-earth, pragmatic way. One only has to read the annual Old Girls' Journal to see how this has been carried over by so many people into their everyday lives. In the news section, Old Girls mention in passing their involvement in their communities – driving for the local hospice, working as a Samaritan or serving as a JP, helping street urchins in Colombia or as a VSO in Africa. The list is endless.

I am sure that part of this sense of commitment stems from the House system which has always been one of the strengths of Sherborne life. If you felt valued and comfortable in the small House community you gained the confidence to venture forth to contribute to the life of the School as a whole and to the wider world beyond it.

Let us rejoice that we have made our first century and let us go forward with hope into the next, upon the sure foundations built by our predecessors.

Anne H. Dixon

July 1998

Contents

Sources of chapter title quotations: (2) traditional; (6) Peter Rabbit, *Beatrix Potter, 1900; (8) Francis Quarles, 1630; (11) nursery rhyme; (12)* Mrs Worthington, *Noël Coward, and* A Little Night Music, *Stephen Sondheim, 1973; (13) 'To a Louse', Robert Burns; (15) Pete Seeger, 1961.*

Introduction: Sources Cut on the Bias

In writing this History I must declare a personal involvement: I am both observer and participant. Having taught history and given university advice to girls at Sherborne from 1972 to 1992, I am well aware that a large number of sixth-form historians will be reading this and marking *my* 'essay' according to the advice: research the sources, evaluate them and communicate your findings.

School sources are excellent though patchy, if rather factual and formal: the *School Magazine* (now *Meridian*) from the first in 1906 to date, and *SOGU Magazine* since 1966; many Prospectuses (the 1915 one was particularly illuminating); minutes of Governors' Meetings (especially useful on the 1939–45 War and the inflation of the 1960s and 1970s); and the two previous 'histories' – by Beatrice Mulliner in 1929 and the 1949 Jubilee book compiled by thirty-five staff and OGs. Early HMI Reports proved productive (those of 1905 and 1910 are in the Public Record Office at Kew, and the School archives contain the full 1926 Report), as were Dame Diana's speeches in the 1960s defending girls' independent schools, and her Blue Book recording the Queen Mother's visit in 1974. House chronicles are very variable – some almost non-existent, others (W, K, AE) provided great detail but with yawning gaps. Much depended on the energies of the Head of House and the Housemistress – perhaps one has to be of a certain character to record patiently the minutiae of existence for future interest!

Historians would be in difficulty without the subjective accounts of private satisfactions and frustrations. Appeals to OGs and staff for diaries, letters and memories brought interesting responses from all over Britain and as far afield as Stockholm and Vancouver, Sydney, Harare and Buenos Aires, as well as from every decade (yes! one from a 98-year-old). Despite apologies ('I'm no Samuel Pepys' and 'far too embarrassing') I built up a wealth of material. Persis Wingfield (DH 1913) and Ruth and Elisabeth Walwyn (DH 1951 and 1956) kept all their letters, both ways; Jane Welch (AW 1983) and Henrietta Bulley's (DH 1977) diaries were full of interest as this book will attest. Letters to me ranged from one to ten pages, many being extraordinarily colourful and outspoken. The story of the Canadian 'evacuation' of 1940 would have been impossible to write without the Bursary records of finances and also Elva Parkinson's (T 1946, now Mrs Carey) book of memorabilia which she published in 1990. Many staff too have been eloquent, particularly Iain Stuart Robertson, David Horsfall, Jean Stewart, Ruth Haslop, Jean Burton, Caro Macintosh, Joan Burchardt and Augusta Miller.

Of the many published works on education two were especially valuable: *The Doors of Possibility – A Life of Dame Emmeline Tanner* by Susan Major (Lutterworth 1995); and *The Best Type of Girl: a History of Girls' Education* by Gillian Avery (Deutsch 1991).

'To make sense of the past' is a favourite description of the historian's task. Evaluating these sources presented all the usual problems: gaps in the record, human errors of fact, distortions and blurring of the memory among many. (I was pleased when Dame Diana said she had her original speeches – 'You don't want my recollections – they're distorted by what's happened since!') And I had to take account of the pitfalls of anecdotal evidence. The biggest task was not to let the *School Magazine* and its images of a contented united community take over – was School life *always* like that? But there were the supremely honest OGs' letters to restore the balance; even though many would pen a paragraph concluding 'better not put that in', I fear I ignored the advice in places. This History, published to coincide with the School's centenary, has tried to avoid what Gillian Avery calls, 'melting into nostalgia about lost innocence' which such occasions generate. And what of those who fell foul of the system or have ambivalent emotions about the School? Would they join SOGU, write to me, even read this book? Pervading all is the bias of self-selection.

In putting this book together I made personal decisions and so must offer some apologies as well as acknowledgements. The tradition of school histories being chronological, based on a sequence of Heads, seemed inappropriate here as I wanted to include the 'voices' of girls as much as of those in authority. So I opted for an analytical approach, with an abundance of quotations, logging each girl by her maiden name, House and last year, e.g. Margaret Woodcock (K 1939). The first apology therefore is to the conspicuously absent husbands; with the minefield of modern relationships, married names are only included in special cases. The second apology goes to the many OGs not mentioned: I could have written twice as much, but the economics of modern publishing decreed a book of 60,000 words; so my sincere regrets to all those whose particular talents are unrecorded here. Please accept that your efforts are there in the generalities.

Finally, I owe an immense debt to the scores of OGs, staff and Governors who have helped in so many ways. But especial thanks go to Richard Sargent for unfailing support; to Derek Willis for his financial researches; to Anne Legg for her help with the pictures; to Keith Geary for his cartographic expertise. And not least to those who have undertaken the onerous work of proof-reading – my daughter Jane (E 1979) and Patricia Brewster (T 1948, now a governor) – and to my wife, Ann, for 'computerising' the manuscript.

Gratitude also to *all* my 'Correspondents' – by letter, telephone or interview:

Old Girls

Maria Aitken (AW 62), Jo Baker (E 79), Cicely Ballard (DH 30), Ann Barrett (W 45), Sara Barsley (AE 59), Clare Bayley (AE 60), Vanessa Beale (W 63), Rosa Beddington (AW 73), Barbara Bennett (W 33), Shirley Bloomer (AW 52), Joan Bonsey (K 36), Patricia Brewster (T 48), Alison Brown Douglas (E 50), Henrietta Bulley (DH 77), Joan Burchardt (DH 36), Lucy Buxton (DH 65), Ann Cantrell (K 59), Pauline Carter (AE 35), Ruby Cassels (E 41), Jeannette Casson (E 64), Katharine Charlewood (DH 38), Elsa Christie (A 32), Margery Colborne (DH 25), Joy Courtney (AE 40), Christine Cree (K 68), Phoebe Cresswell (A 42), Jean Crombie (T 38), Rosemary Custance (A 36), Rosemary Day (K 42), Alethea Dew (Ald 32), Jaquetta Digby (DH 45), Anne Dixon (T 49), Susan Ferard (AW 49), Diana Forman (E 36), Sheena Forman (E 37), Georgina Foss (K 60), Josephine Gardner (AW 37), Elizabeth Gibson (E 69), Betty Gilbert (E 37), Diana Gorsky (AW 76), Felicity Greene (A 34), Diana Grove (Ald 27), Audrey Hamilton (T 36), Lorna Harman (AW 36), Mary Hallam (W 49), Patricia Hartley (W 46), Rachel Harvie-Watt (DH 62), Lucy Hayne (A 31), Juliet Haysom (T 96), Ann Hoblyn (AE 50), Philippa Hodgson (DH 66), Claudia Horsfield (AW 75), Anne Hotblack (T 46), Vanessa Howe (K 74), Anne Hubbard (DH 51), Susan Kent (AE 46), Emma Kirkby (E 65), Pippa Lawrence (AE 55), Diana Lentaigne (E 58), Juliet Lock (AE 76), Brenda Livesey (AE 32), Pamela McCloughry (AW 42), Sheila MacFeeters (T 75), Candia McWilliam (AE 73), Fiona Morrice (AW 59), Jenny Morton (AW 75), Judith Mothersill (E 68), Jill Myers (W 48), Elspeth Nicol (T 53), Anne Norris (Ald 26), Nancy Ollivant (Ald 28), Rosamond Owen (A 38), Veronica Owen (W 42), Elva Parkinson (T 46), Doreen Payne (K 40), Hilary Peterkin (W 64), Rosalind Phillips (DH 44), Elaine Radcliffe (K 47), Joy Rathbone (W 31), Diana Reader Harris (DH 30), Felicity Rebbeck (DH 43), Ann Rew (DH 47), Valerie Richardson (A 38), Susan Robinson (A 45), Jacqui Rose (DH 64), Wendy Ross (A 57), Tessa Rowland (DH 56), Hilary Ruston (E 55), Cynthia St Quintin (A 26), Peggy Shackleton (T 27), Cynthia Shepherd (W 60), Ruth Sherman (AE 34), Barbara Slade (T 41), Vivien Spooner (W 36), Sarah-Jane Stancomb (T 66), Nenagh Staunton (AW 77), Jean Straw (AE 45), Margaret Symons (W 38), June Taylor (W 61), Elizabeth Thompson (AW 34), Beth Tricker (AW 98), Margaret Tunbridge (A 46), Rosalind Turpin (AW 64), Elisabeth Walwyn (DH 56), Ruth Walwyn (DH 52), Jennifer Warrington (AW 52), Cynthia Webb (A 49), Fiona Webster (W 66), Jane Welch (AW 83), Paula Whitehead (W 47), Ruth Whittingdale (DG 07), Jane Williams (E 79), Joan Williams-Thomas (DH 36), Caroline Wilson (AE 58), Margaret Woodcock (K 39), Melanie Wray (AW 78).

Governors, Headmistresses and Staff – past and present (excluding OGs)

Lorna Allen, Cecil Armitage, Anne Bjornseth, Jean Burton, Sue Cameron, Elizabeth Coulter, Nancy Downing, Polly English, Keith Geary, Ruth Gee, Rosamund Hall, Ruth Haslop, David Horsfall, John Jenkins, Helen Keating, Wendy Laid, Anne Legg, Caro Macintosh, Sally McConnell, Donald Mathewson, Augusta Miller, Jenny Newman, Venetia Peake, Angela Pitt, Anthony Pitt-Rivers, Sheila Powell, Hassan Qasrawi, John Rees, Iain Stuart Robertson, Janet Robson, Anne Rushworth, Richard Sargent, Romey Schofield, Patricia Scott-Moncrieff, Yvonne Shorland, Charles Simpson, Jean Stewart, Carolyn Taylor, Christine Valeur, Daphne West, Derek Willis.

1
1899: A Dubious Undertaking

Late in 1898 the landlady of an inn near Sherborne Abbey received a guest, who had arrived on the London train. She gave her name as Miss Maynard, and very soon a carriage arrived to take her to dinner at Sherborne Castle. For Miss Maynard was the Mistress-Principal of Westfield College, London University, and she was here at the invitation of Mr and Mrs Kenelm Wingfield Digby, whose family had been linked with the Castle since the seventeenth century. They wanted to ask two questions, the answers to which would form the first link in a chain of far-reaching consequences. Mr Wingfield Digby, MP for North Dorset, told Miss Maynard that he felt keenly – 'a sacred duty' in fact – that a girls' school was needed in Sherborne, independent of, but similar to, the long-established King Edward VI boys' public school adjacent to the Abbey. His wife, Charlotte, felt equally strongly: a Christian school on evangelical lines was a priority, for the only alternative place in the area offering a boarding and 'secondary' style education for girls was a Catholic school – and neither approved of this.

The two questions put to Miss Maynard were how to set about starting a school, and did she know of a likely headmistress. The answer to the first emerged over a long conversation after dinner that night; to the second the brief answer was, 'Yes, but I do not think she will come as she already has a pleasant post at Cheltenham Ladies' College, and anyway she is writing a book – but you could try!'

Charlotte Wingfield Digby, c.1900.

The project was set in motion in February 1899 when a public meeting was held at which several local dignitaries offered support to Mr Wingfield Digby. He was pleased that Canon Westcott, the Headmaster of the Boys' School, led these supporters. With much cold water being thrown on the enterprise such help was sorely needed. There were practical difficulties – suitable accommodation for a school, plus financial backing – and contemporary prejudices were not easily overcome. 'What is the use of spending money on a girl's education?' was a common attitude. As Miss Sara Burstall of Manchester High School for Girls said, 'The majority of English people have a dumb conviction that education is a necessary evil – a feeling not confined to the labouring classes.'

Many middle- and upper-class parents had two specific reservations. They had heard the oft-expressed fear that too much study, especially of classics and mathematics, could unhinge a girl's nervous system; and, even more pointedly, there was the spectre of social embarrassment at having a clever, strong-minded daughter – such qualities were known to deter some potential husbands. So the sort of school the Wingfield

Digbys had in mind, one that would even encourage girls to go to university, was perhaps not wholly desirable. Such attitudes were entrenched in segments of Victorian society, and were not new. Efforts in the seventeenth century to educate girls were treated disparagingly – 'they are but women' was a Jesuitical mock; a century later a critic wrote of the 'norm' for girls – 'the encouragement of that indolence and inactivity which we falsely call delicacy'. The patriarchal sentiment of the nineteenth century was well expressed by Tennyson,

> Man with the head and woman with the heart:
> Man to command and woman to obey:
> All else confusion.

Kenelm Wingfield Digby, c. 1900.

The effect of these attitudes was highlighted by the suffragette, Lady Constance Lytton: when she surveyed her early life, she wrote, 'I was one of that numerous gang of upper-class, leisured-class spinsters, unemployed, unpropertied, unendowed, uneducated – driven through life with blinkers on.' Florence Nightingale, too, felt huge frustrations – 'Behind man's destiny woman must annihilate herself.' The medical profession was particularly hostile to women in education. A letter in *The Times* referred to the 'fact' that 'the mind of woman is always threatened with danger from the reverberations of her physiological emergencies'; and it was commonplace for doctors to regard women as deviant from the (male) norm, regarding anything they could not treat as 'hysteria'. When Elizabeth Garrett gained admission to Middlesex Hospital medical lectures in 1861, a petition against her was drawn up: 'We consider that the promiscuous assemblage of the sexes in the same class is a dangerous innovation.'

All this might have daunted lesser mortals than the Wingfield Digbys. But Charlotte in particular had a special character trait: once she had chosen her course her tenacity of purpose was remarkable. For two months in the early spring of 1899 she argued and cajoled. The need was there, she said. Despite all the prejudice, social emancipation of women had made significant progress in the past three decades. Victorian middle-class feracity too was a bonus, for families were seeking ways of escaping the trammels of numerous unmarried daughters, and many were not attracted to the 'finishing school' type of establishment. The majority of these only offered genteel, feminine accomplishments such as music, drawing and needlework in their prospectuses, providing what amounted to little more than coaching for success in the game of matrimony.

It was already clear that daughters of the well-to-do were looking for occupations outside the family. Charlotte Digby had certainly heard of a number of schools which had been anxious to establish education on the same footing as that of boys. Over 30 day schools had been founded by the Girls' Public Day School Trust, and several boarding schools had good reputations. Cheltenham Ladies' College and North London Collegiate had been set up in the 1850s, but it was Roedean which appealed to Mrs Digby. Founded in 1885 by the three Lawrence sisters, its particular ethos was attracting attention: housemistresses who also taught, competitive house games and a prefect system clearly imitated boys' public schools. Significantly, it had a grid-iron woven into its insignia, symbolic of the desire to 'stretch' the girls academically, to university standard if possible (St Leonard's and Wycombe Abbey were already moving along these lines). Higher education lectures for women and even all-female colleges were developing: Girton and Newnham at Cambridge, Somerville and Lady Margaret Hall at Oxford, and the Royal Holloway and Westfield Colleges of London University were already in existence.

In her campaign Charlotte Digby also used the works and speeches of influential writers and academics: the Victorian self-help enthusiast, Samuel Smiles, had pleaded in 1878 for the 'instruction of women to enlarge their mental freedoms'; and Edward Thring, the pioneering Headmaster of Uppingham, addressing a conference of headmistresses, commented: 'You are fresh and enthusiastic and untrammelled – we boys' schools are weighed down by tradition.' A very persuasive person, Charlotte Digby felt the opportunity was there, and she had the vision to grasp it. However, she and her husband were realistic enough to appreciate the considerable difficulties that lay ahead: in balancing the prejudices against the more encouraging signs, the setting up of a girls' school in Sherborne still seemed to Charlotte a 'somewhat dubious undertaking'.

By April 1899 enough support was forthcoming for a small council to be formed – the Wingfield Digbys were joined by Canon Westcott. The idea of raising money by offering shares in a company was discussed, and Kenelm Wingfield Digby offered to guarantee interest on £1,000 (about £50,000 at today's values) for two years. Then on the 8 April the Council advertised for a Headmistress – not quite in the late twentieth-century sense! An 'invitation' was drawn up and sent to a few would-be candidates, with Miss Maynard's suggestion at the top of the list.

Miss Beatrice Mulliner, aged 30 and an assistant mistress under the formidable Miss Dorothea Beale, Headmistress of Cheltenham Ladies' College, remembered very clearly the invitation to come and discuss a girls' school. Some years later she wrote:

> I received this letter which puzzled me not a little. It invited me to come and stay for a few days in Sherborne – at a castle of which I had never heard, and it was signed with the name of a total stranger. More pointedly it said, 'The Council are anxious that it should be clearly understood that the school is at present non-existent and any salary agreed could only be guaranteed for two years.' Though mystified, in the spirit of adventure, I went.

Over dinner on the first night she was told all about the prospects for the new school. She had already been disarmed by the charm of the Castle's occupants.

> The children appeared at their usual hour. I do not think Venetia will remember it. She was about seven, and her only interest was in the stranger joining in 'Cuckoo' – a wild form of 'I spy'. Having played all over an old Elizabethan house with secret doors, blind alleys and steep mysterious stairs, it was difficult to feel shy and constrained.

Also, she had been captivated by the beauty and what she termed 'the extraordinary vivacity' of Charlotte Wingfield Digby. Following her death in 1935, Miss Mulliner spoke at her Memorial Service:

The School's first home: Ransome House, from Greenhill, 1899.

> She introduced me to her own happy home life. I can see her still as she met me that first night in the old drawing room, surrounded by memories of Raleigh and Stuart times. She had unerring taste.

On the second night the visitor was offered the post of Headmistress. Over the next 30 years, her 'reign', Beatrice Mulliner was fond of quoting 'a non-existent school', 'a dubious undertaking', and particularly 'a salary guaranteed only for two years'.

The intention was to have a school in being by September. With the capital from the sale of shares building up, suitable accommodation was quickly sought; there was little available. Only an ancient house on Greenhill seemed possible. Tradition had it that it was built by Abbot Ransome, who had, in his medieval days, done much to restore the Abbey. Later it was acquired by the Boys' School, and a house-master had built a large extension at the back, as a boys' common room. Later still, the School sold it to a landowner who used the large room as a stable for his hunters. Eventually he gave them up and the property stood empty, the garden becoming a wilderness, and the old house took on a derelict appearance. Now known simply as Greenhill House, a three-year tenancy at £80 per annum was obtained and some hasty renovations put in hand. The smelly horse-boxes were removed and the stables cleaned and turned into classrooms ('very chilly', as Miss Mulliner recalled); the garden was quickly made tidy by some gardeners from the Castle. An 'Opening' was announced for 20 September 1899, when the new Headmistress would be 'At Home'; to confer some dignity to the occasion silver, cups and even footmen were sent up from the Castle. A distinguished speaker too was produced at very short notice – Sir Edward Clarke KC, who had once been in the government as Solicitor-General, and was by happy chance staying a few days with the Wingfield Digbys.

Formalities observed, 'the School' assembled a week later; prayers were said and work began. There were 14 pupils at the initial roll-call, only seven of them of 'secondary' school age (one of them was technically a 'student' preparing for her teacher's certificate, and another came only half-time); the other seven were kindergarten and, in Miss Mulliner's words, 'Alas! six of them were little boys and therefore unpromising.' One of these 'unpromising' boys, Jack Whittingdale, later became the School doctor! His 6-year-old sister, Ruth (Day Girl 1899–1907), was the only little girl, and can be seen sitting on Miss Mulliner's lap in the first-ever school photograph. Ruth recalled later (much later, when she was 97) one of the Headmistress's earliest tasks in that summer/autumn of 1899:

> An unenviable job was to call on families in the area with children suitable for this type of school. She must have been given a list, for as she was not a Dorset woman it can't have been easy.

Nor were the working conditions satisfactory that first term. The tenancy agreement dated November 1899 lists over seven pages of further renovations: 'Strip and paper walls' appeared for every room; the need for shelving and other basic fitments indicated how spartan the working environment must have been; phrases such as 'the piggery – ten tiles broken – very dilapidated', were typical of the general state of the place. The landlords even agreed to contribute £52 towards getting the place into something decently habitable – a considerable sum in those days.

The money was well spent, and by the beginning of 1900 things looked promising. Charlotte Wingfield Digby's vision and Beatrice Mulliner's sense of

The whole School, in the summer of 1900, taken at rear of Ransome House. On Miss Mulliner's lap sits Ruth Whittingdale; of her brothers, Tom in white socks leans against Miss Moore, and Jack (later the School doctor) wears a dark sailor suit.

adventure were paying off. Numbers crept up: 21 when the second term opened, and 36 at the beginning of the second year – 26 of them in the Upper School. Crucially for the School's reputation, its declared academic bent gained swift success. Miss Mulliner, equipped with a 'First' from London University and a distinction in her teaching diploma, had been joined from the start by Kathleen Moore, with a French degree from Westfield College. The two of them were well pleased when six girls – out of the eight entered – passed the Cambridge Local Examination, with Evelyn Blanch (Greenhill 1902) gaining a distinction in French. Two girls also passed Royal Academy of Music examinations.

Talk of enlarging the premises was now current among the Governing Body, some saying perhaps the tenancy of a second house near by should be considered. But the Governors' web of social and clerical connections, added to Miss Moore's paternal links to parishes in south-west London, were bearing fruit. Applications were growing and within two years the number promised to be over 60 – what if a year later they approached three figures? After some hard talking in the Council, some more Wingfield Digby generosity and a major act of faith, a momentous decision was reached: a new building would be erected on fields on the outskirts of Sherborne. Roedean had begun, like Sherborne, with a minute number – 'six paying pupils and four for show' – in a Brighton town house; its act of faith in laying the foundation stone for a splendid new school for 200 on the cliffs east of the town had occurred after ten years, in 1897. What Roedean had done in '10', Sherborne could do in '3', though perhaps not for 200 – yet!

It was certainly a second act of benevolence by Kenelm Wingfield Digby (the last before his early death in 1904) which underpinned this stage of the enterprise. His first had guaranteed the interest on the £1,000 share issue which had resulted in 'Greenhill'. At that time he had, on the advice of Miss Maynard, followed the example of Cheltenham, St Leonard's and Wycombe Abbey, and set up a public company, a kind of joint-stock business. Called a 'proprietary school', Sherborne operated under its own 36 articles:

COMPANY LIMITED BY SHARES
Memorandum
&
Articles of Association
of the
SHERBORNE SCHOOL FOR THE HIGHER
EDUCATION OF GIRLS COMPANY
LIMITED
Incorporated the 27th Day of October 1899

Now, less than three years later, Mr Wingfield Digby offered a gift to the school of a piece of land, about an acre in size, on the south side of Bradford Road. On 20 May 1902 the Countess of Ilchester laid the foundation stone for a large hall and classrooms. The Governors meanwhile had increased the site by the judicious purchase of another 4 acres, and plans for a boarding house (Aldhelmsted) were drawn up, whilst Greenhill would be retained for extra boarding. The Hall and classrooms were formally opened in March 1903 by the Marquis of Londonderry, the first President of the new Board of Education in the government. Aldhelmsted was in occupation the following September, with the school roll already at 99.

At the 1902 'Foundation', Canon Westcott had spoken of,

> times not so far distant when it was considered a sufficient education for girls if they were taught a little wool work, to play the piano (indifferently), and to acquire a smattering of foreign languages – enough to be able to ask in an indifferent accent 'Have you seen my grandmother's red cow?' [much laughter]. But today it was recognised that women have both bodies and minds – and what theologians call 'souls'. It might be well therefore to extend to girls the same education as given to boys.

Miss Beatrice Mulliner beamed. From now on she would have no worries about her 'salary being guaranteed only for two years'; clearly all this was no longer 'a dubious undertaking'.

Postscript

Over the years the name of the 'School' has had some idiosyncratic usages. The early legal documents maintained the 'company' terminology: 'The Sherborne School for the Higher Education of Girls Company Limited.' The press in reporting various events wavered between 'The Higher School for Girls' (1900), 'Sherborne High School for Girls' (*Bristol Mercury* in 1903), and ' Sherborne Girls' School' (*Dorset Chronicle* 1903). When Miss Stuart came in 1930 she was bemused. Financial ledgers clearly called it 'Sherborne Ladies College', whereas the towns-people seemed divided over common parlance: some said 'The Girls School', others, according to Miss Stuart, 'were determined to raise its position by referring to "The High School"'. Occasionally the word 'public' would be used. So in 1935, when a legal reconstruction took place, ridding the School of its old 'Company' image, the opportunity was taken to establish formally the name by which it has since been known: Sherborne School for Girls. Today though the observant can view some preserved history; 'SLC' is fixed on the weather-vane above the main school roof.

Other eccentricities have permeated even House terminology: see Chapter 2 for the time when Aldhelmsted 'Senior' and 'Junior' had nothing to do with ages or rank, and when East was west and West was east.

DISTINGUISHED OLD GIRLS

AMRIT KAUR

(Ald 1905)

Rajkumari Amrit Kaur was Secretary to Mahatma Gandhi for 16 years, before becoming the first Minister of Health in Nehru's government from 1947 to 1957. Her task? To initiate (with meagre resources) a welfare service for India's vast population – well described as 'the biggest job of any woman anywhere in the world'. Her father, the Maharajah of Kapurthala, a convert to Christianity, sent Amrit to Sherborne in 1902 'for a Christian education'. A small, fragile girl, unused to running or playing games, she was to become Head Girl and School Games Captain (both winter and summer), and later proved a brilliant tennis player, winning the All-India title. She nursed in the 1914–18 War, and helped found the Indian Red Cross. Launching herself into politics with courage and determination, her passions were votes for women and the overthrow of the Indian caste system. Gradually, through her work with Gandhi, she was drawn into the controversial issue of Indian independence – even being imprisoned by the British Raj for three years with her fellow campaigners for 'Quit India'. In government in 1947 she reverted to matters of health; regular milk for children and home nursing for TB patients were two hard-fought victories. Amrit also moved into international work: she was at UNESCO in 1946 and, arguably her greatest achievement, became President of the World Health Organisation in 1950. Three years before her death in 1964, she was awarded the René Sand Prize for distinguished social service on the world's stage. She never lost her affection for Britain and particularly her School. A gifted speaker, she returned regularly to talk to the girls – in Jean Straw's (AE 1945) words, 'a fascinating lady'.

Amrit Kaur, taken c.*1955 when she was Minister of Health in the Indian Government.*

2
'She Sleeps Well o' Windy Nights'

Provision of congenial surroundings to live and work in has always been high on the School's agenda, and from the start Miss Mulliner emphasised the natural environment. In speeches and brochures she advanced its attractions to potential parents:

> The buildings stand on a ridge 260 feet above sea level, and command extensive views of Dorset. The foundations are all on rock, the oolitic limestone of the County; the climate is dry and healthy. Sherborne is an ancient town possessing perhaps the most beautiful Norman Abbey in southern England.

Its rural environs certainly impressed many an OG and staff as well. When Emmeline Tanner (later Dame Emmeline, Headmistress of Roedean) came in 1904 to be interviewed for the History post, she noted,

> I feel a little thrill as the train brings me in sight of the Castle grounds. And to walk up Digby Road till one comes to the beautiful Abbey and the Almshouses, then up Yeatman Road and peep through the gateway towards the boys' studies, chapel, and library – all pure joy.

For the girls a further, even magnetic, appeal has been the ten-minute saunter from the School to the Boys' School and the adjacent shops and coffee-houses of Cheap Street – though OGs without exception from the School's first half-century remember the resolute efforts of the authorities to isolate them from such distractions.

The School itself in the very early years had a daunting appearance. Miss Tanner's view must have been the same as that of Marguerite Stubbs (DH 1912). Though set on a hill in beautiful countryside, she wrote,

> When I first saw it the School might have been a model for Kipling's *Bleak Houses.* Bare and gaunt, Aldhelmsted, Dun Holme and the School stood among the fields; no trees spoilt the view to the west. The farms came right up to the boundaries and in summer we were kept awake by the corncrakes.

Then the grounds were much smaller than today's 40 acres. The Governors had made salient purchases of neighbouring plots to bring the acreage up to 26 by 1915. Yet foliage and bricks mattered as much as space – to such a degree that when nine HMIs came for a Board of Education inspection in 1926 their Report highlighted, 'the excellent design and furnishing of the seven boarding houses. The various school buildings, grouped round fine playing fields, form a whole of great dignity and beauty.' Clearly, much work had been done to change the School's appearance for the better.

When surveying building projects over the whole century, it is striking how immense has been the concentration in the first and last quarters (roughly), with only a little in between. This suggests consolidation before inevitable renewal, but only in part; the great economic depression of the 1930s and the 1939–45 War with its subsequent austerity give a more complete explanation. One interesting feature was the construction of a 'new' building, which in time came to be altered or replaced by yet another 'new' building; en route girls gave affectionate nick-names to certain features – inevitably many vanished. Few girls or staff, past or present, can explain *all* of the following: the tin-tab, the bunny hutch, the well, the airport lounge.

The first period, 1903–28, had an almost frenetic quality. The Wingfield Digbys had been all too accurate in their forecast of Sherborne's need for a girls' boarding school: the initial surge at Greenhill, from 13 to 99 by 1903 presaged things to come. Within seven years the numbers reached 140 and an 'overflow' in rented houses in the town seemed permanent. In 1915 the Headmistress announced: 'Our numbers have never been so high: 170 and rising. All the houses are more than full, and Ransome has its complete 29.' Three years later the School roll stood at 257; and when Beatrice Mulliner retired in 1929 she declared, 'We are at full strength: 287.'

The housing and teaching of all these girls meant building in response to rapid growth rather than to any considered plan. The Governors counted themselves blessed, with a large compact site at their disposal. When Aldhelmsted was built in 1903 it accommodated 46 girls, all eating together, and with 23 sleeping on each of the two floors – not in open dormitories, but, as Miss Mulliner described,

> in cubicles which have on two sides wooden partitions (2 inches from the floor and 6 feet high), and curtains at the end. The sleeping accommodation is specially arranged to obtain the maximum amount of light and air.

Greenhill had to be retained for the overflow until a new house could be built. An acre to the west of Aldhelmsted was purchased and a second house for 30 girls, Dun Holme, was opened in 1907. The overflow at Greenhill, far from disappearing, steadily increased, and began calling itself 'Wingfield', in anticipation of a third house; soon a fourth was deemed necessary, so in 1910 'Priestlands' was rented and began calling itself 'Aylmar'. With great ceremony in September 1911 these two Houses occupied the new double building built to the east of the main school. Dorothy Birds (W 1912) proudly announced that this 'really ushered in the dawn of the present-day Sherborne.'

She was, of course, premature. A year later, Aldhelmsted's floors, already termed Senior and Junior, were officially separated into two independent 'houses' within the same building when an extra cloakroom was added. (The origin of 'senior' and 'junior' seems unknown, as the names had nothing to do with rank or age.) Plans for two more houses were drawn up, as Greenhill, now formally reverting to its original name of Ransome, continued to fill up. In the summer of 1914 the foundations of Thurstan were laid – then the Great War broke out in August and government regulation raised serious problems of supply of materials. Alice Dove (Ald 1915) remembered the delays: 'the few layers of bricks and scaffolding towering into the air, which were "Thurstan", remained like this for many terms.' The 'Ransome' girls were annoyed at the delay, especially as they had to walk in strict 'crocodile' up to School for morning prayers; but a concession was made giving them a horse-drawn wagonette to return them after morning school and to convey them back again for evening lessons. In January 1916 Thurstan was completed and occupied; but the Headmistress had to admit in a humorous understatement to parents, that even two months later,

> it is still approached from the School by way of a precarious plank! Now that the darkening of lights is enforced and the field somewhat boggy, the journey thither in the evenings is apt to be one of excitement and surprise.

Work was immediately started on the adjoining house, Ealhstan, which was completed with no delays and opened in 1917.

Though pressure of numbers eased in the 1920s, and Ransome was given up (to Lord Digby's School in 1919), the Governors decided to buy some ground to the west of Horsecastles Lane. In 1928 rapid construction produced a new house, Kenelm, in a buttercup field atop some rising ground; a bridge over the lane followed equally rapidly. The first occupants were carefully listed as 'three prefects, three seniors, eight juniors, nine "babies" and several prowling Kenelm cats'.

In the same period teaching and study requirements were as important as Houses. In 1905 the Governors gave money for what Miss Mulliner claimed as 'probably the finest girls' gymnasium in southern England', 25 ft by 60 ft, with a spectators' gallery. In 1910 new classrooms were added, but the proud centrepiece was an

The new School buildings 'bare and gaunt', facing south, c.1904: Aldhelmsted on the left and the schoolrooms on the right.

enlarged Hall – lengthened by a platform at the east end, and opened with considerable pomp in July. It was to have but a short life: seven months.

Disaster struck on the night of 16 January 1911. It was a few days before the girls were to return and Miss Mulliner herself was away. At 11 p.m. a farmer saw some flickering lights but thought it was a party; at 2 a.m. Spot, a gardener's dog, began barking; the fire brigade was called. Kathleen Moore remembered,

> I was dreaming of the Timetable when someone cried 'Fire'. When I reached the School the middle of the Hall was a mass of flames, roaring and crackling like a mighty bonfire. The firemen concentrated on the west end, leaving the east, 'piano' end to burn – the flames seemed to like pianos! The Hall was finally burnt out.

The girls were informed and told to stay home for another week – which elicited a legendary remark from the Boys' School: 'the beastly luck of the Girls' School'. Beatrice Mulliner hurried back to a scene of desolation, but even she agreed with the music staff, who exhibited particular pleasure: 'We possessed eight ancient pianos; sentiment could not disguise their cracked and feeble tones . . . *they were all burnt!*' Little Alice Dove returned to find 'hundreds of water-sodden textbooks piled up in the corridors – rescued by valiant mistresses. We hunted through them to find our own-named books – "souvenirs" of the Great Fire.' Within days next to Aldhelmsted a large iron-framed 'hall' was erected – the 'tin-tabernacle' as the girls called it – to serve temporarily for morning prayers and Sunday services. But it remained for years afterwards; OGs remember games in wet weather and riotous Saturday evenings in the tin-tab.

The School had generous treatment from the fire-insurers, and within eight months a new hall was opened ceremoniously by HRH Princess Victoria, cousin of the new king, George V. Kathleen Goodman (DH 1911) was impressed: 'The oak-panelled walls are a great improvement on the old hall's bricks. With the pictures up and our new organ (given by Mrs Wingfield Digby) built in, the Hall will be a

A familiar view of the School, Tower and terrace taken in 1949.

Above: *1910: the School Hall (east end) also used as an Art Studio, prior to the Fire.*

Above right: *The Hall (east end) 1922 – Miss Mulliner taking a School Service. The 'Bunny Hutch' is centre picture.*

truly imposing room.'

It was soon evident that classrooms, a library, and science rooms in particular were urgently needed, but as with House plans, the War intervened. Shortage of science equipment became desperate; Miss Mulliner told parents, 'The government will not allow anything like our extra science rooms.' She was much irked by the bureaucratic and financial restraints; not until the early 1920s could plans be implemented. In 1926 she could proudly announce, 'at last our beautiful laboratories, science block and Clock Tower are finished.' Sir William Joynson Hicks, the Home Secretary, came to open them, though not before last-minute mishaps – the heating failed on a cold day ('not a new thing in our history,' said the Headmistress) and the train carrying the government minister struck a milk train.

Beatrice Mulliner was pleased to hand over 'a harmonious whole' to the new Headmistress in 1930. Praised by HMIs, the School also appeared in *The Queen* magazine in 1936 as one of the 'Great Girls' Schools of Britain' (with St Paul's, Malvern and Cheltenham). The economic frost of the Depression, soon to be followed by the War, would curtail any major expansion, but did not entirely hinder progress.

Miss Stuart ended the 'Senior' and 'Junior' Floor terminology in Aldhelmsted – 'parents assume a promotion ladder' – and introduced 'West'(J) and 'East'(S) based on who used which cloakroom. Plans were then made for 'doubling' Kenelm to take 'West'. Scheduled to open in 1938, marriage and some attractive plumbing intervened and created a School oddity incomprehensible to outsiders. Miss Ritchie, the popular Housemistress of East (scheduled to stay *in situ*), left to get married. As a consolation the East girls were given a choice: stay or move. They moved to partner Kenelm because the new house had hot and cold water in every cubicle . . . but of course they kept *their* name, so it was West which stayed east!

Physical education was greatly improved. The swimming pool was opened in 1931, and the gym enlarged in 1936, with a platform outside the south end, so that its glass doors could be opened for gym in the fresh air on sunny days. The games field was extended yet again, and in 1938 a squash court was built. These improvements served generations of girls for over 30 years. In the late 1960s a large new gymnasium was built on the ground between Bradford Road and the A30 – to become familiar to many as 'home' for a quarter of a century of not just PE and indoor games, but also parents' meetings, Confirmation 'bunfights', and the airy silence of years of A-levels, O-levels and GCSEs.

As the focus of planning changed slowly from 'houses' and 'general classrooms' to particular educational needs, each subject wanted recognition, and the Governors had to make priority decisions. Miss Mulliner on her retirement expressed a hope for a music block 'in the not too distant future' – it arrived in 1979! Science's growing requirements, admittedly expensive, became pressing after 1945, and Harriet Hamilton, Head of Science for 30 years, used her renowned persuasive eloquence to wrest £12,500 from the Advancement of Science's national Industrial Fund: it went towards an impressive Chemistry block erected between West and Dun Holme in 1957. It illustrated the School's problem funding large capital projects, and several Appeals were to be set up over the next two decades. A new style of building called Colt was used for much-needed Craft and Geography rooms in 1959; History and Mathematics were similarly housed seven years later.

Care of the sick presented special problems, magnified in the early years by the fear of epidemics, which in a close community could be calamitous. The real horrors were diphtheria, typhoid and scarlet fever, with measles and mumps also worrying. Care was one thing, but some thought that, in keeping with all boarding schools, it became obsessive in the interwar years. Many OGs remember 'embarrassing' medical checks, the regular temperature-taking and hair inspection ('no one actually referred to nits,' said one; known as 'flea scratching' in 1956 according to the present Headmistress).

The Chemistry Labs, 1957, later to become the Lecture Theatre when the new Science buildings were added in the late 1970s.

How serious was this fear? To the authorities: 'very' – when faced with quarantine or even closure. Before mid-century, records show worrying outbreaks every few years; after, their rarity is noticeable. In the huge flu pandemic of 1919, Miss Mulliner was pleased that, 'We suffered less than most schools,' but three years later the *School Magazine* records:

> The influenza streptococcus showed great lack of discrimination: not even the Headmistress was spared. The UVI stepped into the breach, correcting the prep. of the lower school.

The School avoided national outbreaks of diphtheria and smallpox in the 1920s, even gaining praise from Ministry of Health inspectors; but epidemics of flu and measles were to become common. Sadly, it recorded its first death in 1932 when a Dun Holme girl, Alison Royle, died of pneumonia. Quarantine was a regular irritant involving cancelled matches and society visits; in 1938 the whole School contracted either measles or chickenpox – nurses even had to be fetched from Barts. in London. In 1951 West had a week's mumps isolation – staff were found teaching senior girls in the dining room or bedrooms. A polio scare in 1955 put Dun Holme into a 17-day quarantine. Elisabeth Walwyn (DH 1956) wrote to her parents,

Officially presented in 1993 by his niece Georgina Robinson (AE 1976), John Robinson's sculpture stands outside the Diana Reader Harris Art Centre.

'Everyone is very sorry for us, guarding us and wrapping us in cotton-wool: no squash or anything energetic, and no ballroom dancing so that we don't breathe at each other!'

Over the next decades the cry, 'The San is full, the Houses must cope' occurred on a number of occasions: 75 per cent of the School caught Asian flu in 1957, and 160 'went down like flies' in the 1995 outbreak, but 'We coped brilliantly' was the usual confident expression.

'Coping' was normally the task of the nursing Sisters in a variety of places. In the early days a small house at Castleton was rented for infectious diseases; then Ashbourne Lodge in the centre of town was purchased; after it was damaged by bombs in 1940 it was sold, and Priestlands adapted. The Houses used to deal with minor problems, but some cottages at the east end of the School were converted in 1932 for non-infectious illnesses; these were the origin of the present-day 'San', which was properly developed in 1954 when Sister Anita Parrott began her 27-year reign.

The fourth quarter of the century had a building explosion which paralleled the first. Wear and tear was having its effect, and new teaching demands coupled with a School population now creeping towards the mid-400s, required a serious, fresh look at the future. A major 'Appeal' was launched in 1974 with ideas for a new Hall and Sixth Form accommodation; it proved massively unfortunate in its timing, striking the rock of the worst inflation of the century – 24 per cent, caused by the OPEC oil crisis. The new Hall remained on the drawing board.

But the idea of 'Mulliner' survived. What used to be The Cottage in earlier decades had been extended in the 1960s as rooms for the third-year Sixth studying for Oxford and Cambridge. Now in 1975, another large extension created a new House for the entire UVI. Their exit from the other eight Houses was greeted with mixed feelings both by the girls and the staff. Yet for 16 'generations' it was to become their home, a kind of pre-university hall of residence with freedom from the juniors; its 'seconds' queue at lunchtime, the airport lounge, the phone queues and the TV rush-hour of fervent soapsters became legendary. When its mongrel architecture and rabbit-warren interior could stand no more face-lifts, the UVI of 1992 lamented its passing; Siân Jones (AW 1992) wrote of it as, 'the last surviving bastion of social etiquette and genteel behaviour . . . the Old Mulliner is now relegated to the dustbin of history.' In its place, a mere 50 metres away, rose a new structure, still called Mulliner, though better known to the girls as the Sherborne Hilton. Among its comforts are 'a palatial dining room, the spacious drawing room with Jordanian cushions, and lifts to all floors, each with pine-fitted rooms, six showers and four baths'. Old Mulliner, structurally reduced, has reverted to being The Cottage, and is now used for drama and careers.

Elsewhere over three decades building-site images and the jack-hammer noise of construction work made their inevitable appearance. 'Appealing' for money gave way to bank loans, and a huge programme was drawn up. The Hall had already been extended by a large stage, but for Prayers the girls still faced the other way –

An aerial view of the School, 1996.
To identify the buildings see the plan on the back endpaper.

Child's funeral reopens wounds of apartheid
India threatens Pakistan over its support for separatist war

towards the tiered choir area with its 'bunny-hutch' entry; however, in the late 1970s new fire regulations led to the present-day arrangement of a balcony and fixed seats facing the stage. The main school building was modified: a carpeted corridor with lowered ceiling, an extended staff room and refitted Headmistress's study and secretaries' office all produced a well-lit, warm atmosphere.

Major new changes began with an impressive new Science structure on three levels and attached to Mrs Hamilton's Chemistry block, which was converted into a much-used Lecture Theatre. At the same time the importance of music and drama was recognised with the opening in 1979 of the Stuart Centre; at last staff could leave their many teaching points dotted all over the School, particularly in the tiny rooms round the 'well' at the east end of the main building, and move to the congenial base dubbed 'Gussie's Emporium'.

Whilst all the Houses were refurbished in the 1980s, building began again in 1986. Art and Craft had for years existed in cramped areas; a striking light and airy building now offered the imagination a proper creative base. And as an integral part a new Design Technology course was launched with hitherto unheard of engineering equipment in place. The blend of colour, artistic talent and technical wizardry attracts parents at Commemoration, as iron filings to a magnet. This impetus towards space and equipment, which the old chalk-and-talk in 25-seater classrooms could ill-provide, continued apace. Home Economics spread its wings, and a three-storied Modern Language and Geography building rose from the levelled debris of the first Colt structure put up 30 years before.

The Humanities had been pleading for many years for improved library facilities. The first proper library had been attached to the Tower; opened in 1926, it served generations of senior girls and received large regular additions – in 1960 new books, including the *Encyclopaedia Britannica*, totalled 270. Bice Crichton-Miller spent much of her time as Librarian establishing formal library rules: long after her retirement it pleased her to be told that her 'ghost' still held sway in her old bookish domain. Yet the passing years revealed two serious problems. First, junior books were meagre, and were dependent on a County Library van in the early 1950s; the School's own collection in 1952 was, admitted the Librarian, 'some 60 books in nooks and crannies all over the School'. Secondly, the senior Library suffered from the winter cold – draughts, rattling windows and leaks were regular complaints. In 1987 an enlarged, carpeted senior and junior library was planned and the Librarian, Carolyn Taylor, faced the daunting task of arranging the exit, storage and retrieval of thousands of books to allow a year's reconstruction to proceed, whilst giving access to sixth-formers for their basic study needs. A pulley system up three floors, removing and eventually

Elizabeth Coulter and Anthony Pitt-Rivers at the official opening of Mulliner No.3 (below), *the UVI House of the 1990s (between Wingfield and Ealhstan), better known as the Sherborne Hilton.*

Facing page: *The comfortable Mulliner Lounge of the mid-1990s, richly decorative with traditionally stitched cushions presented by HRH Princess Sarvath of Jordan.*

returning all the books was watched with some awe by the girls. Accessions of 700 a year in the 1990s brought book totals to 20,000 (Senior Library) and 5,000 (Junior Library).

Another edifice faced demolition in the 1990s. The gymnasium of 30 years before was now leaking badly; coupled with modern games' requirements this meant a large capital outlay. In 1995 a new Sports Hall provided everything fitness and sporting enthusiasts could wish for.

Mrs Kirkby: she and her husband were the School's first caretakers.

Whilst the Governors and Bursars might oversee the financing of all these building projects (see Chapter 14), the everyday administration and upkeep devolve on a small army: clerical staff, caretakers, gardeners; and the length of service of key figures is striking. Mildred Moore gave 25 years devoted work as School Secretary; on her death in 1943 Miss Stuart referred to her 'gentle courtesy' and commitment to the end: she 'insisted on watching for blackout infringements, even with a temperature of 102 °F'. Sheila Powell came in 1965 and her unruffled but commanding presence was familiar for the next 24 years; she then took over the SOGU Records. The modernisation of the Office (in the form of IT) came under the wings of the blithe Yvonne Shorland and Anne Rushworth: I well remember the looks on their faces when they were told the office would be computerised. Equally composed has been Delia Horsfall as Stores Bursar, who has had to cope with the explosion in equipment and textbooks in the last quarter of the century.

In the early years one whole family dominated the School's caretaking and domestic duties: the Kirkbys. Grandfather was head plasterer during the construction in 1903; father and mother were the first caretakers – the records show their joint salary was '30 shillings a week, no accommodation'; Mrs Kirkby continued after her husband's death until her retirement in 1920, well remembered by OGs as presiding over the buns and milk at break. One daughter was parlour maid in Dun Holme; another began as a nurse in the San, and ended as cook in White Lodge; a third cooked for years in Aylmar; and the youngest used to collect staff books in a barrow and bring them up to School in the 'luxury' days before 1914.

Edward Noake, caretaker for 40 years, whose tall, ram-rod appearance was so familiar to everyone.

Arthur Palmer, caretaker for 16 years: on his death in 1920, Kathleen Moore recalled his pride in 'floors so polished that sliding was a temptation'. Successor Edward Noake: pillar of the School, his 'That's all right, Miss' covered much ingenuity and resourcefulness during his 46 years in charge. The job has massively increased today, as Peter Blake well knows – think of all those buildings, with keys and windows to check! Electrical work too has escalated. Mr Williams came in 1925 and for over 20 years would combine the work of electrician with being the Science 'lab.man'; George Exton stayed for 33 years – so familiar behind the 16-mm projector, before retiring in 1979; Paul Goddard, who had helped him for years, took over and dealt with the plethora of electrical goods in the School's expansion – his world seems dominated by computers and mobile phones.

Gardeners are special – they of course 'front' the School on all occasions – visitors and parents notice! Dycer (whose dog raised the fire alarm in 1911) and Gould dominated the first half-century. Miss Stuart marvelled at the latter's vegetable production in the War and praised him as 'surely the best chrysanthemum grower in the world'. More recently Ralph Wells's 22 years as head gardener has implanted a fresh philosophy, and he much impressed Eleanor Milner (AW 1990) when she interviewed him on his retirement in 1990. He spoke of:

> the ominous Greenhouse Effect, and those politicians – just penguins, all flap, no action! Organic culture needs to come back. And I'm pleased that some A-level girls found 37 specimens of wild flowers in the grounds. Remember we lost 80 trees in the recent great storms – we need lots of Norway Maples and robust poplars.

The School owes so much to these people; clearly without them the girls would not 'sleep well o' windy nights'. Yet one figure has no parallel today: John Isaacs, who came up to Greenhill once a week 'to shampoo the young ladies' hair' when the school was first founded. In the Commemoration Programme for 1931 he advertised as:

Hairdresser by appointment
to
SHERBORNE SCHOOL FOR GIRLS
Expert Shingling
Marcel and Water Waving Hair Tinting
Permanent Waving (newest oil and steam process)

How times have changed.

Ralph Wells, the head gardener, whose ideas of caring for the environment so impressed many girls in the 1980s.

3
An Authority of Headmistresses

The Association of Headmistresses (AHM) was founded in 1874; at its centenary a verdict was delivered on its members: 'by no means tame or tameable'. Characterised as women of strong spiritual conviction and educationally progressive, most inaugurated very personal regimes in their schools. Sherborne's five Headmistresses, some of whom played distinguished roles in the Association's work, were of this mould.

Beatrice Mulliner (1899–1929) was remembered by OGs for her stiffened lace collars, her masterly teaching and formidable, autocratic presence; she had very pale-blue eyes that 'could read your soul'. Some thought her dowdy and old-fashioned, but she owned a car – a rarity for a single woman before the 1920s – and had a reputation for accelerating round corners! She often spent holidays in Switzerland: she skied well, but on ice she unnervingly skated backwards.

A formal portrait of Beatrice Mulliner commissioned in 1930. But Joy Rathbone (W 1931) remembers her differently: 'she wore long coatdresses to her ankles; below were old-fashioned double-strap shoes, and above high net collars with bone supports. Her hats were fastened with ornate hatpins and were weighted down with flowers and stuffed fruit – very Edwardian!'

For over half her time at Sherborne she was known for her vision and energy. 'Progress,' she said in 1905, 'let this be our symbol here.' It was a plea reiterated many times, and she proudly claimed that Sherborne girls went 'out to the world with a vision of a race, a goal, a prize'. She was fond of quoting Plato and especially the classical motto she brought to the School: 'The prize is a fair one, and the hope great.' Miss Mulliner's intellectual curiosity and flexibility of mind impressed everyone, especially when she was confronted by prejudice which saw girls as either intellectually inadequate, or, if educated, as unmarriageable bluestockings. She was determined all girls should have their chance; they must work hard, play hard and be responsible, saying in 1919, 'There is a new world of service opening to girls as citizens of the State, Church and Empire.' To this end she offered a full education: she would create an *esprit de corps* with its emphasis on self-discipline, and proffer a proper academic curriculum, stressing however that her establishment was not merely 'a boys' school plus cookery'.

Not all was sweetness and light. Sir Cyril Norwood (see Chapter 14) criticised her Victorianism with its 'tendency to exaggerate the heinousness of small offences'. She was badly affected by the horrors of the Great War, and sadly missed Kathleen Moore's sense of humour after she left in 1917. Girls in the 1920s found her repressive, and even a teacher recorded bitterly, 'BCM is unspeakable – no one will stand up to her.' She retained to the end the class rigidities of the Victorians. Hers was a school for the daughters of gentlefolk; Ruth Haslop (staff 1938–74) knew of some parents who had to 'wait at the Digby Hotel for two days whilst Miss Mulliner investigated their background'.

1929: a particular Morning Prayers was very dramatic. She was clearly ill. Suddenly she leant hard on the lectern and fell off the stage into the laps of the Lower IV; retirement followed. In 30 years she had built the School up from nothing to become one of the nation's leading girls' schools. She was to recover her health, set up another school and die 'in harness' in 1940, aged 74.

Hilda Violet Stuart at the time of her appointment as Headmistress.

Hilda Violet Stuart (1930–49) came from St Leonard's to begin a considerable Scottish connection. Her eccentric brilliance had an abiding impact on girls and staff alike. Patricia Hartley (W 1946) and Mary Hallam (W 1949) remembered her appearance and preaching ability:

> She wore year-in year-out a shapeless Harris tweed coat and skirt, over which her black gown bellied out with the dignified speed of her progress, passing through the School like a galleon under full sail. She was a great orator – her short, barking delivery in Churchillian fashion made for riveting sermons, outdoing those of the local clergy: wonderful.

'HV' to the staff, 'Stu' or 'Hilda Vi' to the girls, she had a formidable mind and personality, and was devoted to her school and her girls. She brought many fresh ideas. Ruth Haslop says she 'brushed out all that class snobbery with great determination and success.' She loved drama and wrote many productions – her last, for the Jubilee in 1949, she credited to 'the swan or rather the kailyard hen, who will retire with a few strained cackles.' Her introduction of 'Creations' in the mid-1930s is well remembered; lessons were suspended for several days at the end of the Spring term (later the Summer term) to allow for creativity. Ideas ranged from marionettes, a barometer of a lady whose dress changed colour with the pressure, the blood system of a rabbit, original songs, menus for the family, crossword puzzles in different languages to models of Milton's universe and a Chinese house, and a bound and illustrated set of Chaucerian sketches based on Aldhelmsted East. Distinctions were hard to achieve but projects that gained them were quite spectacular. 'Creations' only came to an end when forced out by GCSE course work in the 1980s.

A witty, humorous talker, with a reputation for astonishing kindnesses, HV had advanced educational views. She loved to tell of her interview for the Headship: 'I was asked to promise that Darwin's theories of evolution would *not* be taught . . . I refused, but I was still appointed!' She also had visions of all her girls in careers, though her 'preaching' often fell on stony ground. Elsa Christie (A 1932) recalls,

> Miss Stuart said, 'I am glad there are now more things in the world for women to do than to be efficient man-traps.' We sighed – we longed to be efficient man-traps when we grew up.

In her last years many girls and staff however found her very difficult: 'her moods were unpredictable', remembers Anne Dixon (T 1949), and Gwen Beese (staff 1937–79) said, 'she could be quite caustic and upsetting.' For some time before her expected retirement she had made it quite clear that she did not want to go . . .

Miss Stuart presenting Cherry Williams (W 1947) with the Riding Cup.

Diana Reader Harris (1950–75) was something quite different. She was an OG (DH 1930), she had been a member of staff and as Housemistress had taken girls to Canada in the War (see Chapter 7). On her appointment, one member of staff said, 'the whole atmosphere was transformed by her attitude.' Her beauty and charisma are recorded from the time when she herself was Head Girl – and 'visiting fathers showed remarkable keenness to sit in the front row and see the strikingly tall, dark, curly-haired Head Prefect' – until Diana Gorsky (her last Head Girl) said, 'we were charmed by DRH; she had that wonderful ability of putting people at their ease.'

In her 25 years as Headmistress she faced much social change, political trouble and economic distress. Miniskirts and drugs, the antics of the left wing of the Labour Party and serious inflation were difficult enough as we shall see; but she also had to tackle an intramural 'Independent' quarrel. As President of the AHM in 1965 she presented a powerful vindication of 'schools for girls'. Leaving aside the practical problems of boys dominating discussion and laboratory work in co-educational

NO CLASS BARRIER

On lines similar to the camps for public school and working-class boys, established by the King, when Duke of York, a camp for girls was inaugurated during the week-end at Lower Eype Farm, Bridport (Dorset).

Girls from such famous schools as Roedean, Malvern and Sherborne, and an equal number from girls' clubs, including several from the East End, realised there was no class barrier.

Right: The organiser, Miss Diana Harris (English mistress at Sherborne).

Above: Janet Riddell (Sherborne), in centre, Doris McCarthy, of Millwall (left), and Betty Murphy, of Poplar.

Published in the Daily Sketch, *September 1937.*

schools, she made a rational case: the pace of emotional and intellectual development in boys and girls was at variance. Girls' career patterns (career/break for children/ career) differed, and it was essential that girls develop their poise and self-confidence in part away from the emotional turmoil of adolescent relationships.

Then in 1967 a penetrating wind blew across the Downs from Marlborough: girls were invited to apply for the VI Form of this HMC school. 'Treachery' was the view of many headmistresses; Dame Diana said, 'I was furious because of the motive.' Girls, it seemed, were a means to an end – to civilise the boys. As John Dancy, the Headmaster, said, 'It will help jettison the barbarism associated with the public school ethos.' Oakham School followed with similar motives – 'to end hobbledehoy masculinity'. Dame Diana was convinced that the whole business was untenable when she heard the remark, 'Marlborough remains a boys' school, but it is a better boys' school for having girls in it.' She could not change this attitude but she could find an alternative. In the early 1970s she initiated a plan of co-operation with Sherborne School; parents were canvassed, joint leisure activities and VI Form General Studies were discussed. Favourable responses augured well for the future – the best of both worlds? When she retired in 1975 her ideas were already being implemented.

She died in 1996. Amongst the crowds at her Memorial Service in the Abbey were many who remembered Gwen Beese's valediction in 1975, speaking of, 'her democratic and diplomatic approach to problems, her unfailing generosity and warm hospitality, plus her gifts of wit and repartee.'

Dame Diana Reader Harris at her final Commemoration as Headmistress in 1975 (see also Chapter 9).

Elizabeth Coulter (1975–85) arrived from Princess Gardens School, Belfast, to find, she said, 'a rapidly changing social and economic situation'. Her last school equipment order in Northern Ireland had been 2,000 yards of barbed wire; her first predicament at Sherborne was the oil-crisis hyperinflation which caused such alarming fee problems for parents that 'empty beds' were a serious possibility. To fill the School's 438 she found that 98 new entrants were needed, but only 42 were taking Common Entrance. So a VI Form entry was promoted (18) and another 22 pupils came from Malaysia and Hong Kong (though it soon became obvious that a number were academically weak, and some had inadequate English).

An immediate programme of reform brought pleasing results. Miss Coulter, softly spoken, intensely shy and notoriously unable to remember names, showed a particular talent: she was 'good at bricks and mortar!' Refurbishment was set in motion, aided by the arrival of Derek Willis as Bursar – his own 'good housekeeping' talents complemented the Headmistress's ambitious agenda, which included new Science and Music accommodation. She encouraged the joint activities with the Boys' School which Dame Diana had promoted; within a year General Studies courses (over 100) were under way on two afternoons a week. Attention to careers took the advice service, Miss Coulter said, 'from an optional extra to an integral part of School life'. 'Mulliner' – a separate UVI House – was fully developed as what she regarded as 'that essential bridge between boarding school and the open world of university'. She also inaugurated Staff–Parent meetings twice a year which

Elizabeth Coulter in 1975 on her appointment as Headmistress.

were much appreciated. All this helped bring the numbers back in what she admitted was the 'new, fluid and competitive world' of public school entry. Standards were reinforced – the cosmopolitan element was maintained but at a higher academic level (very high in many cases!); a tougher Common Entrance policy was adopted; and the Scholarship examination was revised to concentrate the awards on the under-13s.

Elizabeth Coulter retired in 1985. She had endorsed Dame Diana's central tenet, that it is the individual girl that matters, but left with one regret that she voiced at the Commemoration Service of that year: 'Much of the change in society today is at the expense of the individual and of individual values. The tendency to increase our efficiency at the expense of our humanity has accelerated sharply.'

The fifth, June Taylor (1985–99), will retire at the Centenary. She followed the DRH path: Head Girl (1961), Housemistress (14 years in Wingfield), and now Headmistress. She fiercely wants the best for 'her girls' – and makes a point of knowing all of them by name (a talent which miscreants do not find appealing!). She has been variously characterised: by a national schools' guide as 'tall, imposing, snowy-haired and elegant'; and by Sheila Dickson (AE 1950, Chairman of SOGU in 1985) as 'Vigilant and untiring – always finding time to arrange flowers, lead a sponsored walk, organise the props for a drama . . . and always wears a hat for occasions.' Once, when athletics points were short, she was seen running to encourage Wingfield girls who were flagging in the 1500 m! Her Head Girl in 1989, Emma Lewthwaite, discovered two other characteristics: 'June is a fantastic cook, and shares, to my immense relief, a singing standard similar to mine – *very* unmusical'.

June Taylor herself comments, 'You need to "enjoy" teaching and the contact it brings with children.' She told one girl, 'I assure you that if I have fantasies of a nine-to-five job in a bank with no girls to worry about, they are not frequent and last about three seconds.' She follows a policy of 'being accessible' – an open study door every Sunday afternoon invites girls, parents or staff to come and talk.

She is pragmatic. Whereas the first two Headmistresses might have run their school as commanders-in-chief, the next three are better identified as diplomats. As Headmistress in the educational climate of the 1990s Miss Taylor has to combine a whole range of talents: leadership in a forward-looking school with a strong ethos; pastoral care and some teaching; awareness of the brooding influence of the State as well as the media (the National Curriculum and League Tables are two such features); sympathy with the financial problems of parents; and finally, an authority which confident and articulate girls do not accept, as in previous decades, unquestioned.

She certainly welcomed the verdict on the School in one of the Press reviews in 1995: 'A work-hard, play-hard ethos; the girls are friendly, supportive and high-spirited; all-in-all a distinguished, civilised establishment.'

How independent is Independent? The right to diversity had long been recognised – the State was in fact a reluctant convert to intervention in education until well into the twentieth century: the real costs seemed too great a burden for the taxpayer. However, very early in the School's existence, Beatrice Mulliner decided that one particular association was necessary: the School must be 'recognised as efficient' by Her Majesty's Inspectorate. Full inspections followed every decade or so, and complimentary quotations from the Reports were included in the Brochure to enhance the School's status and attract able, qualified staff.

By mid-century, full inspections had given way to occasional visits from HMIs; such was the School's academic reputation that some even came to seek advice on particular matters. In the 1990s OFSTED (Office for Standards in Education) replaced HMIs and in 1995 its officials arrived at a week's notice to see some 'core' subjects – English, mathematics, science and foreign languages. 'I had reservations at first, but came to have great regard for some individual members,' June Taylor observed later. A particular example of public school suspicion of state inflexibilities occurred with the Children's Act of 1988; giving state Social Services a statutory obligation to inspect boarding schools it had an immediate impact. One instance revealed the difficulties: children, it was urged, should have 'access to the phone at all times' – this cut across the very real problem of the homesick child. Miss Taylor's verdict was that the whole operation became 'a learning experience on both sides'.

June Taylor in 1996.

The question of political intervention, even control, was not a serious issue until the 1940s. Charging fees, for instance, was as much a feature of state grammar school education as of independent schools before the 1944 Education Act. Thereafter, certain central concerns began to invade educational arguments: fee-paying was one of them, but the 'selection' controversy brought the question of public schools into sharp focus. Discussion of 'sheep and goats' roused powerful political passions, and the debate assumed rollercoaster proportions, hurtling from one extreme to another. Miss Stuart, and then Dame Diana, became closely involved.

It all began essentially with the Fleming Report of 1944. Fleming's remit was to consider the 'association' of public schools with the State's educational system. There was some favourable response from the independent sector, but also caution and reservations. Miss Stuart was invited to comment: the School was much interested in the principle of association, but the devil was in the detail: 'I emphasise the necessity of freedom and flexibility; also there must be safeguards against the danger of public schools being a depository for the uneducable.' The Report required 25 per cent of places to be set aside for state pupils, whose fees would be paid by the local authorities. In 1946 Dorset wrote to Miss Stuart for some places; her reply showed concern for a few, self-conscious, unhappy girls, but 'there are, unfortunately, no vacancies until 1951.' The Scheme nationally fizzled out as few counties were willing to face the expenditure.

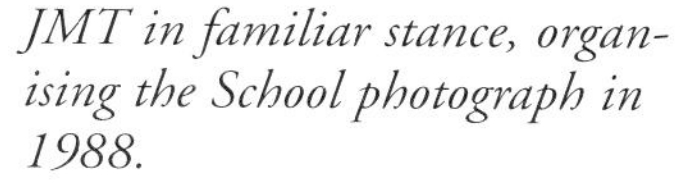

JMT in familiar stance, organising the School photograph in 1988.

In the mid-1960s Dame Diana faced a fresh state initiative – one potentially far more dangerous to independence. The Labour Government set up the Newsom Commission in 1965, 'to advise on *integrating* the public schools with the state system. It pressed for 50 per cent of places to be reserved for state pupils on a co-educational basis, and with it a socially mixed entry of wide-ability range. It was a clear effort to get public schools to adopt the Labour Government's policy of comprehensive schools; if the independent sector was not persuaded, statutory compulsion was proposed. In this context 'integration' went far beyond the Fleming 'association', though not as far as the 'abolition' policy of Labour's left wing. Some comfort was taken from the admission of the Labour minister, Anthony Crosland, that there was 'no intention of making fees for education illegal'.

Immediately the School was propelled nationally onto centre stage. Now President of the AHM, Dame Diana had to confront, she said, 'the political threat to public schools of extinction or take-over'. Over many years she wrote pamphlets for the Newsom Commission to consider, led delegations to the government, appeared in television debates, and made speeches in London, Winchester and Sheffield and as far afield as Australia and the USA. She voiced in a most effective way the Independent case, whilst accepting the need for a closer liaison with the maintained sector.

> We press for variety, not in the quality but in the type of provision. Children vary in their needs, and parents differ in what they want – remember under Section 76 of the 1944 Education Act, 'the child is to be educated in accordance with the wishes of the parents'. Education is too important to be a monopoly of the State. Many parents choose an independent boarding school for the opportunity their child will have to learn to live with other people, to learn tolerance and mutual respect – all day, seven days a week.

She regretted that education had become 'a party political issue' – children, she argued, 'should *not* be used for social engineering.' She gave a clear definition to the Newsom Commission: 'Integration suggests an organic whole in which differently run schools can co-operate.' Her detailed argument contained three points:

> First, central Government (not local authorities) must make public money available so that the best of the private sector is not confined to those who can afford full fees.
>
> Secondly, the Labour Government's assumption that public schools 'exert a divisive influence' distorts the issue; girls' schools do not themselves create discord – they reflect existing social divisions. And in the world of education I have found far more that unites us than divides us in working with the maintained schools.
>
> Thirdly, I must underline the serious problems of the 'all-ability' policy. Most girls' public schools are small: of the eighty members of the Girls' Schools Association only ten exceed 400 pupils, and only one has over 600. Such schools are not large enough to be 'comprehensive' – the traditional academic Sixth Form would effectively disappear.

The Newsom Report was published in 1968. It remained shelf-bound: the government shied away from the costs implied in the Commission's recommendations. But, crucially, it accepted the impossible predicament of Dame Diana's third point: the girls' schools were too small; Newsom would have annihilated their acknowledged excellent education. The incoming Conservative Government of 1970 agreed: 'We must concentrate on keeping what is good,' said its Education Secretary.

4
Matters Academic

Girls in my Sixth Form discussion groups may recall my using the maxim, 'education is what's left when you've forgotten what you learned' as a peg on which to hang investigations into the purpose of education. T. S. Eliot put it another way – 'Where is the *wisdom* we have lost in acquiring all that *knowledge*?' One thing is certain: the issue is highly controversial. From Dickens's Mr Gradgrind ('We want nothing but Facts, Sir, nothing but Facts!') to Muriel Spark's Miss Jean Brodie ('Education is the leading out from the soul of the child'), to Mary Warnock, philosopher, Mistress of Girton College, Cambridge, and Classics mistress at Sherborne School for Girls in the 1940s ('Education should encourage a child's imagination so that she is not a slave to the present or in chains to the environment') – the arguments on purpose have been long and often discordant. They have embraced aims, methods and content; and as they moved from educational circles into the political arena entrenched positions were adopted on matters such as selection, streaming or setting, 'general' versus 'specialist'; pejorative language, such as 'sheep and goats', crept in. Sherborne could not be immune from all this.

Beatrice Mulliner brought substantial educational baggage with her. She was enthusiastic about some radical thinking published in 1898 by the Headmistresses of Wycombe Abbey and Cheltenham: that a balanced curriculum be sought of 'Humanities, Mathematics, Science, Aesthetics and Exercise, supported by moral education pervasive through staff example and attitude and backed by Bible Study.' She was dismayed by some of the poor practice typical of many schools at that time. Arithmetic was 'doing sums' with little understanding; 'Bible work' meant learning by heart; 'domestic economy' was often studied from a textbook, with a kitchen or a laundry nowhere in sight; science was an expensive appendage. Everything seemed just memorising a host of rules, dates and formulae.

She faced formidable difficulties. Specialist teachers were rare, and in the early days there was little money for equipment or library books. But supported by Kathleen Moore and Emmeline Tanner ('Fuss' and 'Tannie' to the girls), the trio proved a powerful intellectual force. The academic ethos was soon established. It was crucial to prove that girls could match the boys; to this end girls studied and were examined in the same subjects. Character-building – Miss Mulliner's 'Code of Honour' – was a key feature, and Miss Tanner argued that it was 'far more important to train the girls' powers of reasoning than merely deliver a load of facts.' To teach the girls to think became a central tenet over the coming decades – and has remained so to the present day. The School's overall success was rewarded in an HMI Report of 1926: 'There is a tradition of hard work and respect for scholarship.'

From then onwards, the forces of change were many: fresh thinking on content and subject teaching-method; examination syllabuses and university requirements; society's perceptions blurring with parental ideas of what was 'important'; and pupil pressure in the choice of subjects made. Sherborne's reputation as a successful academic school meant traditions already established were not easily amended; new 'fashions' awaited proven practice. Proof of that reputation came in 1937 when Miss Stuart took pleasure in telling the Governors that of the 43 girls entered for School Certificate, 40 had succeeded – it was 'the largest number of successes attained by any girls' school'.

One feature that staff strove hard to maintain was a balanced curriculum. Music, sport, drama, community life all entered the equation, but within the academic sphere there were strong pressures. The influential Crowther Report, commissioned by the government in the 1960s, was fulsome in its praise of girls' schools (particularly with boarding facilities), which were 'leaders in developing general studies and programmes of broad educational content in minority time'. Sherborne was certainly one of them. Chapter 8 features much of the range – from lectures, debates and societies to General Studies with the Boys' School and Cultural Studies.

A major problem in achieving this balance has been the increasing demands of classroom subjects. The 'quart-into-a-pint-pot' syndrome has made sensible educational choices by the girls thorny and demanding, bearing in mind requirements of university entry. Dame Diana sat on many national committees favouring the extension of the traditional A-level trio to a possible five-subject package. To no avail – university fears of academic dilution fused with politicians' reluctance to forgo the talisman of 'three'.

One advantage of a balanced curriculum has been that many girls of middling academic ability were not overawed by the strong élite group of high-flyers. Also, it has been staff philosophy that to consider only the gold standard ignores the possibility of other precious metals. Since the mid-1970s parental concern and

Below: *Miss Margaret Mason taking a Sixth-Form lesson in 1911.*

Below right: *A Biology lesson in the laboratory in 1911.*

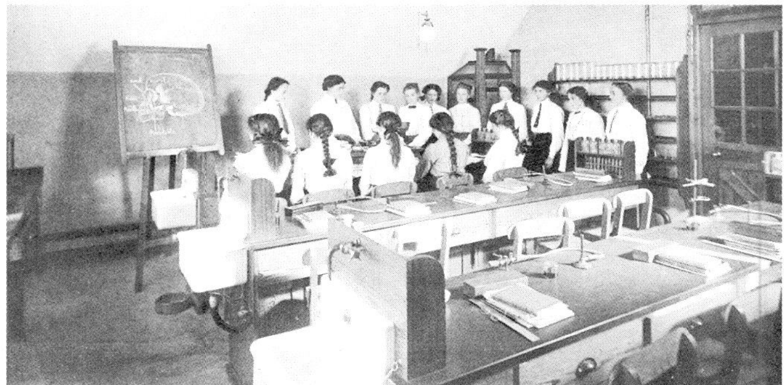

peer pressure amongst girls to achieve university and occupational status has meant a well-nigh complete three A-level pattern to Sixth-Form studies. A judicious mixture of staff chivvying and coaxing has often borne fruit: girls assessed at C/D level have raised their standards to B/C – with many happy faces on meeting entrance requirements to university. En route, the pathway was often troubled. Jane Welch (AW 1983) recorded in her diary on 16 November, 1982:

> Absolute work crisis: geography field-work and essay, plus English essay and text-notes, history essay and notes . . . lax match interrupts (lost 9:1 to Aylmar) – wash hair – elocution (Noël Coward), plus Joint Orchestra. Worried about Andrew . . . not feeling too happy.

Prior to the mid-1970s university ambitions were more muted. A dozen or more girls might stay on in the Lower Sixth to take the one-year 'Course'. Introduced in 1945, it was a sweep of studies, free of the exigencies of a public examination syllabus, covering intellectual, artistic, practical and physical work, including St John's Ambulance and Royal Life-Saving tests. Expeditions were a key feature. Fiona Morrice (AW 1959) says, 'it was the year I enjoyed most' – particularly:

> English with Mrs Egan – she really inspired me – I could have listened to her all day; the History of Everyday Things with Miss Crichton-Miller – she opened my eyes to architecture, china and furniture, and we went on field trips to Stonehenge, Stourhead and many more; and Musical Appreciation with Miss Keir – she taught us to listen to classical music.

Letters from numerous OGs reveal the excellence of many teachers. Their vitality and inspiration, and their insistence on accuracy and proper essay-writing technique were prominent. Their impact is often deeply embedded, though many OGs make a clear distinction between the merit of the teaching and the manner of its delivery! The kindly and the helpful blur in the memory with the eccentric and the dragon. Elisabeth Walwyn (DH 1956) wrote home to her mother about her Classics teacher:

> She is ghastly, Mummy. She has sharp, poky features, a steel-like voice which goes through you and she never smiles. Never! There is nothing to be said for her – *except* that she is a very good teacher. She makes us learn – not 'alf.

With few exceptions in the first half-century, staff were all spinsters; married women in numbers appeared during the Second World War, and the first male, a senior music teacher, came in 1945. Men were still a rarity when Iain Stuart Robertson came as Director of Art in 1963, but by the time I arrived in 1972 we were viewed by the girls as part of the furniture! Like some Housemistresses, many academic staff were characterised by their longevity of service. As familiar fixtures of OGs' childhood it may surprise many that over a dozen staff taught for more than 30 years, with four in the 40s! – Gwen Beese and Marjorie Heywood – 43 years each, Violet Barnett – 41 and Harriet Hamilton – 40. Equally familiar were the idiosyncratic expressions: Anne Dixon's 'Henry the Nav. and William the

Above right: *A LVI 'Course' visit to London: the official photograph with Simon Wingfield Digby MP (Civil Lord of the Admiralty) at the House of Commons in 1953.*

Above: *The unofficial version of such a visit: Ruth Walwyn's (DH 1951) cartoon of the 'Course' crossing Westminster Bridge.*

Conq.', Margot Willmott's 'If you can't get an essay in on time, how will you be able to prepare your husband's supper?', and 'Non-Flopsy Bunnies' were Iain Stuart Robertson's nudes in Renaissance art.

'Shall I ever forget . . . ?' OGs' indelible memories of just a few spanning the century:

> Mrs H. O. Hamilton – we called her 'H_2O' – taught us Chemistry. It was terrifying and explosive, but fascinating. After a two-hour lesson we were wrung out for the rest of the day.
>
> Joan Burchardt (DH 1936) and Anne Dixon (T 1949)

> Margaret Beese and her sister Gwen, 'Baby Beese' and 'Big Beese' to us all. Gwen would gallumph into the classroom trilling 'Salvete Puellae' and we'd morosely respond 'Salve Magistra'. From then on I can't tell you how much fun it was learning *The Iliad.*
>
> Elspeth Nicol (T 1953)

> A magnificent figure for a Gauguin picture – black hair, large dangling earrings and exotic coloured dresses . . . Only a few weeks to go to the exam – Bice Bannerman Crichton Miller took over the Divinity Class. She took the class by storm saying we were all dim and knew nothing. In a panic, we snapped out of our laid-back boredom. She crammed into weeks more than we'd learnt in years . . . I remember her cry of 'My dear old bird', and the awful threat of becoming a shop girl in Bourne and Hollingsworth if one did not attend!
>
> Lorna Harman (AW 1936), Pauline Carter (AE 1935), Rosalind Turpin (AW 1964)

> Mr Norman Simpson taught me in the Sixth. He was a 'Mr Chips' figure, an unlikely object of interest for adolescent girls, elderly, scholarly and modest; he seemed unworldly, yet his lessons were a wonderful forum for ideas on politics, philosophy and human behaviour. They gave us a breathing space of civilised thought amidst all the pressures and trials of life in the Sixth.
>
> Judith Mothersill (E 1968)

Inevitably, there were imperfections over so many years, so many studies and so many teachers. Two subjects illustrate a generality which, judging from OGs' responses, was infrequent. Cicely Ballard (DH 1930) found her history teacher's technique 'deplorable – blackboard dates of kings, battles, wars which we duly copied: that was it'; and Claudia Horsfield (AW 1975) resented her Housemistress telling her she was 'not clever enough to do A-level History' (she was eventually to study it at Bristol University!). The 'Remove' was also intensely disliked: 'humiliating,' said Fiona Morrice, 'especially as my teacher scorned my two out of seven O-levels.' Mechanical copying, the bugbear of so many school-days, soon disappeared, whilst today a more sympathetic ear is given to girls' academic progress. In Science, criticism was of restrictions. In the 1950s Caroline Wilson (AE 1958) says, 'I arrived in the LV – as Physics was introduced in the UIV I missed out!' Cynthia Shepherd (W 1960) also complained: 'I never had a Biology lesson in my life, and sex education was non-existent'; this last was not a new complaint: 'I knew nothing about sex. It was only from the *Bible* I got hints of the adult world. I spent hours surreptitiously looking-up words like "womb" and 'conceive' in an encyclopedia,' said Joy Rathbone (W 1931).

Over the century subjects have witnessed sea-changes as much in the method of teaching as in content, especially in the Sixth.

The first-class teaching of Mathematics, referred to in the 1926 Inspection, removed old prejudices that the subject could lastingly damage the female brain! In the ensuing years it acquired a rigorous, scholarly reputation with girls achieving the highest standards both at School and university – in the 1950s and 1960s there were three Cambridge mathematicians in the Department. John Rees (staff 1980–90) argues, 'it is a naked subject from which there is no escape', stressing staff virtues of great patience and endless encouragement needed to overcome junior apprehension. Janet Robson (staff 1993–) says the real change has been the exit of the 'tricks-of-the-trade' approach and the arrival of a proper understanding of mathematical processes. 'Sooner or later all of us meet a problem we cannot immediately solve, underlining the importance of precision, logic and proof.' Information Technology, now an integral part of the curriculum, has opened up a new world of resources, but Miss Robson stresses, 'students must be critical in their use of it.'

Science, encouraged early on, had more effort put into getting equipment and fine laboratories than into persuading girls to continue their studies. 'There is little time allowed,' criticised the HMIs, and 'almost nothing in the Sixth.' This changed as Mrs Hamilton (staff 1923–63), made her mark. By the late 1920s many girls were studying Science in the Sixth and pursuing it to university level. New staff brought new ideas. Christiana Burchardt (staff 1941–73) prided herself on being ahead of her time and brought in 'hands-on investigations' in Biology to counter the prevailing 'tell-them' approach. In Chemistry most OGs remember 'bottles' predominating until the 1970s when greater emphasis on skills took over. 'Salters' Chemistry was introduced by Donald Mathewson (staff 1983–94): whereas traditional examination syllabuses were 'top-down', to prepare children

A page from the Physiology and Zoology Sixth-Form notebook of Alice Dove (Ald 1915), the first OG to qualify as a doctor at University College Hospital, London.

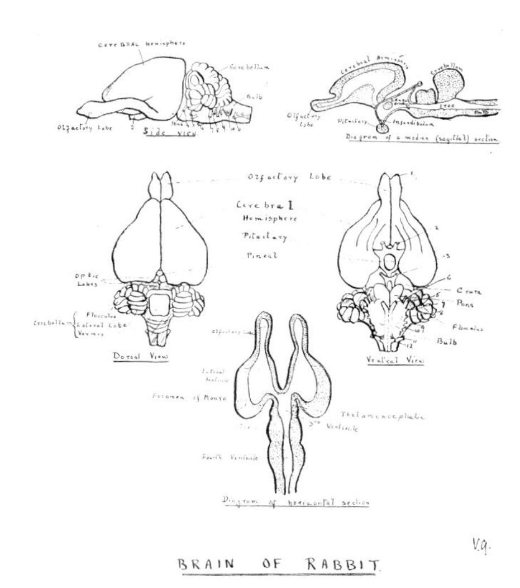

From top to bottom:
Delphi: part of a 'Classical Civilisation' visit to Greece, 1990;
The German 'exchange' visit to Calw in the Black Forest, 1994;
French' girls stayed with families while visiting Paris in 1995.

for possible university study, this worked 'bottom-up' from a child's own experience of, say, carrier bags and clothing, then on to polymers. It was an interesting experiment. The arrival of Hassan Qasrawi (staff 1973–), 'Dr Q' to the girls, brought a new balance to the sciences. He ended the 'Biology-for-the-less-able' image in 1978 when everyone took the subject. At the same time Social Biology appeared in the Sixth Form, with its attraction for Arts girls. The Sciences are expensive, their costs have mushroomed, and he says that even without capital expenditure, the annual budget for everyday teaching at Sherborne is £10,000.

By the mid-1920s HMI thought that English Literature was taught with great enthusiasm, though the amount of formal grammar was considered excessive. English retained its widespread appeal through the decades to come with the main thrust today on literature. There is much scope for individual reading, though where to find the time in a crowded curriculum is a chronic difficulty. Oral assessment came with the arrival of GCSE in the mid-1980s as did course work; Angela Pitt's (staff 1978–) verdict is, 'Much more rigorous'.

Classics formed a major academic study from the beginning, and HMI comment in 1926 centred on the problem of 'how to set a brisk pace without loss of accuracy'. The 43-year reign of Gwen Beese (staff 1936–79) gave it vigorous continuity, but since the 1970s curriculum pressures have made change inevitable. Latin and some Greek *are* taught today, but with the emphasis more on literature than language. Charles Simpson (staff 1972–) seized upon the broad appeal of Classical Civilisation (over 20 students at times in each of the sixth forms), so that Homeric poems and biennial visits to Greece became much appreciated!

The Modern Languages Department, too, has always been a strong one. Of the five French staff in the 1920s three were of French nationality. HMIs praised the oral work and how 'well-arranged lessons rounded-up the stragglers'. German, Italian and Spanish were taught, but to very few. Today Russian and Italian are taught at A-level (with some Japanese being introduced), to add to French, German and Spanish on offer throughout the School. Equipment abounds, with a sophisticated satellite system in operation; listening and speaking now form half the examination marks; and in 1997 literature questions were answered in the vernacular. Daphne West (staff 1978–97) says, 'I'm pleased that the spoken language reigns supreme.'

Exchanges and visits have proliferated. UV 'German' girls regularly go to Calw in the Black Forest; return visits were planned in 1997. An important Russian connection was established in the 1980s, when some Soviet teachers, nervous and watching the 'Party line', came to the School; visits *to* the Soviet Union began in 1982. Daphne West's memories are of 'the courage and generosity of Russian friends merged in with harrowing dealings with Soviet bureaucracy.' Student exchanges became regular in the post-Soviet era – deep into Russia at Perm in the southern Urals. Close friendships remain – and frantic visa problems, though Dr West says, '*Now* we can fax directly and not go through the Moscow phone operator!' Ten Perm girls for a week at School has always been an interesting experience, not to say cultural shock. My memory is of Russian teachers and girls coming to UV History lessons when I was teaching the Russian Revolution; '1917' saw no difficulties, but 'Trotsky and Stalin' provoked awkward moments in the 1980s.

Geography, History and Scripture paralleled each other over the century. All three featured strongly in the early curriculum. Miss Mulliner took the whole School for Religious Teaching – classes of 60 'admirably taught but with overemphasis on the Gospels', declared the 1926 HMI Report. Both Geography and History tried hard to escape from the rote-learning inheritance of the nineteenth century, when History also seemed riddled with moralising over the doings and misdoings of kings. Emmeline Tanner (staff 1904–49) had to write her own history textbook in order to 'promote thinking rather than memorising'. In the early 1920s the subject was praised for its skilful questioning and the girls' note-taking. Geography at that time (under Miss Langridge, the first woman to gain a double First in Geography at Cambridge) was adjudged to be the best-taught subject in the School, acquiring spectacular university results. Yet by mid-century, all three subjects with their 'chalk-and-talk' approach, had diminishing appeal: few pursued Scripture to examination level; Geography O-level had a handful of candidates in 1973 and its fieldwork was minimal; History's larger numbers faced routine questions ('Describe the achievements of Gladstone's First Ministry') – their answers would have pleased Mr Gradgrind!

The 1970s and 1980s witnessed transformations. Religious Studies under Ruth Gee (staff 1986–95) introduced challenging work depending much more on understanding; and a Christian Ethics paper at A-level increased the candidates from one to over 20! 'Chalk' in Geography and History gave way to video and computer work, but more importantly problems and investigations became central to studies. David Horsfall (staff 1974–97) says, 'there were fewer neat answers'; the expansion of fieldwork was critical – 'girls in their local studies test assertions, examine arguments and investigate problems such as Sherborne's traffic congestion.' In the end something understood is what matters – pursued in History through detailed patch studies and original documents with their inherent bias. 'What happened' is still important, but 'why' is now pivotal in making sense of the past.

Two Sixth Form subjects, Economics and History of Art, had quite startling beginnings. The first was introduced in the early 1980s, its popularity (29 candidates in 1990) reflecting booming national financial services, but by the mid-1990s had subsided to a normal ten. History of Art used to be an appendage of Art syllabuses until the arrival of Iain Stuart Robertson (staff 1963–96). He said, 'Then, I had one candidate'; within five years it became an independent A-level with 33 girls clamouring for the course. Rigorous in his academic approach, 'Daddyo' had an infectious love of the subject, so that Sara Williams (W 1977), a mathematician by instinct, was heard years later expounding to travellers on a London Underground platform on the significance of a painting chosen to advertise a forthcoming exhibition. A particular appeal has been the thesis – themes have ranged from jewellery of Ancient Egypt, the sophistication of African Masks and the gothic glory of Fan Vaulting to the architecture of shopping – from stall to mall – and

From top to bottom:
A Sixth-Form Russian visit to Perm in south Urals, 1991;
40 'History of Art' girls visited Italy in 1995: sketch pad example.

Wren's London churches, bombed and unbombed.

Art and Housecraft were praised by HMIs in the 1920s, but seen as restrictive – 'drawing but little craft', and only Needlework was compulsory with Cookery a Saturday 'extra' for many years. Both subjects have seen changes. 'Home Economics' became more coherent, and syllabuses were developed to ensure that, 'a grounding in science was as important as the ability to make a charlotte russe.' Art spread its wings both physically and in content. So many girls knew only cramped accommodation until the new Art Studio of 1988. Jean Burton (staff 1985–94) remembers, 'In order to reach girls in the corner, I had to climb over desks.' Pottery and textiles had long been added to drawing, but now windows, doors, mirrors, cartwheels and rusty tins replaced the still life of fruit and pots, whilst nudes appeared in the life-class. Mrs Burton's philosophy: 'Art is full of risk and emotion – girls feel vulnerable, thinking and manipulating materials. I keep the adrenalin flowing.'

Jenny Newman (staff 1994–) agrees. The range of opportunities has widened and much impressed the examiners: life-classes are weekly; visits to Amsterdam and Paris regularly scheduled. Meanwhile, Anne Legg (staff 1987–) set up CDT – with £42,000 worth of equipment – but is never quite sure whether her design technology work puts her in 'Art' or 'Physics'. The recent spectacular impact on Art of these two staff may be seen in the various colour pictures throughout this book.

'Pick up your pens – you may start writing *now.*' Comprising so many routines central to School life, examinations were, and are, seen as necessary evils by both staff and girls. Miss Mulliner stressed in 1910, 'the gaining of certificates is not the aim of teaching', and today many staff regret that national pressures – particularly the National Curriculum and League Tables – make education so examination-driven. Girls though recognise that they *do* need paper qualifications.

Rituals are legion: frenetic question-spotting, leisurely revision when sunbathing on the lawn or Old Mulliner roof, frantic last-minute swotting outside the examination room – the staff, despite decades of persuasion tactics, have never been convinced of the value of any of these.

The formalities begin early. Common Entrance, developed in 1947, has to be negotiated; perhaps a scholarship attempted, with its attendant nerve-wracking interview (I'm sure that in 1975 Katie Howells (W 1979) interviewed *me* – I failed to get in a word: she got her scholarship!). Then comes the mark-grubbing of the November tests, to be followed by the annual examinations. By the UV girls are seasoned examinees, awaiting School Certificate (1917), O-level (1951) or GCSE (1988). The last was a revolution: it required more thinking and less recall, with the girls being required to do something with what they knew. For the staff it was both exhilarating (we had pressed for years for this) and exasperating (the politicians brought it in at speed). Parents were suspicious – 'My daughter's a guinea pig,' said one, 'I should have conceived her a year later!'

Patterns of Sixth Form work have significantly altered. There were only six girls in the Sixth in 1916; by 1934 there were 23 in the *Upper* Sixth; 60 was the usual number by 1970. Today that figure is around 80 and every girl takes three A-levels because of university and professional requirements. Until the 1960s these were not always needed: a solicitor's training did not require a degree, and only a handful of O-levels was needed to teach small children. The academically inclined tried Oxford and Cambridge entrance directly, ignoring Higher Certificate. These girls paved the way for the School's rising academic reputation. Winifred Dixon went to read History at Westfield College in 1906 – the School's first university entrant; only three more followed before 1914. In the ensuing 12 years 66 gained places, five of them getting Oxford or Cambridge 'Firsts'. In 1932 Miss Stuart proudly announced, 'Two Sherborne girls were the only successful women candidates in the Chemistry of Cambridge 1st MB.'

In these early years the girls focused on a limited number of universities. In 1922, 38 girls were at university – ten at Oxford, seven at Cambridge, 20 at London and one at Durham; by 1944 Edinburgh, St Andrew's, Bristol, Exeter and Reading universities became 'acceptable'.

The mid-1970s saw huge national changes. Oxford and Cambridge colleges went mixed, and new universities and new-style courses were attracting greater numbers (a mere 50,000 entry in 1939 became 140,000 in 1965 and 280,000 in 1995). For girls at Sherborne the new opportunities seemed exciting and endless, and parents wanted to be more closely involved in decision-making. As university adviser in 1972 the task was relatively straightforward, with around 35 successful applicants each year. By 1980 it had risen to 50 and in 1991 I recorded 83. Choices became complex. The style and reputation of a university or course mattered to both girl and parent; preferences were shown – 'Oxbridge', 'Redbrick' or 'Glass-façade'; and the number of interesting, non-school courses meant adventurous decisions, as did the merits of immediate or deferred entry. Parents had to be persuaded: citing 60 per cent of degree-level occupations *not* being related to the degree studied and the case of Jane Williams (E 1979) – with French, Greek and History A-levels, an Oxford degree in Hebrew and Arabic, who then went into computing – was usually sufficient. The whole effect was a broadening of horizons.

A-level performance improved from an 82 per cent pass rate in 1975 to 96 per cent in the mid-1990s; in 1988 a quarter of all these results were Grade A, twice the national average. The choice of universities and courses became more varied.

In the 1980s, 478 girls took degree courses at:

Oxford	43 (6 to The Queens, 6 to St Anne's)
Cambridge	29 (7 to Trinity)
London	61
Durham	37
Bristol	36
Manchester	32
Edinburgh	28

(universities which were the traditional 'Ivy League' focus of girls' ambitions)
Also, among others: Leeds, Southampton, St Andrew's, Reading, Sussex, Birmingham, Nottingham and York.

Courses, single and combined:	
Foreign Languages	185
includes Russian, 48	
Classics, 17	
and Chinese, Hebrew, Arabic and Anglo-Saxon	
Mathematics and Science	101
includes Medicine, Dental, Veterinary, 26	
and Biological Sciences, 28	
Psychology	13
Engineering	7 (none in the 1970s)
History, Politics, Law	66
Geography & Land Management	34
Economics & Business Studies	38
History of Art	47

Sherborne girls mirrored general trends. The days (1965) when only a quarter of university undergraduates were female and a mere 480 women studied with 20,000 men in Applied Science were long gone. Girls are well aware of their 'employability' in IT and the service industries, where their 'presence' and oral skills are valued. But the pace of change in the politics of equal opportunities is still very slow.

Finally, advising the girls on university entry produced its own rituals. First, the UCCA form – the niceties of which order to place the preferences; the inability of highly intelligent girls to get elementary facts right (their date of birth even); positions held at school? 'House Baby' wrote one; the dread of the Headmistress's reference – 'will she remember when I disgraced myself . . . ?' Secondly, the Interview – 'remember to smile and keep eye-contact' . . . how to deal with probing questions ('What makes *you* think you could fit into a college community of 300?' and 'Define corruption') . . . and what to do with the easy chair and the glass of sherry?

> I consciously sat upright and ignored the sherry; then came the awkward question, so I took a sip whilst I searched my brain for the fourth cause of the French Wars of Religion . . .

. . . and Tina Hippisley (E 1981) was in at Trinity, Cambridge.

DISTINGUISHED OLD GIRLS

MARY LASCELLES
(A 1918)

Mary Madge Lascelles, English scholar and Vice-Principal of Somerville College, Oxford 1947–60.

Amongst Sherborne's many OGs pursuing an academic career, Mary was clearly outstanding. An English scholar, she made Oxford University her spiritual as well as her actual home for nearly 40 years. What she enjoyed most were her tutorials in Somerville College, where she had a formidable reputation as a great teacher – though many of her students remember her just as vividly for her standards of integrity, precision and punctuality. 'Books and food on the same table: that is my definition of squalor,' she informed one girl; others 'suffered' from her disapproval over slang. Exact timing was her most memorable trait: one unfortunate rang the bell of Mary's rooms three minutes late for a tutorial to be greeted, 'You have come at last; I shall just go and re-heat the scones.' Known as 'The Lass' to generations of students, one said, 'she always left you with the impression that literature was exciting.' It was this reputation which mattered – far above her professional promotions from Fellow to Vice-Principal of her College, and to the prestigious Readership at the University. She was quietly proud of her election as Fellow of the British Academy in 1962, the result of her scholarly writings. In 1939 she wrote *Jane Austen and her Art* which was widely reviewed and applauded for its fresh insight; still in print in the 1990s it is quoted as one of the key authorities to study. Her *Selected Poems* was published in 1990 – in her 90th year.

5
Nine Houses

In the 1971 Staff Revue, *Those Were the Days*, a performance was given of 'A Trumpet Voluntary for Housemistresses', sung to the tune 'British Grenadiers'.

> Inside that noble building, some Amazons you'll find,
> A race of eight fine women, the ablest of their kind;
> From early in the morning, 'til after night does fall,
> They watch their little darlings, and answer every call.
>
> They solve all parents' queries, they tot up 'washing slips';
> They hold their court in drawing rooms, with problems come to grips.
> You can see them on the games field, on fair days and on foul,
> For like the hosts of Midian, they're always on the prowl!

Unlike OGs, who are expansive, even candid, Housemistresses are notoriously guarded, even reticent, about *their* views of the realities of House life. However, Anne Dixon (A 1966–83) gives a personal insight saying, 'Housemistresses are a very powerful species; they must exercise care to prevent their reigns becoming ego-trips. In my experience we had to jolly girls along and give them something – us! – to kick against.' No personal commentaries survive from the first half of the School's history, but snapshots of more recent years can be seen in accounts by two of East's Housemistresses. Jean Stewart (1969–78) writes:

> I took over a House in good order, which responded well to the inevitable changes of a new regime. The day began with a ship's bell (mine!) rung by the prefect on duty at 6.40 a.m. – breakfast at 7.15. Then I discussed the day with Head of House and Games Captain, before the girls went over to school. Getting to know new girls was best done in 'drawing room' before supper – round the open fire, trust and confidence were nourished while talking or playing 'racing demon'. Prayers before supper with the whole House was a quiet gathering of thoughts. Meals were at round, eight-seater tables, with a rota of places to ensure mixing – crucial to my ambition of creating a sense of family and friendship, with thoughtfulness for others, courteous behaviour and honouring of commitments key features of our unwritten rules.
>
> I shared good times with my prefects, and a particular pleasure were the musical or discussion-focused December suppers with Lyon House prefects from the Boys' School. End-of-term suppers were lively: the 'Stair Race' followed in which the House 'baby' battled it out with the Housemistress (baby up, me down), the whole house shouting encouragement. I ran 27, only winning one! In the summer we had picnics

near Abbotsbury – always happy occasions.

Some sadnesses however: the deepest wounds a girl could receive came from the separation of parents – it was my privilege through faith and experience to give counsel.

Aldhelmsted East
after 1st Bishop of Sherborne
Ald.1903; Ald. Senior 1912; East 1938 – *Faciendum Est* – Violet
House of: BCM–30; Ritchie–7; Heywood–15; Stewart–9; McConnell–5
Legend: HJ's electric clock to remedy East's fabled unpunctuality.

Aldhelmsted West
after 1st Bishop of Sherborne
Ald.1903; Ald.Junior 1912; West 1932 – *Not for oneself but for all* – Pink
House of: BCM–30; Drever-Smith–19; Egan–11; Ashe–11; Downing–9; BJ–14.
Legend: sleeping in the School corridor in 1941 after the air raids.

Key: House name; origin; date of foundation; *motto*; colour; long-serving Housemistresses.

Sally McConnell (1989–95) added her own slant:

> I was the 'new girl' – even to private education. It took time to absorb well-established traditions and a bewildering geography; I had been there some time when I wandered through a 'cupboard door' to discover a dormitory I didn't know existed! Whirlwind activities: lectures, matches, bonfire parties, the trauma of November tests . . . the jolly, under-rehearsed Christmas 'entertainment', and the 'Ghost Train' (why did nobody warn me of its horrendous noise?).
>
> Keen House spirit is shown at its best in that most competitively atmospheric occasion, the Dancing Competition, with its frenzied rehearsing. Then in the summer the girls giving way to Wimbledon ambitions on our grass courts, the end of term barbecue, swimming . . . I feel proud of the House, seeing everyone getting on so well, playing silly games and enjoying each other's company.

Emily Armitage (Ald 1910), the first OG to be appointed Housemistress.

All this had well-established foundations. A brief anthology of Housemistresses from the first six decades shows the stern to the benign. Margaret Mason, the great all-rounder in Dun Holme – teacher of Mathematics *and* Classics, coaching hockey *and* tennis . . . the frail Muriel Davis, who ran Classics, the *School Magazine* and Dun Holme for 21 years . . . Augusta Perry, in control of Ealhstan for 20 years, remembered affectionately for understanding the girls' need to let off steam ('wild hockey games in the attic on wet days,' said one girl). Frances Hoyle had 18 years at Wingfield – she was so steeped in Classics that *The Times* obituary said of her, 'she never used a short word when she could use a long one; a train was never shaky, it oscillated' . . . Emily Armitage Sherborne's first OG Housemistress had 13 years in Aylmar revealing a cheerful, generous-minded spirit – 'how thankful I was to send my daughter into her care,' said one OG . . . 'Tags', Frances Taylor, ran Wingfield for 20 years; formidable and devoted to her girls – she even apprenticed herself to a carpenter in

Dun Holme Sitting Room, c.1910.

Facing page: *Juliet Haysom (T 1996) in the Art Studio: for an exercise in tonal contrast and proportion, she created this charcoal-and-chalk work by enlarging to 7ft (2m) a small, 6in (15cm) box full of organic and inorganic objects.*

order to start woodwork classes for them! . . . Marjorie Heywood, 'Fuss', who was in East for 15 years, always busy with her embroidered cushions. Ethel Williams, 'Willy' the Irish hockey international, was mistress of Thurstan for 28 years – 'fierce, but how she could bat' – remembered also for her lack of prowess behind the car wheel ('we were a healthy House – *no one* wanted to be driven to the San by her') . . .and her friend Cecil Armitage, 24 years in neighbouring Ealhstan, both to be seen striding to the pool every morning.

'Below-stairs' provides another interesting vantage point for life in House. Nellie Webb came as No 3 Housemaid to Aylmar in 1934, aged 14.

> Hard work was no stranger to me: I knew how to scrub, polish and clean. I worked with Ivy the cook, Violet the parlourmaid, Iris the 1st housemaid, Molly the kitchenmaid and Mrs Bryant the cleaning lady. My days began at 6 a.m., tidying the Matron's sitting-room, doing the grate: then I brushed the front stair-carpet, scattering moist tea-leaves once a week to bring up the colour (no vacuum cleaner!). The 'Young Ladies' – we all addressed them as 'Miss . . . ' – would come rushing down to breakfast. Afterwards I started on Matron's bedroom, before going to 'my' dormitory with its 18 cubicles, two bathrooms and a toilet. Mopping, dusting and polishing the wooden floor once a week with a heavy weight covered in cloth . . . taking 'little packets' from the lockers to be burnt and being teased by the boiler-man . . . a quick change of uniform to wait at table. After lunch I helped in the kitchen . . . then two hours rest in our large attic. We had one halfday a week and one Sunday a month off.
>
> I was a keen observer of how 'the other half' lived – some of the young ladies were very friendly, others rather condescending. The Matron was kind, even taking me to my aunt during the holidays in her two-seater, bull-nosed Morris. I was fortunate in my two years at the School – with good food and comfortable quarters, I felt superior to factory and shop girls. I earned ten-shillings a week.

Aldhelmsted Dining Room, c.1910.

LIFE
DAYOF
greatest
Juliet

Examples of the creativity of the Design and Technology Department; all work is fashioned from raw materials. Except for bottom left, these were GCSE projects.

Above: *Hannah Clarke's (AE 1994) American walnut and silver communion bowl for use in Bradford Abbas Church (her grandfather had been vicar); the design is based on motifs and carvings to be found in the church.*

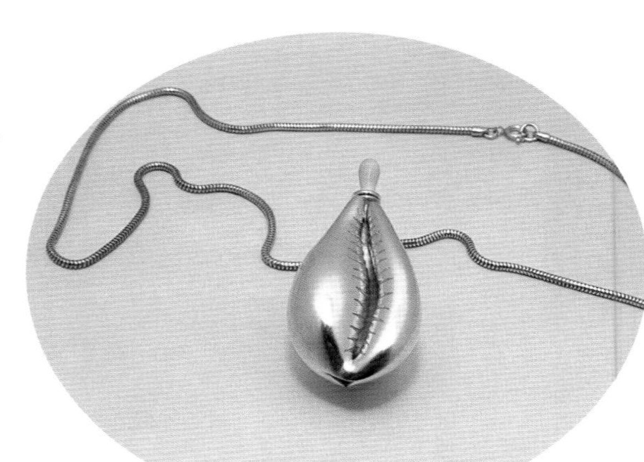

Right: *Joy Green's (AW 1994) 1½-inch (42mm) sterling silver and bone kohl or perfume-holder necklace, based on a Kenyan cowrie shell design of her aunt's tribe.*

Left: *Alison Ebdon's (K 1994) firescreen, 2½ft (75cm) high, is made of elm, sycamore and lime, with the dragon inlaid.*

Below: *Florence Lau's (DH 1996) jewellery box, with its Chinese-design silver motif, was made for her mother in 1994; 7ins (18cm) high, it is made of English walnut and sterling silver.*

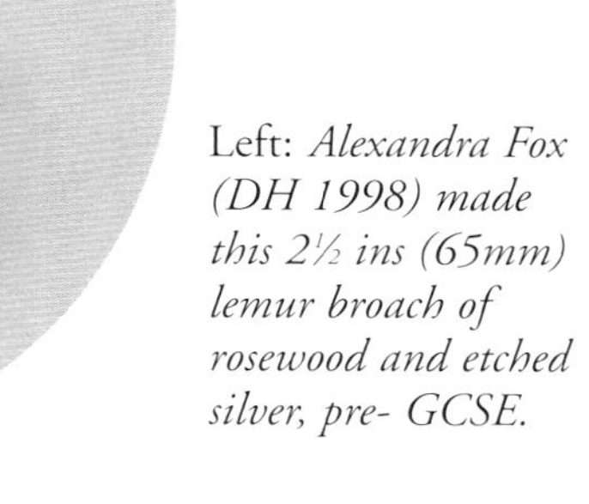

Left: *Alexandra Fox (DH 1998) made this 2½ ins (65mm) lemur broach of rosewood and etched silver, pre- GCSE.*

DUN HOLME
after Bishop of Durham's cathedral hill – 1907 – Blue
House of: Moore–10; Mason–9; Davis–21; Downing–20; Guinness–6; Bowyer–9
Legend: a blue ghost cow on DH's tennis courts on moonlit nights.

Look. Here is Dun Holme: red-bricked, moon-licked,
much-kicked building. Cars vrrooming by. But Dun Holme
sleeps. Suddenly a flickering light interrupts the night. See
the shadow, writhing, wriggling against the bath-room wall,
of Matron preparing for bed . . . Peace at last, toasting
in front of wood fire, sipping steaming mug of coffee . . .
(cat-like creeping, sneak-like peeping, ape-like
leaping, prefects keeping . . . ORDER)

Henrietta Bulley (DH 1977)
(apologies to Dylan Thomas's *Under Milk Wood*)

What of the girls? The newcomers first. 'It's all so BIG, everyone so hardworking, so tall,' said one.

School train from Waterloo: bewildering for the new girls – valiant attempts by seniors to relax the tension – give up: old hands go off to restaurant car for hot buttered toast, a final, boisterous unsupervised fling.

Margaret Woodcock (K 1939)

Aylmar in 1922, taken from the edge of the main School.

> I came from a sheltered, rural home, with a visiting governess. I felt overshadowed by the forbidding, massive figure of Miss Mulliner.
>
> Margery Colborne (DH 1925)

Homesickness inevitably affected some:

> I arrived in 1947 – a year of misery. I was small but at 11 got a scholarship. Homesick and insecure I became insufferably bumptious – ostracised and made to go around with the plain, brainy girl of House. I got wiser, then loved living in Thurstan.
>
> Elspeth Nichol (T 1953)

> I suffered the pain of separation from parents at 12 – a clever, older sister didn't help. But I learned to cope and it toughened me up.
>
> Claudia Horsfield (A 1975)

The dormitory and the cubicle left deeply imbedded memories. Fiona Morrice (AW 1959) remembers the jargon as if it were yesterday:

> West had seven dorms: on the top floor were Top West 8, White Dorm, Top 5; on the first floor, Bottom Far 8, Bottom 5, Bottom 7 and The Slums.

Summers were marvellous, but the winters before modern central heating were rugged. Elsa Christie (A 1932) says,

> Heating was only one pipe running along the outside wall. Our cue windows *had* to be open top and bottom; no hotwater bottles were allowed then – only bedsocks. There was ice in our water-jugs in the morning. I grew up tough!

Patricia Hartley (W 1946) also recalls the 10-inch open windows: 'we put overcoats on the bed, and before it was time to dress we pulled our underclothes into bed to warm them up.' Sheena Forman (E 1937) remembers the morning exercises in the dorm: 'swinging our arms and legs, it must have been some sight to watch with all our shapes and sizes.' Today, after the stampede down the stairs for breakfast, the far-distant East exhibits an ambiguous pride.

> 7.55 a.m. Set off for School; come wind, rain, sleet or snow,
> Eastie Beasties are expert.

The closer Dun Holme however claims with self-satisfied smugness:

> 8.10 a.m. DH pack runs to School; it is obligatory to be late
> and provide a feeble excuse.

In the evening, Margaret Woodcock (K 1939) records, 'the "babies" left the drawing room at 8 o'clock, followed by status at half-hourly intervals', though even today the Pres' 10.30 bedtime 'tends to stretch'. Something akin to 'fagging' used to exist but not by name: '"cueing" we called it,' said Elizabeth Gibson (E 1969), 'it was a kind of genteel fagging. I was allocated to Helen in the UVI, and filled her hot-water bottle every night!' The luxury of a hot bath is well remembered – except in 1974 during the Miners' Strike and coal crisis. Diana Gorsky (AW 1976) wrote home, 'They've turned the heating off in House, and we're only allowed a 3-inch bath, three times a week.'

Sleeping outside on the lawn, impossible to imagine for today's security-conscious generation, was pleaded for in the hot summers. Fiona Morrice recalls,

> begging Mrs Egan: then the bedsteads were put out in the House garden and after supper we dragged out mattresses and bedding. Later we went out in housecoats and curlers amidst junior giggles.

For others there was pleasure *and* pain: earwigs and cockcroaches in the cold mornings . . . or the inevitable chaos if it rained.

WINGFIELD
founder's family name
1911 – *Possunt Quia Posse Videntur* – Yellow
House of: Hoyle–20; Taylor(F)–20; BBCM–22; JMT–14; Glasby–10
Legend: Miss Hoyle's 'crocodile' walking across the fields on a rainy afternoon.

AYLMAR
after a Digby family name
1911 – *Determined, More determined, Most determined* – Red
House of: Rowe–25; Armitage–13; Kershaw–19; Dixon–17;
Scott-Moncrieff–15+
Legend: Nurse Alsford who first made the School's djibbahs.

The camaraderie was often close, intense even. Housemistresses striving for a family spirit were well rewarded. In 1992 West girls described the period after the prep. hour:

> 8.00 p.m. Freedom! The atmosphere between the years is very friendly – time for chatting, laughing, drinking coffee, eating loads of biscuits . . . practising, rehearsing, playing games.

Housemistresses' 'Drawing Room' time could be relaxing, though some found conversation 'stiff'. Josephine Gardner (AW 1937) thoroughly enjoyed being with Miss Boughey – 'most motherly! it was a great change to sit in mufti and silk stockings in real armchairs and talk in a civilised way.' Many OGs mentioned the discussions or being read to round a roaring fire; or happy summer Sunday afternoons – 'no cricket, writing home, a good book – a new Ian Hay or Dornford Yates and a boiled sweet – then dripping for tea' (Lucy Hayne, A 1931). More recently, access to the phone has been vital: most Houses in the 1970s had two phone nights for incoming calls, but there had to be 'a gentleman's agreement not to hog the coinbox phone for outgoings' (Jane Williams E 1979).

Weekends, especially Sundays, could 'drag a bit', but there were always the Games, the Plays, the Films and Jaunts. Margaret Woodcock (K 1939) remembers, 'consequences, jacks, racing demon and the newly invented Monopoly'; and Phoebe Cresswell (A 1942) enjoyed 'Murder, Sardines and Charades on winter evenings'. The House play – everybody involved, including the Housemistress as producer,

Cecilia Leete's (AE 1977) design for the House play programme.

Wingfield, 1961: Bice Crichton-Miller (middle row, centre); on her right is June Taylor, Head Girl, and to follow BBCM as Wingfield Housemistress ten years later.

stage manager and i/c make-up all in one – was a major activity from the 1930s through to the 1970s; in 1941, 17 plays were put on competitively. The range was considerable, from *The Merchant of Venice* (Wingfield, 1961), to numerous productions of *Alice in Wonderland* (Kenelm 1947 and 1953, East 1976). The *en masse* exit to see a film on Saturday evenings was much enjoyed: occasionally to Sherborne's town cinema in the 1930s, but regularly to the School Hall from 1940 onwards. *Richard III*, *The Conquest of Everest* – 'rather uplifting films in the early days,' said one girl, but 'I saw every James Bond in my five years,' records another.

Everyone anticipates with glee the end-of-term supper and entertainment, of which the Ghost Train can be a spectacular feature. It appeared regularly around mid-century in Thurstan and Dun Holme. Ealhstan certainly followed suit in 1953. Here the Middle V usually plans it; the rest of the House, 'Baby' first, has to ascend to the attic and down again in the dark, negotiating slimy hands, wet tights and jam on door knobs . . . the noise is fearful. Outings were also enthusiastically welcomed. In the 1920s and 1930s when half-term exeats were unknown, horsebrake picnics or charabanc visits were arranged to places such as Stourhead, Lyme Regis, Glastonbury and the swannery at Abbotsbury. Later, post O-level/GCSE girls would go further afield for several days, to London or camping perhaps.

Inevitably, there are those who want to be alone, who bless the 'cue' and its privacy, or the quiet of the Library, and who, like Candia McWilliam (AE 1973), express thanks for 'the tolerance extended to mild eccentrics like myself. One of the many benefits of Sherborne was its trimming of affectation whilst sanctioning "differentness".'

Inevitably, too, there have been tragedies. The House good-fellowship has often been needed with the loss of a much-loved parent or grandparent, but never more so than when a *girl* dies – 'there was always a fine line between hysteria and comfort', as one OG says. In recent years the deaths of Head Girl Carolyne Henley (DH 1984) in a car crash, Becky Harries (AE 1985), Charlotte Simpson-Gee (E 1989) and Anna Douglas-Pennant (A 1993) after long struggles with leukaemia, cancer and cystic fibrosis, evoked much misery and anguish, to be alleviated by the supportive atmosphere within their Houses.

THURSTAN
after 11th Abbot of Sherborne
1916 – *Non sibi sed toti* – Brown
House of: Oxley–21; Williams–28 ;Tremellen–9; Taylor(C)–5; Franks–11
Legend: 1943 blaze! (mattress airing in front of a fire, gas-masked Matron dowses it.)

EALHSTAN
after 9th Bishop of Sherborne
1917 – *The Ship is more than the Crew* – Green
House of: Perry–25; Armitage(C)–23; Boxwell–5; Cameron–6;
Legend: 'Tuck', 20 years Matron, who helped lay House foundation stones.

Food: over ten decades in nine Houses, it was a tale of infinite variables. Aylmar has always claimed a starred cuisine, but it is difficult to prove. Lucy Hayne described a typical 1927 menu:

> A magnificent lump of roast beef carved by our West Indian housekeeper for our three round tables, 11 girls at each. Pudding was a square of hot cake and golden syrup. Tea in summer would be spread out under the trees – inch-thick bread with lovely dripping. Then excellent fish cakes for supper.

Below left: *Rosemary Day (K 1942) remembers Mrs Harriet Hamilton's (hatted) 'fine reputation for organising half-term outings' – no exeats then: this one for Kenelm by charabanc to Lyme Regis in 1939.*

Below: *House informality in 1966 – Kenelm girls leaving for a celebration picnic after O-levels.*

Yet Wingfield at break time had delicious warm doughnuts, whereas Aylmar had only small currant buns; Lucy said she held her bun towards Wingfield hoping some weight-watcher would do a swap!

Amazing favourites emerged: in the 1950s chocolate semolina in East, called 'Thames Mud' (but known as 'Ganges Mud' in Thurstan); it was sugar sandwiches and Fry's Chocolate Spread in West. Kenelm in the 1930s liked banana custard with lashings of soft brown sugar ('No freezer, so no ice-cream . . . '). In the 1990s, 'chick fric.' and apple crunch are widely favoured. In Mulliner the regular 'seconds' queue tells its own tale, with the UVI endeavouring to prevent the academic staff pulling rank.

Matron and cook have always been key figures in quality control. Caroline Wilson (AE 1958) writes,

> Mrs Whitfield came and everything changed for the better. Food improved out of all recognition. She fired the cook and taught a 14-year-old kitchen maid, Angela, to cook: marvellous fresh bread, no lumpy porridge, soft fried eggs, and chicken and mushrooms.

Set against these were plenty of dislikes: 'inevitable fruit pie and Cream Topping' . . . 'dreaded the boiled fish', . . . and Elspeth Nicol (T 1953) tells the story of Sunday lunch:

> The sweet was always rhubarb pie and 'froth' (whipped evaporated cream). This was not liked. Once we asked for small portions: Willy's stentorian voice echoed around – 'They're *all* small.'

There were of course restrictions – East was not allowed butter *and* jam (1932), but Kenelm could have both *only* after a House match victory (1939). The Second World War years were very difficult. Rosalind Phillips (DH 1944) wrote home in 1941: 'Jam is rationed! What are we to do? Matron says we now use 40lb *a week*; with rationing it will be 25lb *a month*.' Meat quality was poor. Patricia Hartley (W 1946) remembers her turn,

> to sit at Tags' table. There was so much gristle, but she said it was 'edible – nothing should be left'. There was a great deal of manipulation of napkins to dispose of it.

'It is customary . . . ': there were many of these. Not being allowed to *ask* for anything, but wait for a neighbour to offer the butter/salt etc. Ingenious ploys: 'With *you* the butter . . . ' in East in the 1950s. The curiosity of coloured sugar: Ann Hotblack (T 1946) tells of House Match Lunch – sugar, coloured that of the opposing House, was liberally spooned on to the dish, and then the pudding was squashed on top of it.

KENELM
after founder's family name
1928 – *Res parvae concordia crescunt* – Peacock blue
House of: Hamilton–20; Willmott–20; Gillingham–5; Walker–7
Legend: only House in Nikolaus Pevsner's classic *Buildings of England.*

Some House customs arose from traditions, others bordered on the bizarre. Margaret Tunbridge (A 1946) recalls one:

> There was 'Journey-Money Sunday' – the last but two before the end of term when we asked our parents for the train fare; then 'Button Sunday', the last but one when we sewed a button on our letters; finally 'Puff-puff Sunday', anticipating the train home, when we drew a train to remind our parents!

Everyone wrote letters on Sunday afternoon – only to parents, of course – which had to be left on a silver tray for inspection by the Housemistress – an authority-imposed custom which continued until the early 1970s. Other customs: House ties slung over cues on the day of a House match . . . Aylmar's Teddy which the House Baby still takes to matches . . . 'Hannibal', Ealhstan's stuffed penguin, for years a revered mascot.

Lucy Hayne remembers visits to

> 'Nana', a chilling aproned woman, armed with a bottle of purple permanganate of potash and a thermometer. She would paint sore throats with 'tar' and seemed preoccupied with who was not playing games.

Then there was House fire drill. Elsa Christie (A 1932) loved coming down the shute, but 'Miss Rowe would shout "Duffer, Duffer, Duffer" if we didn't land with knees-outwards-bend-upward-stretch accuracy.' Melanie Wray (AW 1978) admits West were always slow, so:

> Miss Downing and Mrs 'Nick' used to light a bonfire in a dustbin at the foot of the stairs to add some realism. I hold the dubious distinction of being the only Fire Captain to sleep through an entire practice.

Defying authority in some way was always a fiercely guarded tradition. Alethea Dew (Ald 1932) remembers Miss Mulliner's slippered evening prowl:

> We got fed up and tied our eight enamel water jugs to the door handle of our dorm. A very satisfactory clatter-bang ensued – a wonderful chance to scream . . . No subsequent visitations!

The midnight feast has a long history, but Margaret Woodcock (K 1939) says, 'the planning and logistics were not always efficient, though a codeword did ensure secrecy.' The reality in the 1970s was crisps, cocoa and a Mars bar at the top of the stairs. The Babies' Dorm in Kenelm had the great game of leaping from the top of a cupboard onto a bed, always interrupted by a furious Housemistress rushing up the stairs. Rosamund Owen (A 1938) remembers the half-term custom of going to bed with paper curlers in her hair and arriving at breakfast with a most odd appearance. Melanie Wray concedes:

> We tried Mrs Nick's patience on the first day of each month with our 'rule': first words must be noisy, 'Black Hares, White Rabbits'; then we'd walk backwards down the stairs, promising to kiss the first person there – inevitably Mrs Nick, shouting up to behave ourselves.

MULLINER
after first Headmistress
3 incarnations: 1967, 1975, 1992
The youngest House with the oldest inhabitants (UVI only)
House of: Maxwell-Scott–10; Morton–9
Legend: Betty Maxwell-Scott's bruised ankle (chasing a BS intruder?).

1992: the last brood of Mulliner (of the second incarnation), despite their embarrassed admission that alarm clocks were an unknown concept, despite their often embarrassing redefinition of the ethos of the skirt (culottes, pyjama bottoms and worse) did get their priorities right. Siân Jones (AW 1992) and her friends pinpointed Saturday nights when 'the quest for elusive pink mugs' proved far more meaningful than the male attentiveness 'rupturing the sanctity of the airport lounge'. Dora Morton, its last Warden, also exercised by the Boys' School presence, might have been heard singing to the tune of 'Green Door',

Midnight, one more night without sleeping,
Watching, till the morning comes creeping,
Mull'ner what's the secret you're keeping?
There's a lot of movement, and a lot of noise
All over Mull'ner . . .

DISTINGUISHED OLD GIRLS

CANDIA McWILLIAM
(AE 1973)

Candia McWilliam: portrait in The Independent, *June 1994.*

In 1993 Candia was listed among the 'Best of Young British Novelists', a once-every-decade trawl to find the 20 outstanding contemporary fiction writers. She joined the likes of Ben Okri and Jeanette Winterson; the judges included A. S. Byatt and Salman Rushdie. With her first novel, *A Case of Knives* (1988), she had clearly arrived on the literary scene. It is a highly wrought thriller, in 'Rashomon'-style, with four people telling the same story, their points of view revealing that nothing is quite as it seems. It won the Betty Trask Award and was short-listed for the Whitbread First Novel prize. Reviewers praised it for its elegant writing (clothes cupboards are 'tall lozenges of space, obscure and cool, cathedrals of sartorial labour') and its wry social comment. Candia's view: 'It's really four different truths; I wrote it to show how arcane we all are.' Two more novels have followed, and in 1997 her *Wait Till I Tell You* was the year's most widely praised short-story collection; she also writes literary reviews for *The TLS*, the *New York Times*, *The Independent on Sunday*, and *The Scotsman*. She is never far from controversy. At School she admits to being 'eccentric and bad at games', and won the *Vogue* writing competition in 1971. At Cambridge: 'I was amazed: so many invitations to dinner – I wish I had really scholarly habits' . . . yet she got a First in English! Her literary critics ('I even had to sustain *Private Eye*'s malice') focus on her intellectual vocabulary: the second novel, *A Little Stranger*, includes 'ahent', 'graminivore', and 'zenana'. 'I'm surprised at the fuss,' Candia says, 'I don't write books whose bank-account of words is that of *The Sun*'.

6
'But *Don't* Go into Mr McGregor's Garden'

The School was only a few years old when Miss Mulliner warned a new teacher: 'Most of our girls are high-spirited – they require careful and tactful management.'

She was voicing the chronic school authority problem: how to square the circle of freedom versus restraint. Teachers, especially housemistresses, are all too sentient of the appeal of 'forbidden fruit' to the young, yet aware of their responsibility of being *in loco parentis.* The freer atmosphere of today contrasts with that of the first six decades when some OGs say they were very conscious of a determination to keep them out of mischief – they seemed to be constantly watched, tired out on the playing field, guarded from the opposite sex and allowed little privacy. Others though were happy to fit in. Authority's tone was to alter slowly. Alethea Dew (Ald 1932) remembers that, 'After Miss Mulliner retired the regime gradually became more user-friendly'; and Katharine Charlewood (DH 1938) recalls 'a spirit of relaxed enjoyment – certainly not prim regimentation.' Mary Hallam (W 1949) wrote in 1995: 'We did not expect the freedom that girls do today. I never felt hemmed in by the rules; they seemed pretty reasonable.' A number of OGs said they actually preferred school to home, and some admit they needed control! Ruth Walwyn (DH 1951) said her previous school had regarded her as 'a little Indian savage', whilst Felicity Rebbeck (DH 1943) says her vicar father was seeking a place for 'his unruly daughter'.

Rules pertaining to safety outside the School are usually seen as sensible, though in the first 50 years perhaps overprotective. 'We were closely shepherded', said Patricia Hartley (W 1946), whilst Brenda Livesey (A 1932) hated 'that archaic crocodile arrangement!' Lucy Hayne (A 1931) had a particularly unpleasant memory of

> Walking Lists: like an old dance, we each had a card to fill in one's partner for the croc. to the Abbey. Popular girls rushed to fill these lists in no time, but the dull ones had a miserable time.

The total ban on Cheap Street was eased a little in the late 1930s, but with specific restrictions. Margaret Symons (W 1938) is still amused by the Tea at *The Three Wishes* Rule:

> Both Schools patronised the place – the girls had the upstairs room and the boys downstairs. If any girl's parents had the temerity to take her there during the BS Commem. a screen was discreetly placed around their table.

Gradually rules were modified: going out in fours, then threes, and cycling in groups in the countryside were permitted; even the young ones were allowed down Cheap Street on Saturdays in 1971. Miss Mulliner's strict 'No exeat is allowed' changed, but as many miscreants have found since, the exeat privilege was easily withdrawn. Ruth Walwyn, in her last year, wrote to her mother about her little sister Elisabeth (DH 1956):

> Mummy: a Very Important Fact. If you write to DRH asking for Libeth to go home by train she will say 'no' because of infection: but if you ask for her to go by train to see a Harley St. specialist she will say 'yes'. It's just the way grown-ups' minds work, you see.

It was the early regulations *inside* the boundaries that vexed so many girls. Miss Mulliner brought with her from Cheltenham 'The Silence Rule: no pupil shall speak in cloakrooms, passages or on stairs.' She admitted it was old-fashioned, but defended it vigorously – 'Miss Beale would say what a splendid thing it is to learn to control a tongue.' It lasted until the mid-1970s. The rule also applied to the swimming pool on Sundays: Valerie Richardson (A 1938) says, 'swimming was hugely popular, but we had to be silent so as not to disturb Dun Holme's housemistress.'

Many OGs remember Miss Stuart's conventions. Ruby Cassels (E 1941) writes, 'HV filled us with awe. We had to flatten ourselves against the walls as she sailed past; in the grounds we had to hasten to talk to her – if she started to hum you knew she was bored.' Elizabeth Thompson (AW 1934) says, 'we didn't have any freedom to wander; we had to have a purpose!', so going for a stroll in the grounds was frowned upon. And being in the wrong place at the wrong time has always incurred authority's displeasure – from Beatrice Mulliner's hand on a shoulder, 'It's only me, my dear . . .' to June Taylor's, 'My child, pray where do you think you are going?'

Control of reading matter existed in the early decades. 'Only the Bible and poetry were allowed in cues – no novels,' said one girl; in the 1930s Cronin's *The Citadel* was listed as 'unsuitable reading'; and several girls were amused when a housemistress, who was reading some Compton Mackenzie to them, left the book open and they saw some passages marked 'not to be read to the girls'. The social revolution of the 1960s and especially the national publicity given to the Profumo Affair and to the trial of Penguin Books over *Lady Chatterley's Lover* presented authority with fresh difficulties. Today Miss Taylor engages the support of parents over what she calls 'fire-tong literature – to be kept at arm's length'. One piece of censorship from the 1920s looks curious when viewed from the 1990s. Peggy Shackleton (T 1927) remembers her 'extra':

> In my dancing class the mistress was forbidden to teach the foxtrot – Miss Mulliner thought it was immoral. But we did learn the Black Bottom: our teacher said, 'it has

just come in and hasn't been heard of in high places.'

The support of senior girls was sought from the start, with the introduction of a Cheltenham-style prefect system, though many OGs commented, 'little power, much responsibility'. And Housemistresses to this day rely much on Heads of House and the 'pres'. Cordelia Wintour (DH 1931), long-time friend of Dame Diana, gave her appraisal 60 years later:

> I liked being Head of House as I was a priggish, bossy child. The one snag was *no time* to oneself – endless piffling chores, supervising people, making lists, ticking people off – ugh! (I actually enjoyed it).

Many a later Head of House lamented the list-making chore, which doubled if also a School Games Captain. Supervising became more onerous as the in-awe-of-prefects syndrome melted away in a progressively liberal ethos. Nenagh Staunton (AW 1977) kept a list of punishments – 'drawn up one night in desperation and despair by West's pres – but never enforced!' It began,

> If after 'quiet' bell any girl is found out of bed, she will be SENT DOWN to stand
> - in the middle of the hall or
> - in the dark sitting room or
> - in the dark cloakroom or
> - in the Pres' Room, being ignored by 5 pres.

But Ealhstan prefects in 1979 *enforced* 'sitting on the stairs' for the same offence.

Uniform has always been central to the 'thou shalt' philosophy, but attitudes are complex. The School argues the pride factor, but also sees uniform as a social leveller, an escape from designer-labels and peer pressure; today's *Clothes List* is also proffered as a balance of the practical, economic and aesthetic. Parents acquiesce in this, but also aim for a 'larger' size at the start in the hope that girls will 'grow into it'. Tessa Rowland (DH 1956) says that her daughter, Caroline Wells (DH 1997), 'has managed to get through with the original set of uniform', although confesses, 'buttons on shorts are now on bits of elastic, but she refuses a larger pair.' The girls have been rather ambivalent about the uniform factor: 'stuffy conformity', said one; 'jolly easy to throw on in the morning rush', said another; 'not much concession to the battle of the bulge(s)', said a third.

Changes in School attire: 1910.

Uniform did not exist in the School's earliest years, but from the First World War onwards the *Clothes List* has been lovingly preserved by many OGs, beyond any other memorabilia. Peggy Shackleton remembers the 1920s' list: 'Formidable – with such items as Liberty Bodices (2) and Combinations (4 pairs). Our school hats were a disaster – not charm-friendly, possibly on purpose!' Margaret Woodcock (K 1939) has a memory for detail:

> Uniform ranged from the new, beige bandless hat a-top, to like-coloured lisle stockings, with thick wool knickers intervening. Shirts, skirts (knee-long), so-called djibbahs and shantung, long-sleeved dresses were the outer-wear, plus cloak, green suit and overcoat (soon to be replaced by beige Harris tweed – more usable in holidays). White

> piqué, shorts with integrated blouse and black crêpe-de-chine tunics (for massed gym) were extra items.

Over the years girls expressed strong opinions on particular features, none more so than hats and knickers. 'The awful, brown, squashed-felt hat' (Ann Hoblyn, AE 1950), and of course 'HV's order: no curls must peep from under the brim' (Ann Barrett, W 1945). The *School Magazine* of 1936 contained an appeal: 'SJM complains that her green knickers are expensive, a bad shape and very thick – remedy, please?' And even in 1950 Ann Hoblyn complained, 'my meridian knickers always shrink'; whilst 35 years later Sarah May (AE 1989) could say:

> Merids are always too baggy
> And whilst you are jumping and reeling
> They often fall off and are flung through the air
> And sometimes get stuck on the ceiling.

Djibbahs were looked on more favourably: Mary Hallam said:

> We loved our green djibbahs with a passion. They covered a multitude of sins – thin or fat, bosomy or flat, we all looked the same!

Formal wear for concerts in the early days meant a white Tussore silk dress and a white shawl – 'totally impractical,' said Brenda Livesey (AE 1932). 'No cardigans allowed – very frumpish! We used our shawls as cushions,' recalls Joan Burchardt (DH 1936). 'I felt very odd in my shawl – it was the one I'd worn as a baby,' said Elizabeth Thompson (AW 1934). White had given way to green in the 1950s – 'sacks, we called them,' said Fiona Morrice (AW 1959). 'Brown Cows' ('Harris Tweed, remember, never mere tweed,' commented Elisabeth Walwyn) looked smart but were unpopular and uncomfortable, yet appeared on the *Clothes List* for several decades before succumbing to rising costs.

Changes in School attire: 1949.

More liberal ideas gradually took over. Dame Diana amazed the Sixth in 1955 by allowing lipstick – 'only after supper for two hours; but at least we're out of the Victorian era,' Elisabeth Walwyn told her mother. Lucy Buxton (DH 1965) remembers the famous mufti concession; she too wrote home in 1964 about, 'the big news: DRH has announced that the UVI needn't wear uniform *at all* out of school.' Three years later parents were warned, 'Hemlines – some girls are shortening their school skirts unsuitably: no more than 3 inches above the knee is the rule.' In the early 1970s Dame Diana agreed to 'trousers on Saturday afternoons' – 'to our great delight,' recalls Diana Gorsky (AW 1976). June Taylor brought in a new everyday uniform in 1987, though perhaps the real revolution came in 1996 when the School Rules stated: 'During the working day all sixth-formers may wear their own clothes, including trousers.'

How many girls actually broke the code . . . how far would disobedient Peter Rabbits venture into Mr McGregor's garden? Expulsions over the century have been remarkably few; Dame Diana said she could only remember four in her 25 years as Headmistress, 'and three of those were officially for smoking, though what made me so angry was their persistent lying.' There were, in the staff view, good and bad years, but girls by reputation are not transgressors on a grand scale. Jane Williams (E 1979) echoed many others:

> We conformed – if there'd been a prize we'd have won it for being so conformist. Any really anti-social girl we viewed as a strange creature, living on another planet.

But there were plenty of naughty girls – those who kicked over the traces, as many Housemistresses well remember. One occasion authority did *not* hear of: Head of House Stella Ingram (AW 1939) recalls reprimanding girls for sneaking down the fire-escape, dressed-up and made-up, to enjoy Pack Monday Fair's dodgems – 'though, being a bit of a rebel, I admired them really!'

The loosening of social conventions from the 1960s onwards presented Headmistresses and Housemistresses with unwelcome challenges. Of the four real 'horrors' – drink, drugs, sex and smoking – the School escaped reasonably well; only the last has proved chronic and stubborn, perhaps reflecting the national problem. Dame Diana's 1971 letter home, 'I should be grateful if parents would give us strong support in our stand against smoking,' was a serious effort at control. By the mid-1980s June Taylor had clarified the matter: £5 fine (raised to £10 in 1988) for first offence, loss of exeat for second, expulsion for third.

Whether or not deliberately to highlight a problem has been a difficult decision. With alcohol Dame Diana opted for parental support in 1967:

> Changing social customs present temptation – particularly the 'bring-a-bottle-to-the-party' tendency – and girls find it hard to cope if adults are absent.

Changes in School attire: 1990.

Elizabeth Coulter tried a 'confronting the horror' approach, when she invited a speaker in 1977: 'I'm Annabel; I'm an alcoholic.' Her life was like some terrible novel come true. 'I used gin-and-tonic as an anaesthetic against hurt; ten miserable years until AA.' Henrietta Bulley (DH 1977) noted at the time that the talk had the desired sobering impact on the listeners.

Drugs mirrored the same focus problem as alcohol. In 1970 Sister Patricia of a local Addiction Centre came to talk to groups throughout the School. This was Dame Diana's direct approach, but she was not wholly satisfied. So in 1972 she asked me to include a talk-plus-pamphlet in the Friday evening UV Current Events lesson on a regular basis, aiming to move away from the 'big campaign' strategy.

Nefarious behaviour took many forms – some bordering on the comic. Samples from the 1950s: little Sara Barsley (AE 1959) and a friend decided to try 'the pleasures of sunbathing with no clothes on – in a forbidden field beyond East; horror! a gaggle of BS going for a run – we lay low, and didn't try that again!' Elisabeth Walwyn (DH 1956) wrote home about the House prefects evading Housemistress Nancy Downing's 'eagle eye' and going for a midnight swim in the nude, and Caroline Wilson (AE 1958, Head of the UVI) admitted

> disgracing ourselves on a visit to Salisbury Cathedral. Beforehand two prefects and I hired a canoe, had a (forbidden) picnic and then capsized the boat! We arrived for the service dripping wet, our friends hiding us.

The proximity of Sherborne School spawned a social revolution in the 1970s, since

Sixth-formers with the Boys' School in the 1990s – the social graces on the curriculum?

when joint activities have burgeoned. Full-scale music collaboration was followed by major drama productions; a Sixth Form General Studies programme on two afternoons a week developed; dances became familiar features of the social calendar, and girls joined the CCF. By the 1990s termly discos or dinners were organised; and 'mixed sport on Sunday afternoons has proved a great ice-breaker,' says Susie West, AW Housemistress – mixed lacrosse and touch-rugger were popular arrivals on the scene. In the 1997 Brochure, June Taylor wrote:

> There is close cooperation with Sherborne School, and this means that Sherborne has the advantage of single sex education with many of the benefits of co-education.

All this is in marked contrast to earlier decades. Viewed from today, girls and staff find the old rules strange and behaviour often bizarre. The artificiality of boarding school social life, when all contact with the Boys' School was banned, has been commented on by many OGs. Driven inward, emotional contacts were of the quixotic, sentimental kind; different schools had exotic vocabulary – 'ravers', 'goners', 'cracklets', 'GPs' (grand passions) were variations on Sherborne's own 'crushes' or 'pashes'. Mary Hallam recollects that

> Pashes were the craze in 1945. I worshipped the Head of House; I once arranged to steal her pillow and sleep on it all night. Suddenly I was in the Sixth and had juniors pashed on me! It was hair-raising. But it was very innocent and naïve. Sex didn't enter into it – it was plain unadorned adoration.

Officially, the Boys' School did not exist: 'Look the other way' was the order Nancy Ollivant (Ald 1928) remembers being given if a 'crocodile' met any boys. Not everyone obeyed the rules. Rosamund Owen (A 1938) used the 'tin roof of a disused cattle-shed as a *poste restante*'; others sent letters via home! Hilary Ruston (E 1955) went midnight swimming in the Boys' pool, and used 'bicycle rides to meet up with the boys in the castle ruins or sewage works; once Miss Armitage buzzed around in her car hot on our trail, but never caught us in our illegal fun.'

Valerie Richardson (A 1938) recorded some rather different official thinking – 'we couldn't get over it!' – when the prefects were allowed to go to a dance at Bryanston. But not until 1945 was such a thing permitted with Sherborne School; this was the legendary first contact – the VE Day Celebration Dance. Ann Barrett (W 1945) describes the scene in the School Hall:

> As boys arrived we were told to grab one (in a lady-like manner), get his name and then introduce him to Miss Stuart. All the Housemistresses sat on the platform in basket chairs – watching! Conversation was painful; so was the dancing.

Ann Hotblack (T 1946) said the music was 'strictly Victor Sylvester – not our favourite Glenn Miller'. Jean Straw (AE 1945) did not see much, as 'my Housemistress had me patrolling the grounds for fear one of her girls might misbehave.' Patricia Hartley (W 1946) says, 'there was much excitement when it was rumoured afterwards that the boys had become very broody!' Anne Rew (DH 1947) was too young to go, but tells

> the splendid story of Miss Stuart being accosted by the Headmaster in Sherborne. 'I will not have your girls kissing my boys.' The Headmistress replied with her usual self-possession, 'It takes two to kiss', and swept on.

The experiment was not repeated for many years: 1970 saw the next dance at School.

Since the 1970s the easier mixing of the sexes has of course brought its problems. Responses have varied. Melanie Wray (AW 1978) remembers a Mulliner ploy. 'The dark corner behind the San was a haunt for courting couples. Siân Herbert-Jones and I filled a dustbin with Di Noble's bathwater and poured it out of the window.' Candice Wood (AW 1986) sent a note to *Harpers and Queen* in 1994 about the Sixth Form dances: 'the renowned History of Art tutor would stand at the edge of the dance-floor carrying an ice-bucket to calm down over-excited couples.' On a more serious note Veronica Owen (W 1942) delivered a speech in her last year as Headmistress of Malvern: she warned that advances in contraception 'far from simplifying, have made the problem of moral choice more difficult for girls'.

Controlling the girls was one thing; controlling the staff quite another. Kathleen Moore, Senior Mistress for 18 years under Miss Mulliner, documented the plea of a certain Miss Stokes, the history mistress:

> The real necessity in a girls' school is a man tied-up in the pantry, to whom staff could go and chat when they were bored.

DISTINGUISHED OLD GIRLS

EILEEN ARNOT ROBERTSON
(Ald. 1919)

Eileen Arnot Robertson.

'E. Arnot Robertson', as she was known to the public – author, broadcaster, film critic – is credited in *Who's Who* with ten novels. Her third in 1931 made her a household name: *Four Frightened People*, a dramatic story of a Malayan steamboat journey, was chosen as one (No.15) of the very first batch of Penguin titles, today collectors' items. Six others followed over the next decade, attracting an admiring readership. Her last book, *The Spanish Town Papers*, was completed in 1959, just two years before her death. In the 1940s and 1950s Eileen became one of an influential trio of film critics (with Dilys Powell and C. A. Lejeune). She had a reputation for outspokenness, and her reviews in the London press, characterised by vigour and independence of judgement, brought her into conflict with powerful film magnates. A prominent libel suit in 1948 went as far as the House of Lords; here the verdict went against her, but a wave of popular support set up a fund to help defray her heavy legal costs – the School sending 'a contribution for your fight for freedom of speech for film critics'. Clearly Eileen and the School were back on speaking terms! For she had not been happy under Miss Mulliner's regime, in 'that expensive potting shed of the English rose', as she called the School in 1934, 'which was run on a male system imperfectly adapted to female needs' (see Chapter 10). Eileen admitted in a Graham Greene anthology of that year, *The Old School*, that she was not 'the Sherborne team-spirit type': never obeying the rules, she said, 'I used the morning five-minute silence in the Hall to finish my prep; I smuggled up textbooks in the legs of my knickers.'

7
In the Shadow of War

1914–18 1939–45

On the evening of Wednesday 29 July 1914, Beatrice Mulliner received a cryptic telegram: 'International complications. Arrangements cancelled.' The 'arrangements' were that a father was to have picked up his daughter at the end of term. But 'father' was an Admiral of the Fleet, and on that Wednesday Royal Navy battleships were on action stations. The First World War began four days later. Within two months Miss Mulliner told the girls that 'the shadow of this Great War lies heavy over many.' Of the little kindergarten boys at Greenhill in 1899, two were now in France, one fighting at Ypres, another already seriously wounded. Just before the School returned from the summer holidays, the Dorset Yeomanry were quartered in Sherborne – 51 of them in the School gymnasium. On the girls' return, White Lodge domestic science students had 'invalid cookery' added to their studies, and cooking for the Ypres wounded, who had arrived at the Sherborne hospital, became a priority. The 'shadow' soon struck girls' families. News filtered through of close relations: 'killed in Flanders', 'wounded, then died, on the Dardanelles' recorded the deaths of brothers in the *School Magazine*.

That the whole School was galvanised into a prolonged war effort was manifest from the start. The Headmistress urged the girls 'to do something for those who sleep in Flanders'. The biggest immediate response was a Motor Ambulance. Collections which had been intended for a swimming pool were diverted, and appeals made for an ambulance fund; within three months the considerable sum of £439 was raised. An ambulance was rapidly commissioned, and was in France early in 1915, dealing with gas-wounded at Ypres. The brother of one of the girls drove it for part of its work, and he called it a sturdy and speedy bus. It rendered fine service throughout the War dealing with military and civilian casualties, and accounts of its work were regularly sent to School: in 1916 one told how the ambulance 'constantly ran the gauntlet of "Hell's Corner", a junction of three roads in sight of the enemy.'

Set against this, much patriotic fervour was in evidence. Hilaire Belloc came to lecture to the girls and OGs on the War, and Jean Sorley (Ald 1911) said, 'It was most cheering to find a military authority so optimistic about the fortunes of the allies.' At Commem. in 1915 the concert ended with a spirited singing of the School Song followed by 'La Marseillaise' before 'God Save the King'. All this, however, was before the killing fields of the Somme in 1916. From then on War 'appeals' assumed increasing prominence. Needlework for the troops produced impressive results: an archive document records, '4 dressing gowns sent to Greenhill hospital, and 26 pyjama suits, 14 shirts, and a large number of socks went to Southampton Dock Hospital'. Much was done in the summer holidays – 'an eight-week running accompaniment of knitting and sewing' it was called. In 1916 half an acre of the School grounds was dug up, and the girls planted cauliflower, cabbages and dwarf peas. Money too was collected. Girls regularly paid for '6*d.* War Savings Coupons', and with other appeals in just one year, 1917, £137 went to the war effort (worth over £4,000 at today's values).

In 1917 Beatrice Mulliner told the girls that the School 'has risen to the dignity of a mention in Parliament.' Two years before a 27-page *War Supplement* had been produced by the OG Union, listing relations of the girls 'serving their country', as well as the war work of many OGs. Other schools followed suit. But when a new supplement was proposed in 1917, the School was informed that 'much harm has unwittingly been done by publications of this nature', and their distribution was banned. The government's fear (unfounded, said many contemporaries) was that listings included where regiments were serving. Even *Punch* magazine made merry over 'German generals laboriously ploughing' such literature to deduce the present whereabouts of the British armies! A poignant note though was struck by the Woodd sisters (DH 1910 and 1914), whose brother was mentioned in the 1915 Supplement: in the School archive copy Mollie Woodd has added, 'Woodd, ABP, Lt., West Yorks Reg., killed in action, France 1918'.

OGs moved in numbers into war work. In 1914 Olive Begbie (Ald 1905) went

NEAR RELATIONS SERVING THE COUNTRY.

B.E.F. stands for British Expeditionary Force. Mention in dispatches is marked *. The names of those who have already given their lives for their country are printed in italics.

RELATIONS OF PRESENT SCHOOL.

Name, Initial, Rank.	Regiment or Ship, and where serving.	Relationship
Agar, Hon. F.	Military Remount Depôt	Father
Allenby, R. A., Lieutenant-Colonel	Transport	Father
Anderson, M., Captain	7th Gurkhas, India	Brother
Ansell, G. K., Lieutenant-Colonel	*5th Dragoon Guards. Killed in action near Mons, September 1st*	Father
Anson, W. G., Private	6th Gloucester Regiment. B.E.F.	Brother
Anson, A. H. B.	72nd Highlanders, Canadians in England	Brother
Barnes, S. F., Captain	Dorset Royal Garrison Artillery (T.F.)	Brother
Baylay, Brigadier-General	R E.	Father
Beckton, H., Lance-Corporal	Honorable Artillery Company. B.E.F.	Brother
Bernard, J. L., 2nd Lieutenant	6th Dorset Regiment	Brother
Bingley, D. A , Lieutenant, R.N.	H.M S. "Cherwell"	Brother
Bingley, S. N., 2nd Lieutenant	R.F.A. A.D.C. B.E.F.	Brother
Bird, C. B., Captain	7th King's Own Scottish Borderers	Brother
Bird, H. B., Lieutenant	9th Royal Warwickshire Regiment. Egypt	Brother
Bowman, L. S., 2nd Lieutenant	4th King's Own Royal Lancasters	Brother
Brewis, A., Captain	5th South Lancashire Regiment	Father
Brown, E. F., Private	Northumberland Fusiliers	Brother
Browning, M.E., Rear-Admiral, R.N., M.V.O.	H.M.S. "Hibernia"	Father
Carr-Ellison, R.H., Lieutenant-Colonel	Staff Officer	Brother
Carr-Ellison, H. G., Captain	Northumberland Hussars	Brother
Carr-Ellison, S. F. C., Captain	12th Durham Light Infantry	Brother
Carr-Ellison, O. F. C., 2nd Lieutenant	3rd Northumberland Fusiliers. B.E.F.	Brother
Carrick, Major the Earl of	A.S.C.	Father

Extract from the 'War Supplement' that caused a parliamentary outcry.

straight into Red Cross work, 'nursing Kitchener's army with its pneumonia, scarlet fever and any amount of operations.' Some went into munitions work as the famous 'canaries'. Lilian Beckton (W 1912) wrote:

> I had no idea shells were such complicated affairs. There are 70 different operations before they go to the arsenal. Boring the shells is the best paid work – men used to refuse to do it, 'too hard' – until we arrived.

By 1916 many were in France as VADs. Dorothy Sweet (W 1910) in 1918 was the first OG to be 'Mentioned-in-Dispatches', having nursed there all through the War, and she was awarded the Royal Red Cross. Another OG, Audrey Charlesworth (Ald 1911), drove an ambulance in France for several years. Some did government work: Margery Conder (Ald 1909) became Supervisor on the Raw Materials Finance staff at the War Office.

The School suffered some shortages, but not food: as Miss Mulliner wrote to parents, 'Butter and milk are too plentiful in the rich pastures of Dorset.' Girls, though, found the food monotonous, and one girl was disgusted at 'the invention of margarine – nasty, yellow stuff with oily patches'. Tempers were sorely strained over delays in building plans; the Headmistress recorded her desperate correspondence with the Timber Control Office over getting permits. Sherborne, of course, was 'safe', and attracted an increasing number of girls, yet there were official delays in getting Thurstan built. Hiring workmen was next to impossible; even with Thurstan nearly complete in 1916, the plastering had to be done by one man working 12 hours a day. A year later a note was sent to parents concerning the lack of groundsmen: 'You will be interested that our new "groundsmen" are the girls of the School, who work under Miss Mason, earn a reasonable wage, and thus save labour.' On Thursday, 11 November 1918 the school bell rang and the girls went to the Hall. Christel Trevor-Battye (E 1924) remembered

> an amazing sight. The Headmistress was gazing in astonishment at a figure – Mlle. Orcell, the French mistress – prancing about waving the French flag and singing the Marseillaise. Soon we joined in with enthusiasm.

The Armistice had been signed; the First World War was over.

Now the School could concentrate on its prime function, education. But the staff were to become acutely conscious of the catalytic effect of the Great War on the girls: it had sharpened their awareness of world problems, and a new seriousness developed. The horrors of the trenches set a problem for some staff – the Headmistress, History and English teachers in particular – in the 1920s and 1930s: to shield the child from the world or not? They opted for openness. The poetry of Sassoon and Owen was not ignored; a junior League of Nations society flourished; and in the late 1930s CEWC membership brought excellent 'World Citizenship' pamphlets into the classrooms. Newspapers appeared in the Houses – and were read. Many OGs remember the 'queue for the papers' during the Munich crisis of 1938. Margaret Woodcock (K 1939) recalled it became a moral duty 'to keep up with Chamberlain's visits to Hitler – after all the PM's niece was in our House!'

Miss Stuart proudly announced to parents that 'Sherborne is safe' – yet she bought 2,000 yards of 'the black stuff for windows' as a precaution.

When war came in 1939 the armed forces needed administrative bases, and urgently issued 'commandeering orders' on many civilian buildings – boarding schools were an obvious target. Yet it rankled with many of the girls' public schools that they were first in line, whereas the great boys' schools like Eton, Harrow and Winchester were untouched (OBs in official places!). The School, though, could hardly believe its good fortune: it was one of very few left alone. Staff looked on in horror at what was happening elsewhere: Wycombe Abbey, Cheltenham and Roedean were 'requisitioned'; the first, given only a few *hours* notice to quit, in effect ceased to exist until 1946. The School then found itself 'hosting' some of the girls from these schools, not necessarily receiving grateful thanks! 'We were troubled by Sherborne's silence rules,' complained one Wycombe Abbey girl. However appreciative Miss Stuart felt at avoiding requisition, like her predecessor, she had to cope with a sea of regulations imposed by government officials.

Sherborne might be 'safe', but fear and narrow escapes were unavoidable. Some girls were cheerfully confident, seeing the War as an exciting adventure; others were nervous and tearful. The Staff struggled: air-raid warnings (legion), broken nights and much interrupted days were their lot. Firewatching for incendiary bombs was a particular bane of housemistresses. In late 1940 the School was stunned by the announcement: 'No one will sleep above the first floor. West will partly sleep in the Staff Room and the Prefects' Room in the main school.' Soon brick blast-walls flanked by sandbags appeared in parts of the Houses and along the main school corridor, whilst some ceilings were reinforced with pillars of wood. They were to become such comforting features that when taken down in 1945, Felicity Jackson (W 1945) reflected, 'the open corridor has now an almost indecently nude appearance.' Miss Stuart's 2,000 yards of 'blackout' were in early use – the putting up each evening affording the girls a welcome diversion from prep. Gas masks came, the drill in using them giving, said Felicity, 'half-an-hour of unmitigated if stifled laughter'. Ann Barrett (W 1945) remembers with no affection at all 'the black line painted on the bath in House allowing only five inches of water – and that was at the deep end!' Patricia Hartley (W 1946) though found ways round this: 'four of us in a communal bath – such luxury to fill it to the top and splash about.' Mary Hallam (W 1949) also recalls her Housemistress's 'war effort':

1940–1: Kenelm sitting-room where 'the beds were brought down because most of us were tired from so many disturbed nights' – Rosemary Day (K 1942). Bunks were also put in the cloakroom.

> 'Tags' ensured that Wingfield's loos were lit at night with a murky-red wire brazier high up in the corner – we had to stumble along the landing with one dim overhead light. Of course there was no loo paper, only a bundle of cut-up newspapers.

The girls' war efforts ranged far and wide. Knitting 'woollen comforts' was again an enduring occupation; in 1940 the 'grateful thanks of the 6th Submarine Flotilla to Sherborne School for Girls' was one of many letters received. The most loathed task was charlock-picking – ridding the huge fields beyond Kenelm of the 'obnoxious weed' for local farmers. A particular sacrifice was the School Hall 'kneelers': the rubber in these mats went to make tyres for army vehicles. As before, parts of the grounds were dug up for vegetables; in addition 22 hens and seven pigs were kept next to Kenelm, an unwelcome task being announced by Miss Stuart: 'The pig-swill will be carried up there daily by girls in the different Houses.' National appeals for money were periodic. 'Warships Week' in Sherborne in 1941 produced £1,953 from girls' and parents' gifts, and from girls 'gardening' in the town at *6d.* an hour. Great publicity was given to the School's other effort: the buying and equipping in 1940 of two large mobile canteens for use by the Women's Legion. Both gave excellent service in the London blitz of the following winter, Her Majesty the Queen coming to inspect one of them.

September 1940: the mobile canteen being put to good use after Sherborne's 'raid' before being transferred to London.

Sherborne town had only one serious air raid, on Monday, 30 September 1940. En route for the Westland factory at Yeovil, some German bombers mistook the target and dropped around 50 bombs in a great swathe across Sherborne, killing 17 people. The nearest bomb to the School was two fields away from Kenelm, though the Boys' School quad had one. Rosemary Day (K 1942) kept the letter she wrote home:

> We had just settled down to late-afternoon prep. People near the window saw seven German planes. We were sent to the big-prep-room with some maths. I was in the middle of a sum when there were terrific noises: the floor vibrated, the ceiling shook and the windows rattled. From now on in House we will sleep downstairs in the sitting-room.

Also Ruby Cassels (E 1941) has graphic memories:

> We heard the planes and sirens and came down 94 steps from our form-room to the ground floor with prep books and pens. We lay down in the main passage, and very soon we were a jumble of bodies with arms and legs and elbows and hair and fountain-pens all sticking into each other.

Jean Straw (AE 1945) remembers the walks afterwards to inspect the craters. She also recalls earlier that year crossing the bridge to House and seeing great columns of soldiers and trucks: 'We were told by the maids, on whom we relied for outside information, that they were returning from Dunkirk.'

Among major problems was rationing, though many girls remember with wonder how good much of the food was:

> We had little pieces of butter on wee plates with our names on them to last the week; you could blow it on two slices of bread or eke it out.
>
> (Barbara Slade T 1941)

> Great efforts were made: 'peach tart' was created with carrots and jelly.
>
> (Phoebe Cresswell A 1942)

> Good memories of roast for Sunday lunch, with splendid pies and junkets, and a sort of savoury lentil mixture which came on fried bread for breakfast; also beautiful rice-puddings. Aylmar always seemed to have done well. Then there was 'Bag-Supper' on Mondays (a picnic meal, in a paper bag, which we could eat anywhere).
>
> (Susan Robinson A 1945)

OGs and the Staff were far more involved in the Second World War than the First. Brief lists of those in all the major women's services in 1940 rapidly expanded. By 1942, there were 36 in the WRNS, 19 in the ATS and 38 in the WAAF, as well

Mary Edwards (AE 1937) joined the ATS in 1938. This photograph was used by the Daily Sketch *during the Munich Crisis to encourage women to 'join up'. Mary served throughout the war as a gunner on the Essex coast at Shoeburyness.*

as large numbers of VADs and FANYs (First Aid Nursing Yeomanry). Within a year 194 were listed in HM Armed Forces, and some had been Mentioned-in-Dispatches; of the 58 Commissioned Officers one, Dorothy Potter (Ald 1927) rose to the rank of Chief Commander in the ATS. Another OG, Barbara Frankel-Foster (E 1920), worked for the French Resistance with Col. Rémy, and was awarded the Croix de la Resistance. Large numbers were of course nursing, 11 of them in one hospital, St Thomas's. Cordelia Everidge (AW 1937) died as a VAD – in the words of Miss Stuart, 'the first of us to die while serving her country'. Staff too were listed: Miss Crichton-Miller in the WAAF and six others in the ATS held commissions. Such staff involvement had unwelcome repercussions at School: the Headmistress faced massive difficulties in replacing teachers who had 'joined up'.

A small sideline to the School's history showed that the realities of war in Britain were not fully appreciated overseas; with Dunkirk, impending German invasion, the Battle of Britain and the start of the Blitz all in 1940, the following advertisement was placed in the *School Magazine* by Torfrida Walford (T 1920):

> Wanted to rent, furnished house, South-West England, near sea & golf course, May–Sept 1940. Maids' & 4–5 Bedrooms preferred. Send particulars to my home in Bombay.'

Early in 1940 the British Government announced a scheme for parents to send their children for the duration to Canada, the USA and Australia. Within two weeks the 'lists' were closed: 225,000 applications had been received. Some public schools made their own plans for setting up 'branches' – Roedean and Sherborne looking to Canada. There was a huge demand to get children to safety, motivated by fear of the consequences of invasion, and as Veronica Owen's (W 1942) father said, 'the fewer useless mouths our merchant seamen have to feed the better'. Many parents had connections in high places, and not a few were uncomfortable about their families; Nazi propaganda, rape and links with British Jewry added to the overwhelming sense of danger. One Sherborne mother caught the atmosphere: 'The summer of 1940 was fraught with anxiety and fear for the future' – over a hundred School parents quickly supported the idea of evacuation.

In charge of the Sherborne girls was to be Diana Reader Harris (DH 1930), now a member of staff. She and the Headmistress spent some days in London with Canadian officials organising money and passages. Later she described how urgent but controversial the matter became:

> I only had five days' notice, and I said I wouldn't go unless my Matron in West came too – I was only 27! I was convinced that getting the children out was the right thing, though one West parent thought all this was appalling – 'leaving the sinking ship', he said.

There were certainly mixed feelings about the enterprise. Jaquetta Digby (DH 1945) remembers her mother making arrangements for her to go to Canada, but her sister, Pamela, had recently married Randolph Churchill:

> Winston said to my mother, 'No relative of mine is going to run away' – so I went to Dun Holme instead!

After frantic arrangements a first group of 22 girls sailed from Liverpool on the SS *Duchess of Atholl* on 26 June. It arrived safely in Quebec, though OGs have vivid memories of a very rough crossing. 'Nearly everyone was seasick – fortunately not me; I went around with the basins!', remembers Pamela McCloughry (AW 1942). A second group was to follow to bring the numbers to 150; in the event the 'Sherborne' Canadian contingent never went higher than 47 – fear of German U-Boats was heightened when SS *City of Benares* carrying government-scheme children was sunk and 73 drowned.

Meanwhile, realities of getting settled in Canada immediately surfaced. First was accommodation: Miss Stuart's original intention of founding a separate 'Sherborne-in-Canada' school for 150, financed directly from England, proved a non-starter. A Toronto school, Branksome Hall, was acting as 'a transit hostel for war-guests from Britain' during the summer vacation, and its staff met the Sherborne contingent among other evacuees. The Canadian plan was to scatter them all as day-girls throughout the city; but a cable from Miss Stuart revealed strong opposition to 'her girls' being dispersed. Miss Reader Harris was in a quandary: however, one ray of hope was the immediate rapport she had struck with Branksome's Headmistress, Miss Edith Read. 'No matter,' she said, 'we'll find you a house.'

A second problem, money, or rather the lack of it, proved intractable. The girls found Canadian banks unwilling to change pounds for dollars; the staff found buying furniture etc. for a 'Sherborne' house impossible. Branksome now revealed themselves as wonderful hosts. The girls were invited by parents to their homes or summer camps, and Branksome Alumnae (OGs) generously offered to furnish the house at 40 Maple Avenue; a continuous stream of living equipment, new and loaned, poured in.

Other financial problems proved chronic. School archives have sheaves of letters revealing all kinds of difficulties. Parents thought the initial idea of 'girls educated in Canada, fees paid in England' admirable until complications set in. The British government began blocking the transfer of money. Patiently, letters had to be sent to parents saying that although Branksome fees were $700, only $600 could be transferred from England; the shortfall would build up, and had to be paid after the War. In fact without kindness and loans from Canadians the whole project could have collapsed. At home one irate parent became very unhappy about 'promises', and had to be told bluntly by Miss Stuart that 'if you do not feel that Sherborne's word is sufficient guarantee, you should make other arrangements for your children.' Later the father of Elva Parkinson (T 1946) faced official barriers when trying to pay Canadian bills in dollars: 'My bank finds the permission of the Bank of England will have to be obtained!' Miss Reader Harris too had personal financial problems: in 1941 she wrote a letter to the Sherborne bursar, having just received notice from British government officials that 'employment in Canada cannot be treated as contributory service for a teacher's pension.' Her despairing comment was

> I'm afraid it's all beyond me. I should have thought I was just as much in the employ of Sherborne as when I was at Sherborne. Apparently the Board of Education doesn't think so!

Part of Diana Reader Harris' Canadian Petty Cash records: Elizabeth Riddell's 'extras' for two terms in 1942 (the exchange rate was $4.43 to the £1).

E. Riddell

Spring & Summer Terms 1942

Skirt cleaned	.35
Hair cut	.40
Coat cleaned	.66
Roll-on	.98
Brassiere	.58
Shoes	3.69
Gym Shoes	.98
Shoes	2.98
Skirt cleaned	.75
Socks	.75
Socks	1.05
Anti-moth	.25
Trainfare	22.75
Dress	3.95
Jumper	.30
	40.42

On top of all this she kept up a mass of detailed correspondence, mostly handwritten, on the minutiae of the girls' lives in Canada, including 'extras' lists. Elizabeth Riddell's (W 1944) 'extras' for two terms in 1942 were calculated down to the last cent.

The girls knew nothing of these administrative headaches. Their attention was naturally elsewhere. On arrival: embarrassment at thinking, 'I'm a refugee'. First impressions: the extraordinarily kind welcome ('almost suffocating,' said one), the heat, no blackout, peaches by the basketful; then the homesickness – agony for some. All were kept in close touch with the War in Europe: the Blitz, Churchill's speeches, the invasion of Russia and 'relief that England was no longer alone'. Veronica Owen kept her letters home and rereading them 50 years later was struck by, 'my desire not to grow older in order to seem the same to my parents on my return – I had a need to keep in touch.' Adapting though became a necessity, 'fitting-in' an urgency. One girl wrote to School, 'the Branksome girls all seem terribly grown-up and affected, with all their lipstick and paraphernalia.'

The girls were well looked after: academic standards were maintained, and they did well in examinations; the food was excellent; and opportunities abounded in sport and in the social sphere. Joan Riddell (W 1944) sent an account to Sherborne:

> Basketball, skating in the 'Varsity Arena, skiing every Saturday, and swimming in Branksome's own indoor pool. Saturday: downtown to a movie. The School Dance is the main event at Easter – Third Form upwards are invited by Miss Read to bring their 'steadies' or else get blind dates.

All this, metaphorically and physically, was oceans apart from wartime life at Sherborne. Yet, by 1943, things were changing in Canada. There was now a much closer involvement in the War: oil and petrol rationing had arrived, and there had been massive Canadian Army casualties in the tragic Dieppe raid of 1942. In England, parents were now agitating for the 'war-guests' to return home, as invasion was no longer a fear; 'Canadian generosity has lasted long enough.' A few girls had already reached 17, and had come back to join up. In the summer of 1942 Pamela

McCloughry returned 'on a small French cargo ship which I discovered was carrying high explosives!' In that same summer Veronica Owen and Joan Mack (W 1942) boarded 'a "banana-boat", carrying enough bacon for the whole of Britain for a week, 4000 bags of mail, sanitary towels and nine passengers.' The return over the next year was normally by troopship or cargo vessel in convoys of about 70 ships. The Battle of the Atlantic against the U-boats was still a serious danger, and some journeys could be painfully slow – 28 days for some.

Back in England: to rationing, to queues, 'all rather drab and sad' – so little hot water, dark trains, no signposts. With considerable shock many girls found their parents quite unfamiliar. Others gloried at being home at last – London was 'vibrantly alive' to one, though another OG was 'shocked at the bombing devastation in the capital'. Adjustment proved difficult for some – 'the experience drove me into a shell,' said one; Jenny Horton (AW 1946) commented

> Canada made us grow up quickly. We were used to thinking for ourselves. But I did not realise how exhausted by war people at home had become.

And those who returned to Sherborne found the old, traditional rules very irksome after life in the New World; whilst their peers who had stayed behind envied the self-confidence of the returnees.

Facing page: *Sherborne girls skating at the Toronto 'Varsity Stadium, January 1941, and* (above) *the house that was home for the evacuees for two years.*

Postscript

Sherborne had *its* School Dance, the first ever with the Boys' School, on VE Day in 1945, but that is another story (see Chapter 6). The Branksome Hall link remained strong for over 20 years. A girl from each school was 'exchanged' annually, and the last Canadian girl, Sheila MacFeeters (T 1975), says:

> it was one of the best years of my life, and I will always be grateful for the opportunity, and for the fact that I made it to the Greyhound in Cheap Street without being caught.

8
'Be Wisely Worldly, Be not Worldly Wise'

Beyond the classroom, beyond the gates: some understanding of the outside world and the promotion of confidence to face its challenges have been important aims of a Sherborne education. Through lectures, debates and mock parliamentary elections, through law trials and competitions – the means have varied, but the end result has been in Penny Deacon's (staff 1984–93) words, 'girls with initiative and an independence of mind'.

Lectures began as a staff enterprise, Beatrice Mulliner adapting her own preaching prowess to a series of literary and classical themes. The lure of outsiders, with national or even international reputations, became evident in February 1914 when Commander Evans RN, a key organiser of 'Scott's Last Expedition' to the South Pole, came to talk. In memory of Oates's famous sacrifice the School was given a holiday. In 1925 the expedition was again the theme; this time a Cambridge University lecturer, who had been Robert Scott's geologist, showed spectacular slides of Antarctic scenery and wild life. Of lectures on distant lands none could match the pathos of the 'Everest' visit. George Mallory came in 1922 to tell of his previous efforts and current preparations for scaling the mountain. Betty Robertson (W 1923) took notes:

> It is hard to imagine the difficulties of progress at this altitude, for at 23,000 ft five breaths have to be taken for each step. He and his companions were forced back; they tried again with oxygen despite the weight of the cylinders. But porter illness and avalanches made further climbing impossible.

Mallory had arrived early – in time for a 'hockey tea'– and Margery Colborne (DH 1925) recalled later, 'He was given a miniature brandy bottle from West's splendid Christmas tree. We were grieved to hear in 1924 that he and Irvine were lost in their attempt to climb Mount Everest.'

Emotions were again in evidence in two lectures on Lawrence of Arabia. The first, by Captain Armstrong in 1935 on 'Lawrence and Ibn Saud', was soon after Lawrence's fatal accident; Lorna Tudsbery (AW 1936) wrote excitedly, 'He was only afraid of old age. There could have been no more wonderful ending for him than sudden death on a motor cycle at 72 mph in a narrow Dorset lane.' Then in 1942

Sir Ronald Storrs, who had escorted Lawrence from Cairo to the Arabs in the desert in 1915, delivered a balanced talk on his enigmatic personality to a packed Hall. The Middle East, its history and political problems, often appeared on lecture programmes. General Sir John Glubb – 'Glubb Pasha' as the press dubbed him – was outstanding; his lucid description of the area gave the girls new sympathy with the Arabs in the late 1950s. Another rounded lecture dovetailing all the complex issues was given in 1994 by HRH the Crown Prince of Jordan (see Chapter 13). Colette Clement (AE 1995) was fascinated:

> Suddenly media reports make more sense; the factions are no longer just a string of initials. To talk to us he was taking time out of a schedule that would give us a nervous breakdown, but we now know the situation is a real one: it concerns people and not merely statistics on a page of *The Economist*.

'A speaker with a difference': HRH Crown Prince Hassan of Jordan.

The antiquity of the Middle East had a wonderful illustrator in 1932. Still in the midst of his 12-year excavations at Ur, Leonard Woolley covered many familiar names from the girls' classrooms: Nebuchadnezzar, Abraham and the Flood, and the royal tombs of Sumerian civilisation. Two speakers well known to television viewers, Sir Mortimer Wheeler and Professor Glyn Daniels, were to open up other fields of archaeology with their talks on 'Digging up the Past' in the 1960s.

Adventurers were always the biggest attraction: two already enjoyed massive media popularity. Sir Alec Rose came in 1970 to describe his single-handed, round-the-world voyage; and in 1978 Sir Ranulph Fiennes, the explorer, spoke of hair-raising journeys up the White Nile by hovercraft, parachuting on to Norwegian glaciers, and on preparations for his future expedition to the North Pole.

Russia, too, seems to have enthralled several generations of girls. Sir Bernard Pares, historian and expert on that country, came twice in the early years of the Second World War, providing much enlightenment on Stalin and Soviet ambitions. But he could not have matched the immediacy of the Headmistress. Miss Stuart's account of her journey with Diana Reader Harris through the USSR and into China in 1936 was summarised by Rita Setten (AE 1937), who highlighted the poverty and starvation they saw. She said the audience was riveted by the story of their arrest at the frontier because 'their passports were valid for one way and their tickets for the other!' The School's own Russian expert, Dr Daphne West (staff 1978–97), was not at all surprised by such bureaucratic delays – then or now! (see Chapter 4). In the mid-1980s Mrs Griffith-Jones, the mother of OG Clare (DH 1974) described her experiences when as an adolescent she fled from Warsaw to Russia in 1939, only to be interned in one of Stalin's labour camps in Soviet Asia. She spoke for 45 minutes almost without notes, to an audience stunned that someone at their age could have faced and survived such events.

Literature, the arts and the intellectual world have not been neglected. Herbert Read spoke on 'Painting' in 1935, and shortly afterwards Ernest Raymond analysed the craft of the novelist. Two philosophers made special efforts to reach their schoolgirl audiences. Dr C. E. M. Joad, of the BBC's 'Brains Trust' panel, visited in 1938, and Mary Warnock in 1966 built a lecture on 'I ought . . .,' with such examples as the acceptability in some places of eating your grandmother and in others

DUKE OF EDINBURGH AWARD

Gold
Alex D'Arcy Irvine
Juliet Larcombe
Jane Scott
Sarah Wade
Fiona Creighton

Silver
Sasha Burn
Lucy Ferguson
Elizabeth Blandford
Sumaya El Hassan
Katherine Plincke
Samantha Moralee
Kate Reed
Melanie Copeland
Lucy Jameson
Vanessa Harry
Jane Pakes
Alice Roberts
Claire Wingfield Digby
Sarah May
Camilla Franklin
Sophie Orr
Nicola Schleifer
Emma Bartlett

The 1988 awards.

the moral condemnation of unchaperoned girls! Many OGs remember with affection the distinguished French writer André Maurois coming to talk on 'The English'. 'The Old Vic' was described by Tyrone Guthrie in 1953, and three years later Roger Manvell of the British Film Academy stirred the girls so much that a Film Society was founded in the school. Professor Sir Kenneth Clark, eminent art historian and lecturer, spoke in 1959 on the painter John Turner. John Betjeman, later the Poet Laureate, paraded his famous indolence and good humour, reading from his recently published *Summoned by Bells.* Maria Aitken (AW 1962 – see Chapter 12) had invited him to the Literary Society, promising 'to provide an intelligent audience and an excellent dinner with the Headmistress.' The latter also provided her own fur coat for JB to lecture in because he was cold! Maria wrote to her mother,

> An enormous success: he totally disarmed everyone. The girls and even the most astringent of spinsters on the Staff were enchanted. I adored it.

Dame Ninette de Valois' account of the Diaghilev Ballet on tour was equally entertaining, whilst in the 1970s there were several visits from Margaret Lane, author and broadcaster, whose topics ranged from an earlier Countess of Huntingdon to Peter Rabbit and his origins. In her last year as Headmistress, Dame Diana persuaded two distinguished literary figures to address the School: Lord David Cecil on 'Hamlet' and Dr A. L. Rowse on 'Shakespearean England'. During dinner in White Lodge for the latter, he so cornered the conversation that her renowned reputation as a hostess was much taxed!

Impressive as all these eminent visitors were, none could hold a candle to two relatively unknown lecturers in the 1920s. Beatrice Mulliner had a talent for spotting something 'new' well before it passed into normal household use. In 1921 Professor Bailey demonstrated 'wireless'. Ruth Galletly (W 1922) was amazed at the 'receiving apparatus, which had peculiar interest – it was the only one of its kind in existence'. This was the year before the BBC was founded. Seven years later, two girls wrote an account of the visit of a Mr Denton: the first said,

> We gazed at the platform, full of intense anticipation. On the left were strange things, coils, a vivid light, a wheel, queer boxes. In the middle in full view stood Mr Denton, in evening dress. 'You think you see me, but you are quite mistaken. You do not.' This was the disconcerting beginning of a most fascinating lecture on the romance and wonder of the discovery of television.

The lecturer had been secretary to John Logie Baird whom he described as 'the first actually to demonstrate publicly true television'. The other girl was ecstatic:

> Television is absolutely incomprehensible! As I listened I became incredulous – how

The 1994 Expedition.

> can such a thing be? The faces of two Sixth Form scientists beside me shone with excitement. There is nothing in the world that is impossible now.

Contentious issues were also introduced. One such on alcoholism, in 1926, was couched in scientific form – Dr Weeks brought with him a model of the human brain, and he both entertained and informed the girls on the 'four stages: pleasure, merriment, disorder and oblivion' which alcohol induced in the brain. The range of such lectures reflected the main issues of the day. Industrial and race relations were considered, the latter in the middle of the difficult times of the mid-1960s. Social problems have always been to the fore, none more so than when in 1967 the Revd Bruce Kenrick, founder of 'Shelter', came to talk on his Notting Hill experiences; he stayed long after his 'hour' as so many girls wanted to ask questions.

In the 1960s, extra lectures were put on for the Sixth Form. One was by Sir John Wolfenden, whose recent report as Chairman of the Royal Commission on *Homosexuality and Prostitution* had received much publicity: he spoke clearly and with some humour on the subject of 'Crime and Sin'. Nuclear warfare and defence matters were never far from the girls' minds, especially in 1962, the year of the Cuban Missile crisis. Dr Marjorie Yates of the Ministry of Defence outlined the government's policies, but it was Rear-Admiral Sir Anthony Buzzard who gripped the girls with his lecture on 'The Bomb', covering international arms-control and the moral and practical choices that have to be made to secure peace.

One impact of these lectures on the girls is perhaps best illustrated by Fiona Webster (W 1966): 'I'm very grateful to Sherborne – I've never been afraid to ask questions in public, a practice instilled by all those lectures by famous people.'

BUCKINGHAM PALACE

I hope that in taking part in the Award Scheme you will discover fresh interests and make new friends, and find satisfaction in giving service to others.

There are many worthwhile activities from which you can make a choice and I hope that those which you decide to do will give you pleasure and increase your knowledge of the world and of yourself.

The Duke of Edinburgh Awards have tempted many who later go on the exhausting 'gap' year projects (see Chapter 15).

The emotive issue of Women's Rights emerged on many occasions in lectures and debates. The Suffragettes of course could not be ignored! Winifred Dixon (Greenhill 1903) sent an account to the School in 1908:

> Much to the amusement of my friends I went to a Women's Suffrage Demonstration at the Albert Hall. We could only manage gallery seats in this vast assembly. The programme told us that Mrs Pankhurst was still in prison, but Christabel announced that her mother had been unexpectedly released and so would chair the meeting. I wish I could give you a faint idea of the enthusiasm; amid a storm of cheering Mrs Pankhurst walked down the gangway. What struck me about the speakers was their *saneness*. But though I sympathise with their aims, I do not feel ready to join because of their methods.

Later that year, the Principal of Westfield College, University of London, addressed the girls on the 'Position of Women in the World'. She provoked much laughter when comparing girls of the day (1908!) with those of the eighteenth century, when a girl was advised, 'not to enjoy robust health, for a man likes a sensitive delicacy – and she must never parade her knowledge.'

The girls were not obviously persuaded. In a debate the following year, the motion that 'the Parliamentary vote be extended to women' was lost 28:38. During the debate, much was made of the 'more-women-than-men' problem, together with 'dangers to the welfare of the Empire'. Miss Mulliner too was unhappy with images of the 'shrieking sisterhood'. In 1918, on the eve of the Act giving women over 30 the right to vote, hoots of merriment were provoked at a School fancy dress party. Mary Lascelles (A 1918 – see Chapter 4) described, 'the arrival of a virulent "Suffragette" who attempted to corrupt the morals of the School by disseminating dangerous pamphlets.'

That girls questioned whether 'the vote' was really the central issue in Women's Rights was clear as the century developed. As recently as 1991 a debate 'that Margaret Thatcher had proved that women have no place in politics' was supported by what the Debating Society secretary called 'that in-school feminist, Miss Angela Pitt' (Head of English)! I also found that in the 1970s and 1980s opportunities in the workplace and their relation to childbearing had assumed far more importance. The History Department taught an O-level course for many years on 'Women's Rights in the 20th Century', in which the story of education leading to greater career possibilities, the history of contraception and the demise of the chaperone were perceived as far more relevant to the girls' future lives than the vote. In 1986, Mrs Firth of the *Financial Times* lectured on 'Women in Journalism': she bluntly offered the girls: 'A five-point plan in employment: get in, get on, get pregnant, get out, get back – and my emphasis is on the last'.

The Debating Society has had a chequered career. Formed in 1908 its subjects have ranged far and wide. Controversial issues – the poor, conscription, Irish Home Rule and vivisection (1909–12) vied with entertainments – 'that the modern tendency to rush is to be deplored' (carried, in 1908!). Political themes attracted heated discussion, but at times not much enlightenment. In 1924 'This House welcomes a Labour Government as a step towards prosperity' was carried 48:29, but the Secretary was critical: 'Very few people spoke and those who spoke, spoke rather often and off the point.'

For some years the Society would find little support, even disappearing. But current issues of import and appealing speakers would bring the debaters back: the weakness of the League of Nations (1933), and 'Is democracy failing?' (1938) revived the Society's fortunes for a while. Debates with the Wildman Society of the Boys' School in the 1960s and 1970s injected a much needed animation – as well as becoming, in Candia McWilliam's (AE 1973) words, 'the locus of a certain amount of romantic energy'. 1985 was a good year for The Forum (the Senior Debating Society's new name). One debating theme on 'Arts *v.* Science' had occurred before; in 1920 'Science' had been soundly beaten. This time it involved girls and staff and was publicised as :

The Debate of the Year
This House believes the study of humanities is
more beneficial to society than that of the sciences

Proposer – Mr Barry Williams (Historian), Seconder – Rebecca Bomford (AW 1986)
Opposer – Mr Donald Mathewson (Chemist), Seconder – Caroline Furze (AW 1986)

The Lecture Theatre was definitely overfull and my own memory of it is of a very heated debate; despite the best efforts of Becky and myself (our argument was that the wonderful achievements of science have outrun the ability of man to control them) we had to concede defeat.

Since the 1940s the Debating Society has had to compete for the girls' support with so many other avenues of expression. The 1940s saw an interesting experiment when a series of Parliamentary meetings was held. A full *Hansard* record of a debate was studied, the speeches of Members and ministers précised and semi-learned. Then with great skill and flourishing of notes, the girl-politicians would act out the scene before the School. The government was criticised for inadequate provision of canteens for miners and vital war-workers in 1941; Winston Churchill withstood a motion of 'no confidence' during the dark days of defeat in 1942. A year later, the great Beveridge Report on 'want, disease, ignorance, squalor and idleness', which heralded the Welfare State, was given an energetic and spectacular coverage. This format was extended to the Law: Sherborne Sessions were investigated and full legal procedures and dressing up led to many entertaining and serious cases being heard.

Politics were again the focus of attention in 1945 – this time during the General Election. Local candidates gave lectures on party manifestos, and 'on the day' the School had two 'votes'. One, by the existing straight vote system, gave the Conservatives a large majority; the other, using proportional representation, resulted in a Conservative lead over Liberal reduced to one vote. Later, in 1950, several weeks of campaigning – including £150 deposits of 'Monopoly' money! – swept the Conservatives to a massive 200:20:20 victory, both Liberals and Labour losing their deposits. Things were *not* the same in 1955. An exciting campaign at school gave the Liberals 106 to the Conservatives' 47. Elisabeth Walwyn (DH 1956) wrote home:

> The school looked like a party HQ, with gaudy posters at every turn. The mass hysteria was terrific during speeches. I had strong Liberal feelings and we won! By the real election day we were all worked up; we heard the results would be coming in all night, so nine of us decided to take a wireless to one room with our mugs, pyjamas and rugs; also stocks of cocoa, biscuits, bread and jam. We settled down for hours of listening and filling in the huge constituency map. It certainly taught us the geography of England. Our torches ran out at 3 a.m., but we'd worked up a wonderful atmosphere. We only had two hours sleep: we were absolutely dead in school that day, but as the staff were too, it didn't matter.

School societies have long provided a focus on things outside the classroom. Apart from the Debating Society, the first recorded example was a Natural History

Society in 1910, and it flourished in various guises over the ensuing years. A very successful Current Problems Society was founded in 1942: 80 members pondered the 'Jewish Problem', 'India' and 'Poverty and the Beveridge Report'. Future topics included Russia, the BBC, Conscription of Women and Race Relations. It too flourished for a long time. I inherited its 'Presidency' in the 1970s and by common consent merged it with the Current Events 'lesson', which was voluntary for the UV last period on a Friday afternoon. Very sceptical about its timing and optional nature, I advertised a theme, 'Communism', expecting a quiet discussion with a handful of keen girls. In the event over 60 crowded into the history room, sitting on chairs, tables and crossed-legged on the floor! The 'lesson' ran for 20 years, with annual coverage of issues such as inflation, advertising, and trade unions; the two which drew the largest numbers were the World Population Explosion (this so animated the girls that Housemistresses told me it regularly dominated discussions at supper afterwards), and Northern Ireland, which ran and ran, so that my notes made for 1973 became in effect a historical document to be considered in the meeting of the late 1980s.

Many other societies thrived, with their heyday clearly the 1950s and 1960s. In 1957 society reports in the *School Magazine* covered six sides, and included Bible Reading, Local History, a Literary Society, an Art Club, a Language Society, a Reel Club and Film Society. A Photographic Society had remarkable success – within ten years it boasted a membership of 150. The long-standing Science Society has more recently blended in with BAYS (British Association of Young Scientists) – the Wessex branch meets in Yeovil College or School alternately once a month, and has a subject range for example of artificial limbs, the intelligent robot, pathology and acne.

In 1966 an inter-house public speaking competition produced a very high standard of oratory on European issues – the metric system and reunification of Germany, for instance – with Wingfield emerging as winners of a close contest. By the 1980s this had developed into School participation in the Sherborne Rotary Club competition for local schools. In 1988 teams led by Eleanor Clark (T 1989) and Charlotte Boyle (T 1989) came first and second, and Eleanor's team swept the board in the Wessex finals. In the same decade, the 'Young Enterprise' competition began to emerge. Sarah Griffith-Jones (AW 1991) gave a graphic account of the 1989 combined group with the Boys' School, with its lessons for future business women:

> A mock company with a lot of work. Parents seemed surprised that we actually sold shares, having taken our 'market' into consideration; we also made the product and hopefully sold it. We had to manage accounts, maximise profits, pay back shareholders and pay the workers!

A new style of course and lecture was introduced in 1976, and with modification has continued to the present day. 'A revolutionary change,' recorded one girl about General Studies, which Elizabeth Coulter developed with the Boys' School staff. A huge range of non-examination courses were put on for the joint Sixth Forms on Wednesday and Friday afternoons. 'Impressive, intellectually high-grade

> Church simplicity, fortunately in beautiful surroundings. The sermons were long.

The 'crocodile' had to arrive before 10.30 a.m. so as not to inconvenience the rest of the congregation. Sitting quietly on seats in the aisles from which many girls could neither see nor hear, learning set texts for over half an hour was hugely unpopular. In the 1930s Canon Askwith, the School Chaplain (later Bishop of Blackburn) was dismayed at all this, and for some years organised a special 10 a.m. service out in Castleton Church, but the War and security problems meant a return to the Abbey.

Over the years 'Sundays' embedded themselves in the girls' consciousness. Cecily Ballard (DH 1930) recalls

> walking in 'croc' to the Abbey for 8 a.m. service; back for breakfast, then return for 11 a.m. service. After lunch it was Scripture prep. for an hour, then writing letters home. After tea another service in the School Hall. However Sunday lunch was something special: I still remember a delicious apricot tart and cream.

Nancy Ollivant (Ald 1928) was ambivalent:

> Though enjoying my days at Sherborne, I do think we spent a great amount of time praying . . . small wonder that when I left I wanted to be a missionary – encouraged no doubt by the marvellous preaching of Miss Mulliner.

Hilda Violet Stuart was also a vigorous, impressive preacher, and many OGs remember both her and Dame Diana 'sailing through the Bunny Hutch' for Morning Prayers or delivering the sermon at Evening Service, and holding the girls' attention with ease. There were many striking visiting preachers. Dr Cyril

Augusta Miller conducting the School Choir in Sherborne Abbey, c.1980.

Miss Stuart with four Mienchow Kindergarten children on her visit to China in 1936.

Gayaza, Uganda 1989 – comments by the girls after Gayaza's deputy headmistress visited Sherborne: 'we support them, they are coping well, but they need much more help . . . moving, it hit me how badly off they are . . . whenever I complain at not being allowed new clothes I shall think twice . . . it's so unfair, I wish God could have evened it out'.

Norwood, then Master of Marlborough (later a School Governor), gave the 1921 Commemoration sermon.

> Take the Great War: a gambling stroke to control the power and resources of the world. It was at bottom a struggle of the material against the spiritual, of the self-seeking against the ideal. God's cause prevailed. But do not let us be smug; are we contentedly slipping back into the old grooves, and reckoning national greatness by money, markets and territory? We have to get back to the simple teachings of Christ; we must find some way to inter-communion between our churches, or we must fail.

His final appeal found echoes down the years. In 1944 staff and girls held a 'unity' service. Girls read and sang from the litanies and sermons of the years of the Reformation and Puritanism; when Fox's *Journal* was read all the girls donned their hats in honour of the Quakers. Singing 'The Church's One Foundation' was a fitting finale. In 1959 the School Service in the Hall was taken by ministers of the Church of Scotland, Congregational, Methodist and Baptist churches. Several OGs say the excellence of the preaching by visiting monks and friars from Wessex 'houses' in the 1970s and 1980s was much appreciated.

Both Hall and Abbey provided an ambience which remained in girls' memories far into later life. 'It was with a sense of sadness,' wrote Margaret Woodcock (K 1939), 'that one departed from the Hall for the last time.' And Candia McWilliam (AE 1973) was moved to write: 'The Abbey could be beautiful, so that even we, indifferent children, noticed and felt part of something serious and to be perpetuated.'

The religious life of the School community – the care of its soul – so definitive and fundamental to its existence, has many other facets. Over the century the formality has been tempered, the sheer plethora of tasks reduced and the appeal widened. For instance, preparation for confirmation was decidedly protracted, and not only for the girls. Miss Mulliner took on all the interviewing and the marking of extended scriptural essays; these were such a heavy burden on her that the staff attributed her collapse and illness in 1929 to such overwork. The essays have long gone, and in 1947 Miss Stuart allowed the girls to go bareheaded to the service – 'less dressing up for a special occasion,' she said. Today confirmation remains an essential part of normal school life, whilst the 'Bishop's Bun Fight', when parents, Confirmation candidates and staff meet after the service, is a convivial, corporate occasion.

The teaching of Scripture has always been important to the curriculum – until 1933 it was even a compulsory subject for Higher Certificate (A-level). By mid-century 'chalk and talk' on the Bible only had been expanded to include playlets and the study of modern thinkers. In the 1970s, Jane Williams (E 1979) commented:

> RK was interesting: we were taught in successive years the Bible with Mrs Stewart, other religious movements with Miss Guinness, and then we had Mr Hartley – excellent discussions. I remember an impromptu one on John Lennon's 'Imagine . . . no Heaven' (we were singing it when he arrived).

In the mid-1980s RK became more clearly RS – 'study' beyond mere 'knowledge' – and a quiet revolution gathered pace. The focus was now on the Bible, the Koran *et al.*, plus ethics and social problems, in keeping with the girls' own wider sympathies and sensibilities.

In the last quarter of the century, one abiding staff memory of Morning Prayers must be the orderly 'leading up' by the junior school, followed by the Upper Sixth scurrying like Alice's White Rabbit to avoid being late; another must be the content with its emphasis on collective conscience. Charity, in the strict sense of compassion for others, has always had a prominent place in the life of the School. All kinds of social work in England and missionary work overseas started immediately under Beatrice Mulliner. For this was the outward expression of the School's abiding image as a caring community.

It began in China. Charlotte Wingfield Digby's sister, a missionary in the western provinces, wrote to Sherborne in 1902 saying, 'This is pioneer work: no Christians, and no schools for girls, who still have their feet bound.' She had opened a school and was appealing for help. Soon an annual gift of £100 was being sent to the girls' boarding school at Mienchow in Szechwan Province. There was explicitly no attempt to 'foreignise' the Chinese children, but suspicion of European influence increased. The school had a stormy existence. Throughout the 1920s civil war in China had devastating effects when anti-Christian soldiers seized the school. By 1936 it was rumoured that the £100 gift was going to bandits.

> I went out to see for myself: I found Szechwan quite terrifying. It abounded with gaolbirds called by the local population 'Szechwan rats'. I was told that the last English woman here was found in a ditch without a head! But the school is the one centre of peace: outside no child ever smiled, inside they laughed.

So wrote Miss Stuart after making an extraordinary and dangerous trip to the school. By the end of the 1940s the Communists were at the centre of yet another civil war. In 1949 the Sherborne £100 'was used to buy rice immediately – for our teachers' salaries, money being valueless'. Within two years the controlling Communists announced, 'No more foreign money', the school was abruptly closed, and the 49-year-old link sadly ended.

The Church Missionary Society asked Sherborne to transfer its support to the Gayaza High School for Girls in Uganda, which it did willingly. It has remained an official School charity to this day, and exchanges and visits by girls in both directions have strengthened the link. Uganda too had its political upheavals, so that the safety and functioning of the school became serious problems in the 1970s under the dictatorship of Idi Amin's regime. Gayaza's choir came to Sherborne in 1983: Alice McMurtie (A 1984) recorded the enormous 'welcome' in evidence both ways: 'The concert was thoroughly enjoyed. The songs were in English and Ugandan dialects and there were favourites such as "Moto" sung in Swahili.' The visitors left with a cheque for £1,200 which individual Houses had raised.

The African bond has a parallel in India. Once, Amrit Kaur (see Chapter 1), having addressed the School, said, 'You are going to do something for me.' The girls, fascinated by this dynamic small figure in a beautiful sari, agreed with enthusiasm. So Dame Diana established a second official charity, whereby the School sends regular

Camila Batmanghelidj (DH 1981) – known to all as 'Batman' – a flamboyant character who set up the charity A Place To Be, a kind of 'Welcome Club'. It has helped 1,600 6–16-year-olds in the inner-city areas of London – the tower blocks of Lambeth and Camden for example. Psychotherapists listen as the children tell of abuse, neglect and poverty; Camila encourages them to express themselves through art, whilst she badgers government and other agencies for help.

Commemoration collections for the training of a doctor and nurse at Ludhiana Christian Medical College in the Punjab. Closer to home the School has twice offered help to Europe: in the austerity years following the Second World War toys, clothes and even stationery were sent through the 'Save Europe Now' Fund to German schools in the Rhineland. Letters of thanks emphasised the need to 'bridge the hate'. A decade later money went to the Hungarian Relief Fund – with an interesting postscript for the School. In a lesson on the Cold War Kate Anderton (K 1988) told me of her mother's hazardous escape to England from the Soviet tanks in Budapest during the 1956 Rising – Elizabeth Biro (K 1959) coming straight to Sherborne.

The needs of the destitute in England, particularly those of children with poverty-related diseases, commanded much support in the first half of the century, and some of it lingered well into the days of Welfare State provision. The Welcome Club in London's East End came to Sherborne's attention in 1909 through Miss Kathleen Moore's sister: it was the only social centre in the area run in girls' interests. Its founder, Eleanor Seton-Kerr, offered 'human sympathy, understanding and service' to local factory girls – cheap nourishing lunches and educational classes. In 1910 a Welcome 'holiday home' for these girls was opened on the Sussex coast at Littlehampton. A report to the School stated, 'It is almost impossible to imagine how hard and sad their lives are: one girl – father dead, mother in an asylum – was ill and half-blind working with poisonous inks in a printing factory.' Over the next half century the School supported 'Welcome' with money and clothing.

Miss Mulliner kept the plight of the poor firmly in the girls' minds, in Morning Prayers, in House and in articles. In 1924 she made an impassioned plea on behalf of the children of slums and their lack of fresh air. One practical result was the opening in 1925 of St Christopher's in Marston Road, Sherborne, for 'needy children who want a change of air after illness'. Miss Stuart kept up the attention: in the middle of the Depression of the 1930s proposals to help 'the Distressed Areas in the North' led to the setting up of a holiday camp school at Saltburn on the NE coast. £1,000 was offered to establish it and an annual £280 promised. It was, said Miss Stuart in 1949,

> one of the happiest of the social activities undertaken by the School. Alas it ended with the War when the Government requisitioned the building. Let us hope the need for it is not so pressing in these state-aided days.

A PHAB group of the early 1970s in front of Aylmar and Wingfield.

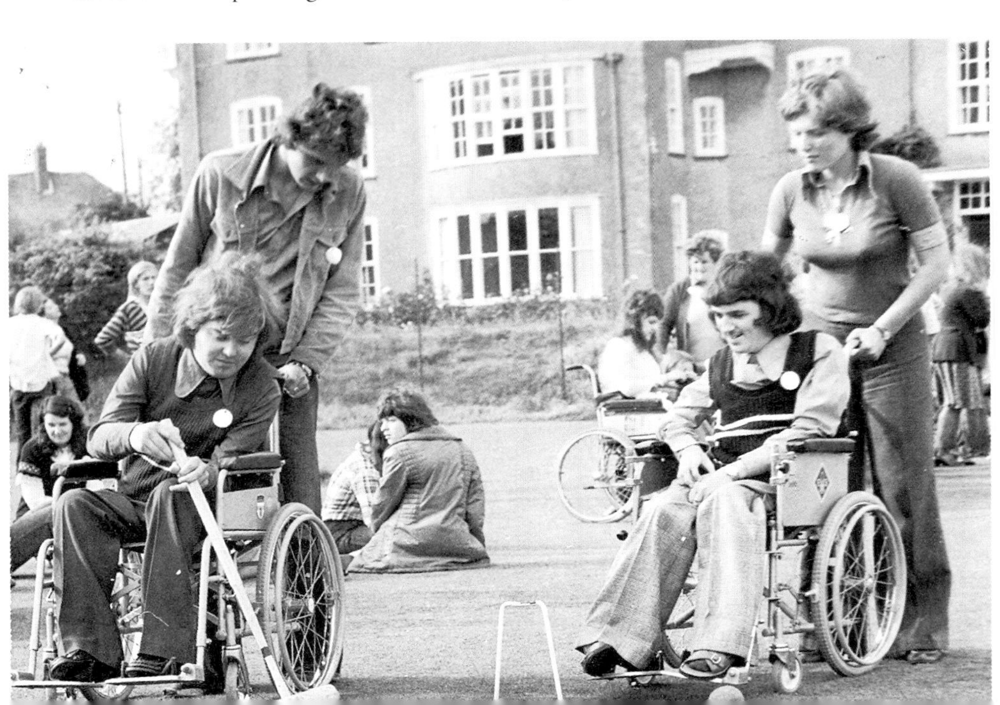

It proved a hollow hope. In Sherborne's second half-century plenty of places and people were to be in need of help. Charlotte Black-Hawkins (W 1965) brought a disturbing report back from Liverpool where she had been on a course for social scientists: 'We walked through some of the worst slums in Liverpool – perhaps the most eye-opening experience of the weekend.' The need for a charitable conscience was still evident. OGs had played their part: back in 1937 liaison with the St Pancras Society had created the Sherborne Nursery School in this deprived part of London. It flourished for 55 years, helped by government grants. But by 1992–3 it had come under Camden Council, and political factors intervened. Despite pleas, the nursery was closed. Sara Stephens (A 1956) said,

> Camden are squeezing hard to save a lot of money. We believe that it was a cost-cutting exercise where very little has been gained and a great deal lost.

The focus of 'good works' has widened considerably since the 1960s. 'Visiting my old lady' began appearing in many a girl's diary. If they were 'dud at sport', as one girl put it, Sixth Formers on games days put their time to good use in regular visits to old people in Sherborne including those in the almshouses. They talked and talked, bringing much needed 'contact'. One OG says she still has a worry: that 'I wasn't sympathetic enough to their aches!' Two Aylmar girls still at School, Kate Home Smith and Charlotte Kerr, said in 1996:

> Every Friday we visit our 'Granny': she is 88 and very blind, but she always manages to keep her spirits high. We take her shopping, read to her, write letters and of course talk – she loves company and we always have a laugh with her.

Charity blurred in with social service, and sponsored active participation was added for money-raising. The School was a founder member of SYCOSS (Sherborne Youth Council of Social Services), and with other young local people set about fund-raising: Christian Aid in 1970 gained £1,440 from a massive sponsored walk; toys to Cheshire homes and money for a lift in the almshouses were other efforts that year. But PHAB Week, sustained by the energies of Anne Dixon (T 1949, later Aylmar's Housemistress), must be something special in recent School history. Set up on a Wingfield/Aylmar base in 1968, it was 'house-full' three years later when 28 Able Bodied from School, the Boys' School and Dorset Youth Clubs lived and worked with 23 Physically Handicapped, the mostly seriously disabled in wheelchairs. A great deal of courage and zest for life was shown. Games and outings merged with courses on photography, music, shadow drama, art and pottery. In 1976 it went international, by air or by Red Cross ambulance to Austria for two weeks; a 'PHAB Club Austria' was later formed in Vienna. Hugh Williams, of the Boys' School, wrote of his experiences in 1980:

PHAB seen at its best: working together.

> Susie's in a wheelchair. She's pretty plump: it took four of us to lift her upstairs . . . the point of our course was to work together, not as a PH or AB but as a PHAB unit. It's a holiday to be experienced. Why go to PHAB? Karina, a sixteen-year-old in a wheelchair replied, 'I come to PHAB because when I'm here I feel as though I'm walking.'

By the 1990s the one or two 'big' efforts had multiplied and splintered. A single

PHAB in Austria, 1976: 'our ambulance once broke down and we journeyed another five long, steep, twisting miles in a breakdown van, clutching wheelchairs to stop them slipping' (Frances Rawle, W 1979).

lecture could generate £1,017 – Charlotte Pyke (W 1995) described how 'Col. Cook touched our hearts with the plight of children enduring the violence and savagery of the Yugoslav war.' A single girl – 'courageous, daring, with a death-wish!', said her friends – could raise £1,063 for Breakthrough Breast Cancer in 1994, as when Sophie Foot (W 1995) went Bungee Jumping:

> This is the ultimate adrenaline experience; I fell from the 160-foot-high crane, and bounced . . . leaving my tummy suspended 10-foot above ground as the rest of me went up.

Individual Houses raised their own funds: in 1996 Kenelm's 'Roses for Valentine's Day' brought in £350; Ealhstan's £259 came from 'toffee, fudge and music'; Wingfield's fete, with the Headmistress showing skill at the coconut shy, raised £524; and Aylmar's pantomime, despite only ten days of rehearsal and no acting talent at all, collected £382, all for varied charities.

Finally, 'walking for charity' has become ingrained in School life. As Zoe Kind (A 1995) said of the major sponsored walk in 1994:

> Hundreds of girls put on tough DM boots, grabbed a few plasters and Mars bars, and set off on a 12-mile hike. Why? The Abbey's west window needs repairing. We raised £4,192.

At the beginning of the School's history girls in crocodile fashion walked to the Abbey; a century later the link remains – however, they now walk *to* and *for* the Abbey.

Charity Walks: the 1970s and 1980s . 'Wellies, hockey boots, trainers, occasional bare feet . . . minds thinking of ice-cold water . . . through long grass, stinging nettles and brambles . . . endless corn stubble . . . feet tired, bodies hot' (Emilie Goodison, AW 1990).

DISTINGUISHED OLD GIRLS

DIANA READER HARRIS
DBE

Diana's 'life' at School encompassed Head Girl, English mistress, Housemistress (of West), the wartime Canadian evacuation, and then 25 years as Headmistress – well documented in this book. Outside, she had so many other 'lives'. Seven years with the Association of Girls' Clubs in the 1940s gave her a lifelong interest in Youth Service, which included work for the Outward Bound Trust. Her 'education' involvement was prodigious: she was a governor of Sherborne's three state schools and several independent schools; on the Dorset Education Committee for 18 years; President of the Association of Headmistresses (1964–6); Chairman of the Royal Society of Arts; and she advised or pressured governments in a range of guises (via the Schools' Council, 1968–75, via Agricultural College committees, via women-at-work for the Ministry of Labour, and via membership of the Independent Television Authority). Her deep Christian principles moved her into work for the Church Missionary Society – being its first woman president from 1969 to 1982 – and for Christian Aid as its Chairman, 1978–83; in her last years she was a lay canon at Salisbury Cathedral. She served the School and the worlds of Education and the Church with such distinction that she was awarded the DBE in 1972. Dame Diana's central, oft-expressed belief was: 'Everyone has something of value to give, a better nature to be appealed to.' At School her passion was for opportunities for girls in education and work – hence her enthusiasm when I told her the title of this book.

Dame Diana Reader Harris (see also Chapter 3).

10
'Run, Girls, Run!'

Mixed hockey was the first game played, though not quite as understood today. Canon Westcott, the Boys' School Head, accompanied a few of his staff once a week to a field near today's Aylmar, to coach and play the game with all six girls of the Senior School. Cricket was introduced in the first summer, coached by a professional. Then, in the autumn of 1900, Miss Creemer Rowe arrived – travelling once a week from Bournemouth to take eight girls in motley attire for gymnastics in the hall at the rear of Ransome House. Apparatus was limited to a double bar, a horizontal ladder and a jumping stand. A tennis court was laid out next to this hall and the girls played for a couple of hours each week in the summer.

In 1903 came the move to the present School site and with it a playing field. Margaret Mason was appointed to the staff and proved a fine coach for hockey, cricket and tennis. She and Miss Rowe organised the first athletics contest in 1904. The School archives have Miss Rowe's own small programme of 'Flat Races and Athletic Sports', including throwing the cricket ball, skipping and obstacle races; it records the School's first 'Senior 100 yds. Flat Race', won in 13.6 secs. by Joyce Clarke (Ald 1905), who also took the Long Jump with 14 ft. 8½ ins. A Games Club was organised in 1905 and soon set up matches with local schools in hockey and cricket.

The advent of Miss Emerson in 1910 had far-reaching effects. 'La Crosse' was added as a major winter sport – the first match took place three years later, lost 8:2 to Godolphin – and having come from Madame Osterby's famous academy in Dartford, she also introduced Swedish Drill. Athletics became a minor affair, disappearing within two years; formal gymnastics with skipping and marching took over and were thought to promote a more graceful and feminine physique. Using Indian clubs and dressed in long black skirts and stockings, junior girls competed with intense rivalry in dignified Inter-House competitions. The upper school pursued military neatness and accuracy in marching and vaulting; in 1915 it was reported that 'straight lines, good corners, with a freedom and ease of movement won the Marching Cup for the V Form.' In 1934 a Show Drill class was formed. It was announced that, 'admission to be allowed only to those who excel in the gymnasium and in general posture. Green tunics, as worn by the Finns, will be worn for this.' At Commemoration in the 1920s, 1930s and early 1940s massed gymnastics and drill formations on the School tennis courts were a popular feature. By the 1960s such formality had given way to more freedom and complex apparatus work.

A massed gym display at Commemoration, 1939.

Out on the playing fields the main sports developed apace. In 1922 the School teams in hockey and lacrosse hit winning streaks (some were marginal victories – Royal School Bath, 4:3; others annihilation – Lord Digby's, 16:0). Six girls won places in county hockey teams; and Dorothy Maguire (Ald 1922) captained Ireland's XI in 1934. Hockey superiority was maintained for many years, encouraged by coaching and lectures in 1927 from an England women's hockey international. Such was the influence of hockey that in the mid-1920s, Felicia Browne (W 1926) composed 'An Aeglogue to honour our most glorious sport' :

> Now rise ye nymphs, mud-daubéd as you are
> In honoured fight . . .
> Speed on, Corinna, speed! now pass! oh! run
> Swifter than light'ning, Phoebe! shoot! well done!
> The time is up,
> And ours the cup:
> The cheers resound unto the shyning sun.

In the same period an Old Girls' Games Club was formed: it decided to cut the School down to size and in 1930 inflicted a 7:1 defeat on the 1st XI. Lacrosse had mixed fortunes in the interwar years. A heavy defeat by Queen Anne's (27:5) in 1925 was shrugged off and better years followed. Yet it was not long before the games staff were berating the school team: 'You seem unable to rouse yourselves to any determined effort.' The arrival on the staff of the England International Betty

Lee-Evans changed all this, resulting in a big fixture list, and in 1936 all matches won: 'lax' could now look hockey in the eye. As a reward the entire school went to Bournemouth to watch England *v.* Wales Lacrosse, and see Miss Lee-Evans score 7 in England's 21:1 victory.

These winter games had not developed by accident: Miss Mulliner had promoted them. In the 1915 School Brochure she castigated old-fashioned girls' schools for producing 'delicate bluestockings' and she detested 'their decorous walk in melancholy crocodile'. She went on:

> The playing field teaches great lessons of corporate action. The healthy pleasure of a good game allows a girl no time for gossip, spite and slander, for that love of small talk and petty narrow-mindedness which is the bane of her sex.

This philosophy was rewarded in the HMI Report of 1926, which spoke generously of 'admirable facilities for games which the girls play with keenness and vigour', and of 'the right degree of control given to the girls'. Miss Mulliner's successor continued to nurture games. In 1936 the excellent sporting standards received national reportage in *The Queen* magazine: in a series on 'Great Girls' Schools of Britain' it wrote of Sherborne, 'The last hockey season was remarkably successful, the 1st XI being unbeaten – the Royal School Bath, Clifton High School, Talbot Heath and Dorchester School were all beaten.'

That the majority of girls caught the sporting fever was shown in all its seriousness in House matches. Dorms were festooned with ties and ribbons; Gillian Hepburn (AW 1938) wrote home, 'I nearly died of agony in our match as we were beaten pretty badly; I really felt quite ill with excitement.' Housemistresses were not excused, even if they 'never really cared for sport', as Shirley Bloomer (AW 1952) wrote of Rachel Drever-Smith:

> She paid a heavy price (and a cold one); poor RDS, wrapped in rugs, furs and with hot water bottles, spent many afternoons in a deckchair on the games field whilst West progressed through rounds of inter-house competitions.

Here, and on following pages: some of Julia Carrow's (AW 1975) sketches used in the School Magazine.

Some girls though were deeply opposed to what they called 'the tyranny of sport' – especially its compulsory nature (playing *and* watching). In the early years Edwardian dresses were too tight for breathing and moving arms, even when the games staff told the older girls, 'leave your corsets off'. The sensitive hated the army-sergeant approach to Swedish Drill. A later complaint was directed at games featuring 'too much rushing about', and the famous St Trinian's image of the 1st XI's hockey match 'scourged by the icy blast of a late March afternoon' put off not a few. Eileen Arnot Robertson (Ald 1919, see Chapter 6) was invited by Graham Greene in 1934 to write an account of Sherborne for his book *The Old School*. She admired the teaching, but on sport under Miss Mulliner she was caustic:

> 'Run about girls, like boys, and then you won't think of them' – that was Sherborne. We were terribly, terribly keen on games – even when unwell. Coddling oneself was two-stars horrid.

Gymnasia 1922 style and 1995 style.

Her reference to 'boys' (who were, of course, 'three-stars horrid', even if their existence were admitted) hints at what many OGs referred to as the hidden motive for games: prevention of devilry. Joan Burchardt (DH 1936; later on staff) writes:

> Two hours of cricket on Saturday afternoons were to keep us out of mischief. These were exquisitely boring and I developed a wonderful faculty for switching off.

Cricket enjoyed over 60 years as a main sport. Although regarded as unusual for girls, Roedean began in the 1890s what became a cult in some schools. Sherborne keenly followed Roedean's cricketing lead. By the 1930s five pages of the *School Magazine* were taken up with Test-Match-style scoring details. It promoted the School's image, and the Girls *v.* Fathers Commemoration cricket matches (with fathers using a specially narrowed bat) 'were delightful, crowded attractions'. One 'father', Hugh Bayley (four daughters and two granddaughters stretching over 36 Commems.), recalls with dismay, 'being bowled first ball by a demon girl bowler'. However, it must be recorded that victories over rival schools, like Talbot Heath and the Royal School Bath, were rare occasions before the Second World War. Matters improved after it: in 1951 the 1st XI won all its six matches. Yet cricket's days were numbered: though it had fostered team spirit, it was seen by staff and many girls as 'limiting except for the very best'. In 1963 cricket gave way to athletics.

Another reason for cricket's decline was the emergence of tennis. Its appeal and success dominated many summers from the 1930s to the present day. Although played from the start, it was of minor importance until more courts and more coaching generated success. Attire too played its part: it has been said that nationally, when Suzanne Lenglen cast off her corsets for Wimbledon, tennis was never the same again. Sherborne dresses too made their final appearance and shorts became *de rigueur*. Girls entered Junior Wimbledon, and Phyllis Hewitt (K 1935) was a member of the winning doubles pair for two years in the mid-1930s. The Schoolgirls' Tournament at Queens was regularly participated in; the first success came in 1936, when Peggy Lane (K 1936) and Virginia Heaton (A 1935) won the doubles. Despite wartime shortages, which meant tattered tennis balls – three per court per term! – the School triumphed again at Queens in 1943, winning the new cup presented by Lord Aberdare to captain Anne Dudley Smith (A 1943). The 1st VI had beaten five schools on the way to the final, itself a very close contest of 33 to 32 games against St Paul's. In the long hot summer of 1947 the honours multiplied: the Aberdare Cup for the Champion VI, the Doubles, the Junior Singles and the South of England Cup. Four years later saw another Aberdare victory: it was getting a habit. But 'tennis' did not mean just the 1st VI: over the next 40 years it was its wide appeal which was noticeable. In 1951 27 matches were played against other schools, in 1991 a record number of 65 girls represented the School and the following year saw 37 matches recorded, with 28 successes. Plenty of courts (27 today), plenty of practice and the chance of coaching had proved the recipe for doing well; as Peggy Lane wrote, 'The real hope of any game lies in the large number of happy and aspiring rabbits.'

Some aspirants did rather well. The name of Shirley Bloomer made its first appearance in the *School Magazine* in 1948, when she won both the Lincoln and Nottingham under-18 singles titles. Ten years later she was ranked No.1 in Europe and No.3 in the world. Shirley records what she owes to the School: its staff 'instilled in me the energy, the confidence, ambition and mental toughness – yet also genuine enjoyment – that are so much a part of high-level sport.' She highlights her debt to her 'shrewd teacher', Evelyn Dewhurst ('Fuz' to the girls), who had come to Sherborne as a coach of national repute in the late 1930s, and had much to do with the Aberdare Cup successes.

Others made good, not necessarily in school-based sports. In 1936 Evelyn Pinching (DH 1932) took part in the World Ski Championships at Seefeld, the results of which were recorded in the *Daily Telegraph*:

> WORLD CHAMPION
> Miss Evelyn Pinching, the British skier, became woman champion of the world in the International Ski Federation Sports here yesterday. On Friday she won the down-hill race, and yesterday finished second in the slalom, winning the combined event on the aggregate of points.

When she died in 1988, her obituary in *The Guardian* noted that she was the British standard-bearer as late as the World Alpine Championships at Vail in 1950.

In golf, Tessa Ross Steen (T 1957) became British Junior Golf Champion in 1958, and the following year joined the English international team. Old Girls took a major initiative with eight other schools in developing an annual Inter-School OGs Golf Tournament to be held at Sunningdale. The cup, the 'Silver Tassie', was won in its first year, 1961, by Sherborne. Trudi Hubbard (DH 1957) was the Chairman of the Tournament for five years; Sherborne won again in 1966 and 1988; by the 1990s 40 teams were competing.

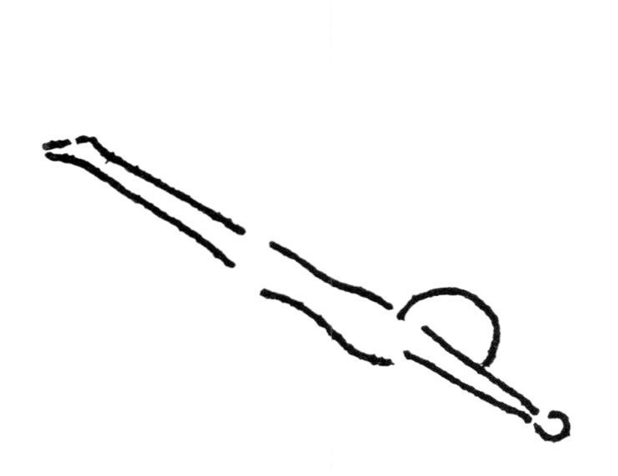

Enter Alison Hollington (T 1982): hers probably the toughest of achievements. Small and hard to catch in long-distance running, she first made a name for herself in 1981, winning the All-England Intermediate Cross-Country Championship

Left: *The hub of the School's musical life is the Stuart Centre, opened in 1979, with 11 teaching rooms and a Chamber Music room. At the heart is the Britten Hall, shown here in 1996: John Jenkins, Director of Music, is conducting the Joint Schools' Sinfonia, a blend of talent from the School, Sherborne School and St Antony's, Leweston.*

Below: *Spectacular national success brought the School Madrigal Society to Vienna in 1981 for the International Youth Music Festival. Merged with six hundred others from all over the world, the girls are here rehearsing for a concert hall performance.*

Above: *Gemma Barnett (T 1994) as Eliza in Rosamund Hall's 1994 production of Shaw's* Pygmalion. Right: *Co-operation with the Boys' School has been a feature of drama productions for 20 years. Beth Tricker (AW 1998) and Tom Beard are seen here in Sherborne School's 1996 production of* West Side Story.

from a field of 400. She was picked immediately for the International Schools' Team and won her event in Italy against strong French, Austrian and Italian competition. Ultra fit, in 1994 she became Britain's Triathlon Champion, a sport not for the fainthearted. Due to become an Olympic event in the year 2000, the Triathlon is gruelling: a 1500-m. river swim, immediately followed by a 40-km. road cycle race, finishing with another half-hour's 10-km. road run.

Lacrosse in 1988.

The impact of the weather on outdoor sports was often severe. *School Magazine* reports in the 1950s for example highlight the plight of lacrosse: season after season heavy rains and floods forced fixture cancellations. Yet if low temperatures and snow led to impossible conditions for games, skating could flourish. In 1932 Barbara Bennett (W 1933) recalls, 'The ice on Castle Lake was wonderful for scores of girls and lots of staff, including Miss Davis and Miss Crichton-Miller.' Many OGs will have a lovely image of Bice on ice. In the 'Big Freeze' of 1941 Ruby Cassels (E 1941) was amazed that, 'we all managed to have skates, including the BS . . . but we were supposed to remain strictly separated!' A similar winter in 1963 had the games field under snow for weeks, so the girls were in the Castle grounds again for skating and tobogganing; even ice hockey became popular.

Swimming suffered in cold summers. Built in 1931, the pool offered an enjoyable pastime for the girls in their long-legged, romper swimsuits, but all too often annual reports referred to 'hardy bathers only', and outside competitions were minimal compared with tennis. Some girls made an official complaint in 1935: 'we beg to suggest that more attention be paid to swimming instruction', to which they received the sharp reply that the games mistress 'does not wish to thrust her services on unwilling learners'! Swimming was regarded as such a minor affair that for many years in the 1950s it received no mention amongst the 'Games Reports', except for the Royal Life-Saving awards. Two things changed all this: the Boys' School indoor pool was offered to the girls in 1976, and in 1981 solar heating was added to the girls' outdoor pool – these made an enormous difference to the amount of swimming and the number of matches. Records tumbled over the years. The Messiter Trophy (fastest over two lengths) had long hovered around 31 seconds. Then in the mid-1980s the special ability of Sian Pomeroy (DH 1984) saw every senior swimming record broken and brought the Messiter down to 28.04; within two years Alison King (AW 1987) reduced it to 27.75 seconds.

The 1960s saw two revolutions: the abandonment of cricket in favour of athletics, and in 1966 the abolition of compulsory games in the Sixth by the new Head of PE, Caro Macintosh. The arrival of athletics in 1963, with its appeal of a range of activities on track and field, was greeted with enthusiasm, though girls were warned they were 'complete beginners'. Ealhstan easily won the first House contest; but such was the naïvety of reportage of the event that the printed winning time of 40.95 seconds for the Relay passed without correction, though it would have won the Olympic final! Progress was impressive. Within two years 18 girls were involved in the Dorset County Championships; Helen Saumarez-Smith (AW 1966) jumped

The 1996 Australian Tour: here the Hockey team, with the Sydney skyline behind.

17'0½" to take her to the School's first All-England Championships. Later, Frances Fanning (K 1970) reduced the School's 'Sprint-100' time to a very respectable 12.4 seconds, and went on to reach the final of the 'All-England' in two successive years – no mean feat. In the mid-1970s Ealhstan ('seemingly unbeatable') dominated the House Finals for three years; in so doing it took athletics out of the 'only-an-individual-winning-an-event' image into the Olympic ideal of 'taking part'. In the words of the games staff, many dedicated captains 'forced' every member of their respective houses, 'kindly but firmly' to get out on to the field and earn a point. Meanwhile, further records were set and the School maintained its reputation as Dorset's leading athletics school, continuing to take part in the 'All-England'.

Miss Macintosh ('Mackie' to the girls) came with a philosophy: 'All physical activity should be enjoyable; it is up to the staff to make it so.' With her proposal in 1966 that team games in the Sixth should be optional, she immediately clashed with 'that formidable band, the Housemistresses, who were convinced that standards would fall.' She was asked to explain her reasons why 67 years of School tradition should go: never were her persuasive powers more needed. A trial period was reluctantly agreed. In fact standards rose.

Almost immediately, on behalf of the girls, she had what she called 'another passage of arms' with some of the Housemistresses over the House Posture Cup. For decades this had been for many a girl, in Ann Barrett's (W 1945) words, 'the bane of my life'. Every two weeks posture marks were awarded and published (2 for 'sitting', 2 for 'standing'). Margaret Woodcock (K 1939) said 'Miss Stuart inspected you through the classroom's semi-glazed doors'; Fiona Morrice's (AW 1959) low marks meant

> standing with our backs against the wall or doing other forms of torture; the worst was having to run round the games field before breakfast.

Caroline Wilson (AE 1958) was 'once muddled with her perfect sister – it was such a luxury not to walk round the lockers with books on my head.' By the 1960s the PE department had responsibility for the awarding of marks, but Miss Macintosh argued, 'as we never saw the girls sitting down except in Prayers, it was impossible to be fair.' The Posture Cup awards were terminated.

The School tradition of Headmistresses appointing first-class sportswomen to coach or run the PE department was continued with Miss Macintosh (she retains her place in the *Guinness Book of Records* with 52 lacrosse caps for Scotland and four for Great Britain). The major team sports flourished in her 24 year 'reign'. School lacrosse teams were outstanding in 1973, 1978, 1986 and 1990, winning the All-England National Schools' tournaments in London and latterly Milton Keynes. Hockey, whose 1st XI were unbeaten in 1995–6, produced excellent players at junior and university levels. But in the last quarter of the century it is the *range* of sports on offer that impresses. Squash is popular: Sherborne had the first court in any girls' school in 1938 – with a plaster front wall and two wooden side walls, worth it was said, 'at least three points a game against visiting schools'. It crumbled becoming unsafe, but two new courts in 1975 and a further two in 1995 give many more girls the chance to play. The School's first international squash player was Anna Craven-Smith (DH 1956), who toured the USA with the England team in 1963. Fencing under expert coaching burgeoned in the 1970s, with girls reaching the National Senior Schoolgirls' Foil Championship. Its appeal – 'a sport of precision, grace and deft movement, not sword fighting', as Nicole Bovill (T 1983) described it – has attracted many, with Tansy Aked (E 1989) outstanding in her 1988 performances as County champion in both Dorset and Hampshire, and with a place in the Nationals. Sailing was added to the range in 1972 and by the late 1980s orienteering, archery, badminton, judo and self-defence, aerobics and volleyball were also available. The 1995 Sports Hall (that 'Palace of Health', said one member of staff) has five badminton courts, two volleyball courts, two squash courts, indoor tennis, trampolining facilities, table tennis and a gallery full of jogging, cycling and rowing machines.

A fencing class in 1988.

The Australian tour was the highlight of the 1996 season for both lacrosse and hockey teams, when Romey Schofield (staff 1989–) took them south – in August! From Perth to Adelaide, from Melbourne to Sydney they pitted themselves against school and state sides: wins or draws in their school contests, but state teams were as expected much tougher, despite the School being cheered on by Australian OGs. Each girl funded her own travel, but at School £6,000 was raised to pay for kit and multifarious activities – including a Perth safari and snorkelling on the Great Barrier Reef.

School Sport (an excusable pun) is definitely healthy.

DISTINGUISHED OLD GIRLS

SHIRLEY BLOOMER
(AW 1952)

Shirley says she feels 'an immense gratitude to the School' for instilling the three Cs – competitiveness, confidence and concentration – and for her meeting with 'Fuz' Dewhurst, who was to coach and influence her from the age of 13 for the next 45 years. At School, Shirley was captain of hockey and lacrosse, being selected for Junior West of England Hockey and Dorset Junior County Lacrosse; in 1950 she won the National 16-and-under Squash title. A member of the School Tennis VI in her first year, in her last she was in the winning Aberdare Cup team. She then moved successfully on to the international tennis circuit, competing at Wimbledon in the year she left school – the first of 19 appearances. Here she was a Ladies' Doubles finalist in 1955, and Singles q/f in 1956 and 1958. She won the British Hard Court Championships in 1957, retaining the title the following year. Overseas, success in the Americas saw her reaching the semi-finals of the US Open Singles in 1956, being ranked in the world's top ten for the next three years. As British No 1, winner of the French Singles and Doubles Championships and the Italian Open, she reached her highest world ranking, No 3, in 1957. Two years later she married Olympic Steeplechase gold medallist Chris Brasher. Tennis Correspondent of *The Observer* for some years, Shirley has remained close to the game by coaching and advising many of Britain's top young players.

Shirley Bloomer after winning the British Women's Singles in Bournemouth, 1957.

11

'Music Wherever She Goes'

Augusta Miller, Director of Music at Sherborne 1973–96, contends that 'Music is one of the most civilising aspects of education.' It is a belief which has been central to the School's history since its very early days. A trio of dedicated, talented staff was the key to early development. Frances Hoyle, housemistress, scholar, pianist and organist founded the choir – a very select group indeed. She worked in close harmony with Archibald Tester, a young master from the Boys' School, who in the words of Kathleen Moore, 'first taught Sherborne girls to sing'. He brought a sense of fun to the School's music – the girls loved singing folk songs to his amusing accompaniments. He taught many of his own compositions, the most liked being his cantata 'John Gilpin', which he described as being 'a grand musical joke' when the girls gave a spirited rendition at a School concert. He was also instrumental in promoting inter-house singing: a House Glee Competition in 1910, won by Dun Holme, was praised by the adjudicator, the organist of Wells Cathedral: 'the delightful quality of tone, so pure and liquid and never forced, proving that good methods are being used in the teaching of class singing.'

The achievement of the third member of staff, Violet Hayward, has lasted to this day: she established in 1912 the School Musical Society, 'to study the lives and aims of the great composers'. At first limited to lectures with musical illustration by the staff, the following year saw an ambitious concert devoted to Bach's works. Mr Tester conducted the School Orchestra augmented by members of the Bath Pump Room Orchestra, and the Choir sang, assisted by tenors and basses from the Boys' School. This was the centrepiece of the Society's first season of concerts (membership: two shillings and sixpence – 25p).

The Musical Society's first programme, 1913.

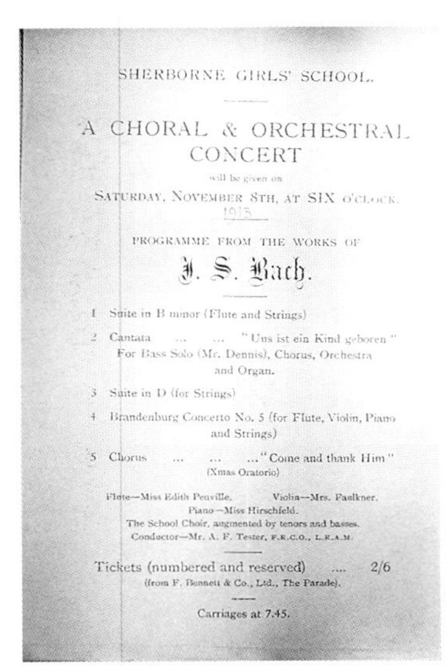

SHERBORNE GIRLS' SCHOOL.

A CHORAL & ORCHESTRAL CONCERT

will be given on

SATURDAY, NOVEMBER 8TH, AT SIX O'CLOCK.

1913

PROGRAMME FROM THE WORKS OF

J. S. Bach.

1 Suite in B minor (Flute and Strings)

2 Cantata ... ... "Uns ist ein Kind geboren"
For Bass Solo (Mr. Dennis), Chorus, Orchestra and Organ.

3 Suite in D (for Strings)

4 Brandenburg Concerto No. 5 (for Flute, Violin, Piano and Strings)

5 Chorus ... ... "Come and thank Him"
(Xmas Oratorio)

Flute—Miss Edith Penville. Violin—Mrs. Faulkner.
Piano—Miss Hirschfeld.
The School Choir, augmented by tenors and basses.
Conductor—Mr. A. F. Tester, F.R.C.O., L.R.A.M.

Tickets (numbered and reserved) 2/6
(from F. Bennett & Co., Ltd., The Parade).

Carriages at 7.45.

Visiting singers and instrumentalists arrived the next season, and Gervase Elwes' song recital from Handel and Brahms started what was to become a long tradition. Some famous visitors so liked what they saw of the School and its atmosphere that they became regular performers. Albert Sammons and Benno Moiseiwitch came in 1917 and their violin and piano playing respectively were to be heard many times in the future. Of one concert Miss Hayward wrote, 'Moiseiwitch gave a long recital, which seemed all too short for his audience who would not let him go till he had added two encores . . . most of us had never heard such playing before.'

In 1924 Myra Hess came to Sherborne: the School was entranced. Marcia Thring (DH 1924) commented, 'I am sure many of us had never appreciated the

Scarlatti Sonatas to such an extent, so beautiful was her delicacy of touch and phrasing.' So began a lengthy relationship with the School, her last visit being in 1950, when the *School Magazine* recorded that, 'In everything Dame Myra played, classical or modern, her interpretation was such that even the youngest listener could not fail to understand.' During one of her wartime visits she was staying in East when the air-raid sirens sounded. Jean Straw (AE 1945) vividly recalls her 'on the floor of the cloakroom with us, playing jacks, and then sitting at our old up-right piano for a sing-song: such a nice woman.' Elisabeth Schumann sang Mozart so that 60 years later Jean Bonsey (K 1936) still has 'happy memories of her voice, so pure and clear'. The Griller String Quartet in 1936 gained prolonged applause. Solomon, the pianist, and Léon Goossens, the oboist, gave wartime recitals.

Then in 1945 came Kathleen Ferrier. At 33 she was just making a name for herself, and Shirley Henderson (A 1947) – herself the daughter of Miss Ferrier's singing teacher – wrote of her 'beautiful tone' and especially of her singing of Gluck's 'Che faro': 'We all felt we were fortunate to have heard her so soon, so that we may hope to hear her many times again.' Within a year Miss Ferrier achieved international status at Glyndebourne in *Orfeo*, and was in great demand in Europe and North America; however she was persuaded to fit Sherborne into her busy schedule again in 1948. The hope of future visits ended with her early death five years later.

After the War the 'lecture' origins of the Music Society were revived and for half a century performances were interspersed with lecture–recitals, often by celebrities themselves. Among these, Gerald Moore was highly entertaining when in 1953 he defended 'the great importance of the accompanist' with his Schubert illustrations, whilst in 1980 Anthony Hopkins proved very popular with his lecture on 'Noises Off'. When in 1987 Evelyn Glennie gave a talk on 'Percussion', Tara Palmer-Tomkinson (A 1990) noted the enormous reception:

> So many people came – staff, pupils and visitors – it was incredibly difficult to fit everyone in. No one left disappointed. She is only 21 and though totally deaf has perfect pitch. She played the marimba with four sticks, and demonstrated the drums, timpani and snare drum – she showed great skill on our school drum-kit!

After Howard Goodall gave a lecture on 'Writing for Television', Olivia Bonner (DH 1996) said that his range of work – Mass in Latin for a Cambridge choir, 'Mr Bean' for Rowan Atkinson and music for the BBC's *Not the 9 O'clock News* – was a great inspiration for her own passion for composition. The next year, 1996, *she* won the Dorset Young Composer trophy.

Between the lectures major concerts continued. Owen Brannigan came twice; many girls fell in love with John Shirley-Quirk's beautiful voice in 1967 when he gave a recital of Purcell, Beethoven and Ravel. Attendance at concerts obviously varied, with 'names' being the biggest draws, but over 200 has been standard. Prior to Evelyn Glennie, one huge attraction claimed over 400: the audience was, according to one girl, 'hanging from the rafters in the Hall' to hear Humphrey Lyttleton and his Jazz Band in 1977. 'I was transfixed,' said another: 'real full-blooded jazz,' exclaimed a third. Henrietta Bulley (DH 1977) noted at the time: 'Gussie kept

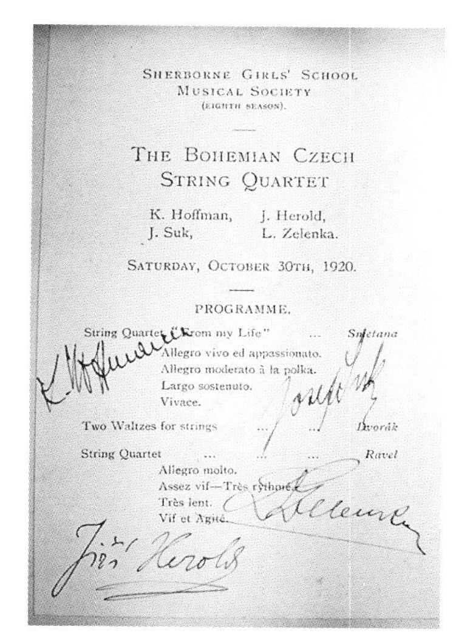

Sherborne Girls' School
Musical Society
(Eighth Season).

The Bohemian Czech
String Quartet

K. Hoffman, J. Herold,
J. Suk, L. Zelenka.

Saturday, October 30th, 1920.

PROGRAMME.

String Quartet "From my Life" ... Smetana
Allegro vivo ed appassionato.
Allegro moderato à la polka.
Largo sostenuto.
Vivace.

Two Waltzes for strings ... ... Dvorák

String Quartet ... ... Ravel
Allegro molto.
Assez vif—Très rythmé.
Très lent.
Vif et Agité.

The programmes illustrated represent a minute section of the Music Department's autographed collection of all its concert programmes since 1913.

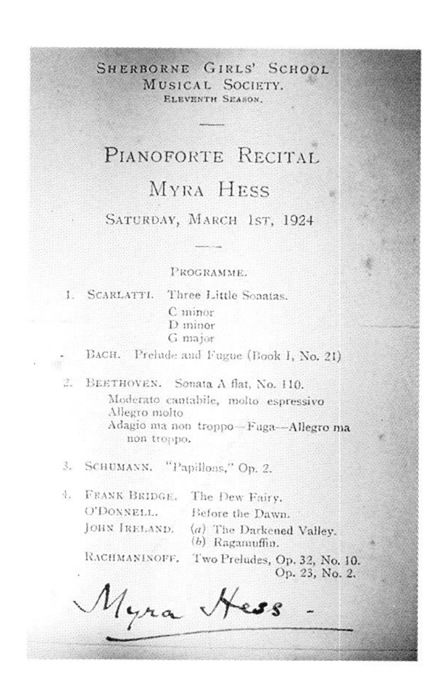

Sherborne Girls' School
Musical Society.
Eleventh Season.

Pianoforte Recital
Myra Hess

Saturday, March 1st, 1924

Programme.

1. Scarlatti. Three Little Sonatas.
C minor
D minor
G major

Bach. Prelude and Fugue (Book I, No. 21)

2. Beethoven. Sonata A flat, No. 110.
Moderato cantabile, molto espressivo
Allegro molto
Adagio ma non troppo—Fuga—Allegro ma non troppo.

3. Schumann. "Papillons," Op. 2.

4. Frank Bridge. The Dew Fairy.
O'Donnell. Before the Dawn.
John Ireland. (*a*) The Darkened Valley.
(*b*) Ragamuffin.
Rachmaninoff. Two Preludes, Op. 32, No. 10.
Op. 23, No. 2.

Myra Hess

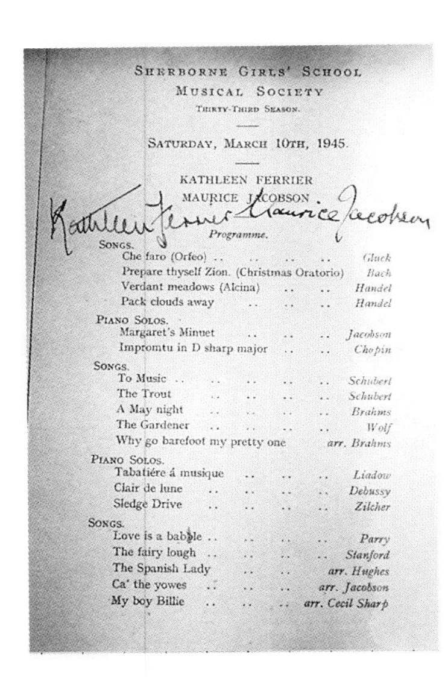

SHERBORNE GIRLS' SCHOOL
MUSICAL SOCIETY
THIRTY-THIRD SEASON.

SATURDAY, MARCH 10TH, 1945.

KATHLEEN FERRIER
MAURICE JACOBSON

Programme.

SONGS.
Che faro (Orfeo) .. .. *Gluck*
Prepare thyself Zion. (Christmas Oratorio) *Bach*
Verdant meadows (Alcina) .. .. *Handel*
Pack clouds away .. .. .. *Handel*

PIANO SOLOS.
Margaret's Minuet .. .. .. *Jacobson*
Impromtu in D sharp major .. .. *Chopin*

SONGS.
To Music .. .. *Schubert*
The Trout .. .. *Schubert*
A May night .. .. *Brahms*
The Gardener .. .. *Wolf*
Why go barefoot my pretty one *arr. Brahms*

PIANO SOLOS.
Tabatiére á musique .. .. .. *Liadow*
Clair de lune .. .. *Debussy*
Sledge Drive .. .. *Zilcher*

SONGS.
Love is a babble .. .. *Parry*
The fairy lough .. .. *Stanford*
The Spanish Lady .. .. *arr. Hughes*
Ca' the yowes .. .. .. *arr. Jacobson*
My boy Billie .. .. .. *arr. Cecil Sharp*

telling me to sit down. It was ridiculous having to sit down – *they* played so much better when *we* were standing up.' Home-grown talent was not ignored. The School's most distinguished OG in the field of music, Emma Kirkby, gave a recital in 1995. Claire Allen (T 1996) thought it 'one of the most awe-inspiring concerts yet, entertaining a vast audience of girls and townspeople. The combination of her soaring voice and Anthony Rooley's lute was an inspiration to the audience.'

These celebrity concerts were the professional backcloth to Sherborne's own musical culture. Participation stands on equal terms with listening and appreciation; and it is the sum of all the elements which has led many, many girls to echo Felicity Rebbeck's (DH 1943) gratitude for 'the excellent opportunities and a lifelong interest'.

Continuous staff dedication provided the scope. The Hoyle–Tester–Hayward partnership gave way to Gwendolyn Harris-Jones, whose lively encouragement spanned 34 years, and who has been superbly characterised by Jean Straw: 'HJ was small, rotund and very forceful – her white hair tied back in a bun, and with two sausage curls which bobbed about when she became vehement.' In the 1950s and 1960s the Misses Keir, Eva and Barnett held sway.

> Miss Eva was the organist, and for filing out of School Service she would often play Walton's coronation march 'Orb and Sceptre', to which the whole school would hum and sway. I always swore I would walk out of my wedding to it . . . and I did.
>
> Caroline Wilson (AE 1958)

The severe but wonderful choir mistress, Ella Keir ('tails in, tummies in', she would decree) whose patience with the clumsy and naïve was legendary, was fatally injured in an accident in 1962. Lucy Buxton (DH 1965) wrote in her diary of

> a beautiful memorial service: 'Barney' had just read from *Pilgrim's Progress* when the organ broke forth in the trumpet voluntary. I imagined Keir marching through the pearly gates.

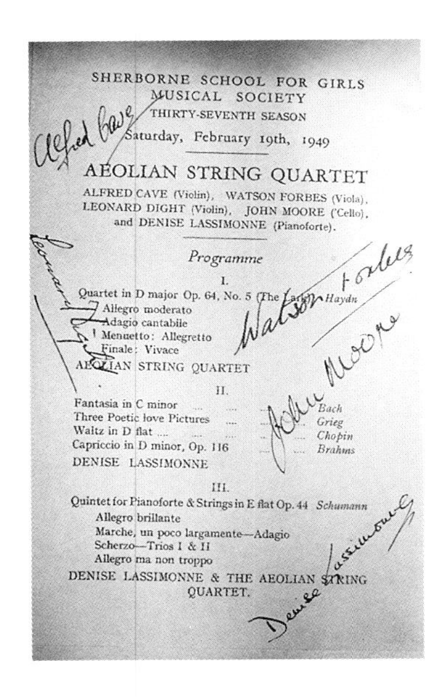

SHERBORNE SCHOOL FOR GIRLS
MUSICAL SOCIETY
THIRTY-SEVENTH SEASON
Saturday, February 19th, 1949

AEOLIAN STRING QUARTET
ALFRED CAVE (Violin), WATSON FORBES (Viola),
LEONARD DIGHT (Violin), JOHN MOORE ('Cello),
and DENISE LASSIMONNE (Pianoforte).

Programme

I.
Quartet in D major Op. 64, No. 5 (The Lark) *Haydn*
Allegro moderato
Adagio cantabile
Menuetto: Allegretto
Finale: Vivace
AEOLIAN STRING QUARTET

II.
Fantasia in C minor .... *Bach*
Three Poetic love Pictures .... *Grieg*
Waltz in D flat .... *Chopin*
Capriccio in D minor, Op. 116 .... *Brahms*
DENISE LASSIMONNE

III.
Quintet for Pianoforte & Strings in E flat Op. 44 *Schumann*
Allegro brillante
Marche, un poco largamente—Adagio
Scherzo—Trios I & II
Allegro ma non troppo
DENISE LASSIMONNE & THE AEOLIAN STRING QUARTET.

Augusta Miller's 35 years at Sherborne, 23 of them as Director of Music, took music far beyond its previous confines – 'when I came to Sherborne, Music was a very ladylike subject.' On her retirement in 1996 she was acclaimed by the Headmistress, who spoke of the energy, fun and that 'streak of the *enfant terrible*', so clearly recognised by generations of girls. Such was the commitment, that 'as far as she is concerned the School exists solely to provide *her* with suitable musicians!' (the School's Director of Music and myself as the School's University Adviser did not always see eye-to-eye about this) .

None of these people, of course, could function without the legions of instrument teachers; by mid-century the piano, oboe, clarinet, violin, 'cello and flute were offered; today this list has extended to include viola, double-bass, piccolo, cor anglais, bassoon, saxophone, recorder, classical and electric guitar, harp, trumpet, horn, trombone, tuba, percussion and even the bagpipes. Though now taught with excellent equipment in the impressive purpose-built Stuart Centre, budding musicians previously practised in tiny little rooms dotted round the School – except for the organists. Caroline Wilson's sister 'dreaded having to practise on this as every mistake could be heard all over the school.' In the earlier days equipment had come under criticism. In 1926 HMIs reported that 'of the pianos, twelve are unfit for use, having the tone of a brass band – these should be replaced. Practice pianos in the Houses are also suffering from senile decay.' After this things dramatically improved. The end result of all this teaching and practice was not just competence, but steadily improving grades in the Royal Schools of Music examinations. Until the 1930s nothing was recorded of these, and even then only a handful of girls tried piano and violin, to reach perhaps Grade 6. By 1942 though, a piano Grade 8 with distinction, the highest possible, was awarded to Joan Salmon (K 1942). Twenty years later, the range of instruments and the numbers of girls had increased markedly: 85 girls gained some level of award; theory had been added and soon solo singing would come. 'Grade 8 with distinction' began to appear regularly. Taking a year at random: in 1989 six girls gained this highest award. In fact Jessica Nightingale (A 1989) achieved two – in 'cello and solo singing – having already reached it in viola two years earlier. Many girls have gone to music colleges, and particular girls have followed Emma Kirkby – Clare Toomer (E 1980), Sacha Langton (W 1985), Madelaine Townley (AW 1987), Thalia Eley (DH 1989) and Holly Pattenden (T 1997), for example – in taking their precious, individual musical talents with them to university and beyond.

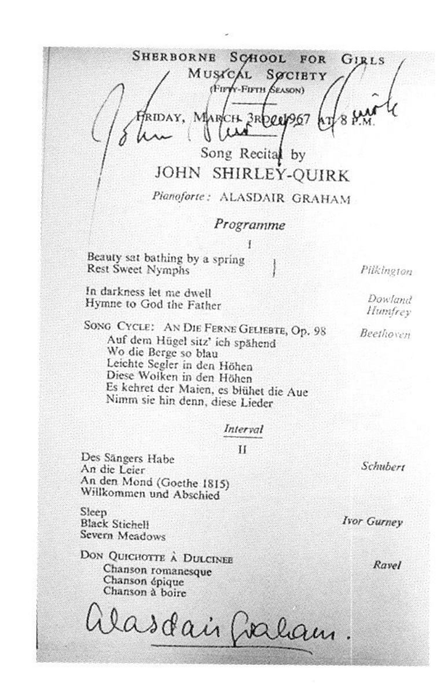

Sherborne School for Girls
Musical Society
(Fifty-Fifth Season)

Friday, March 3rd, 1967 at 8 p.m.

Song Recital by
JOHN SHIRLEY-QUIRK

Pianoforte: ALASDAIR GRAHAM

Programme

I

Beauty sat bathing by a spring
Rest Sweet Nymphs — *Pilkington*

In darkness let me dwell — *Dowland*
Hymne to God the Father — *Humfrey*

Song Cycle: An Die Ferne Geliebte, Op. 98 — *Beethoven*
Auf dem Hügel sitz' ich spähend
Wo die Berge so blau
Leichte Segler in den Höhen
Diese Wolken in den Höhen
Es kehret der Maien, es blühet die Aue
Nimm sie hin denn, diese Lieder

Interval

II

Des Sängers Habe
An die Leier
An den Mond (Goethe 1815)
Willkommen und Abschied — *Schubert*

Sleep
Black Stichell
Severn Meadows — *Ivor Gurney*

Don Quichotte à Dulcinee — *Ravel*
Chanson romanesque
Chanson épique
Chanson à boire

Alasdair Graham.

Listening to music, even learning to play, is one thing, but 'making music' in its full orchestral and choral sense has been pivotal to School life. In the first half of the century, the inter-house singing competitions became a tradition – providing a deal of banter and self-criticism. Margaret Tunbridge (A 1946) remembers how the popsong 'Deep in the heart of Texas' became the setting for:

> West did croon
> A lively tune;
> Flat are the choirs of Aylmar

The Choral and Orchestral Workshop Day of 1995.

FRIDAY PROGRAMME

GOD SAVE THE QUEEN
(*Harmonised by Sharmini Thillaimuthu*)

1. FIRST ORCHESTRA
   La Réjouissance—La Paix—Bourée from Music for the Royal Fireworks ... ... *Handel*
   Concertino, Opus 26 ... ... *Weber*
   Solo Clarinet: Kate Trench
   Conductor: Miss Janet Fortnum
2. FLUTE SOLO
   Allegro Maestoso from Flute Concerto in G ... ... *Mozart*
   Flute: Nicole Barber. *Piano:* Sharmini Thillaimuthu
3. PIANO DUET
   Ballet from Petite Suite ... ... *Debussy*
   Alexandra Kidner and Emma Kidner
4. ENSEMBLE
   Gavot from Symphony IV ... ... *Boyce*
   Violins: Antonia Walden and Clare Sugden. *Viola:* Alison Davies.
   'Cello: Ann Payne. *Oboes:* Catherine Lower and Jennifer Morton.
5. VIOLA SOLO
   Allegretto Pastorale and Presto from Sonata in G Minor ... *Tartini*
   Lilias Lamont
6. DUET FOR TWO FLUTES
   Hoe Down ... ... *Brian Bonsor*
   Victoria Wilson and Sarah Nightingale
7. CHAMBER ORCHESTRA
   Gavotte and Musette: Rigaudon from Holberg Suite ... *Grieg*
   Conductor: Miss Janet Fortnum
8. OBOE SOLO
   Largo and Allegro from Sonata in C ... ... *Loeillet*
   Jennifer Morton
9. PIANO SOLO
   Seguidillas ... ... *Albèniz*
   Alison Davies
10. MADRIGAL SOCIETY
    All Creatures Now are Merry Minded ... ... *John Bennet*
    In Going to My Lonely Bed ... ... *Richard Edwards?*
    Dancing Song (Hungarian) ... ... *Kodály*
    Old Macdonald's Farm (First Performance) *Sharmini Thillaimuthu*
    Conductor: Miss Augusta Miller

1975: for many girls and parents Commemoration Concerts are the highlight of the year.

But at School level, especially after the Second World War, music was taken further afield. Nationally, orchestras, radio and television beckoned; with the coming of cassettes and CDs school musicians had fresh opportunities for recording; tours abroad loomed.

In 1947 the National Youth Orchestra was formed by Ruth Railton, and in her autobiography Dame Ruth acknowledges the 'encouragement and active help' of Diana Reader Harris. Jean Lynden-Bell (DH 1949) and Joy Henderson (A 1950) were selected for the Orchestra in its early years, and Joy wrote of

> an experience not to be missed, when one hundred and ten nervous and excited girls and boys were given the opportunity of playing in a symphony orchestra and working under distinguished musicians.

More recently, Jessica Nightingale gained a place in 1987, and Catherine Strange (AW 1994) described in 1993, 'the exhilaration of stepping onto the Barbican platform for my first NYO concert, later to be recorded for BBC Radio Three.' In that same year, 13-year-old Ruth Rogers (W 1996) was appointed co-leader of the National Children's Orchestra, having been with it for three seasons as a violinist, whilst Emma Backhouse (AE 1993), described her National Youth Choir course as, 'very intensive, each day packed with seven hours of concentrated singing . . . then comes a sense of urgency to meet concert deadlines.'

The Madrigal Society was formed in 1960 and, numbering 22 girls, it is still the flagship of the School's choral music. Its repertoire ranges from madrigals of the sixteenth century to folk music, spirituals and barbershop songs of the twentieth. It performed for the Queen Mother in 1974 and gave a concert at the Hong Kong embassy in 1980; it went to Kensington Palace in 1989 at the invitation of the Duke of Gloucester, and sang Evensong twice in the 1980s in St George's Chapel, Windsor Castle. Recording the Madrigal Society's work for posterity began when a School record of the Commemoration Concert was made in 1971. More recently a Classic FM broadcast in December 1994 was recorded in Sherborne Abbey, and Jo Willcock (AW 1996) noted some of the non-musical problems:

SHERBORNE SCHOOL FOR GIRLS
MUSICAL SOCIETY
(Sixty-seventh Season)
Friday, 21st October 1977, at 8.15 p.m.

Humphrey Lyttleton's Jazz Band

> trying to control coughs – confusion over turning pages for instrumentalists – waiting for the three o'clock Abbey bells to finish – having to rerecord because a heavy lorry passed by!

And in early 1996 some of the Madrigal Society went to make a recording in Oxford with the Christ Church College choir.

National competitions have brought enormous success; in 1977 the girls reached the finals of the BBC's 'Let the People Sing' series, and began a decade of spectacular activity. Within two years they were to win the National Schools Choir Competition which had a thousand entries, and immediately appeared on ITV's *The South Bank Show.* Their repertoire was becoming well known: 'Il est bel et bon', 'I'm going to my lonely bed', 'The Bluebird' and finally the tongue-twister 'Peter Piper picked a peck of pickled peppers' – the last of which was chosen at one point for the BBC's *Pick of the Week.* In 1981 they were off to Vienna for the International

Youth Music Festival. Three 'Madrigals', Anna Robertson (K 1982), Celia Tait (A 1982) and Jo Udal (K 1982), wrote a memoire of the contest in which Sherborne came first in the British entries and fifth in the International (Europe and the USA) competition:

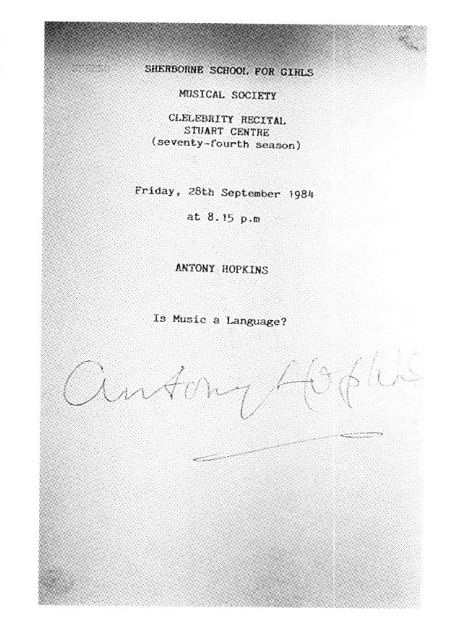

SHERBORNE SCHOOL FOR GIRLS

MUSICAL SOCIETY

CLELEBRITY RECITAL
STUART CENTRE
(seventy-fourth season)

Friday, 28th September 1984

at 8.15 p.m

ANTONY HOPKINS

Is Music a Language?

Antony Hopkins

> All term 'Vienna' rivalled even A-level agony as the most repeated subject, and we knew Miss Miller would be in a panic keeping twenty girls in check for seven days, not to mention Gussie and Aunty Sue [Miss Cameron, Ealhstan Housemistress] having to share a dormitory with four giggling girls. First taste of Vienna: rehearsals with six hundred others and a vast orchestra on the steps of the Hofburg – an exhilarating experience; afterwards smoked salmon and caviar at the Rathaus. The centrepiece was our rehearsing and performing with three other choirs for Gluck's *Orfeo* – a tremendous opportunity to sing in the Vienna Concert House in a professional atmosphere.

Later generations of girls did well in other competitions and appeared on ITV's *Highway* with Sir Harry Secombe (1987) and Radio Two's *Sunday Half Hour* (1990). Overseas tours began in 1989: to Prague for the British Council, to Tuscany, to Belgium, and then by 'Gus Bus' to Meerssen in Holland in 1995. More recent visits to the Continent – including singing Mass at Mont St Michel – have maintained the momentum under the present Director of Music, John Jenkins, who also took the Madrigals to the wedding of Clare Lowther (A 1988) in the Chapel of the House of Lords.

Miss Miller says that 'one of the greatest changes in Sherborne has been the amount of combined music with the Boys' School.' No longer a repertoire 'as adapted for schools', and certainly no more 'adapted for girls' voices', works are now performed as the composer wrote them. Singers from both schools join in Evensong at Salisbury Cathedral, Chapel Choir, Chamber Choir and the Music Society; and there are two joint orchestras (now called Sherborne Schools Symphony Orchestra and The Sinfonia), which involve girls from Leweston as well. The most obvious illustration of all this is 'Dorset Opera'.

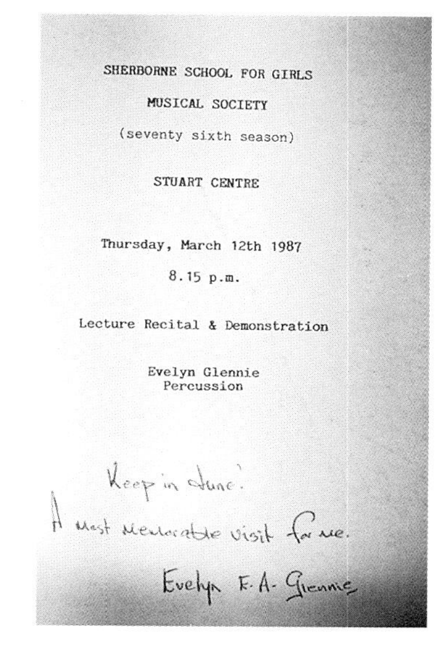

SHERBORNE SCHOOL FOR GIRLS

MUSICAL SOCIETY

(seventy sixth season)

STUART CENTRE

Thursday, March 12th 1987

8.15 p.m.

Lecture Recital & Demonstration

Evelyn Glennie
Percussion

Keep in tune!
A most memorable visit for me.
Evelyn E.A. Glennie

Established in 1974, its object was to put on performances at Sherborne School involving a professional orchestra and soloists to work closely with large numbers of boys and girls as chorus and stage staff, and some townspeople helping with carpentry, catering etc. It has been a huge success. Productions, which are staged in August, began with a series of famous works: by 1979 *The Bartered Bride*, *Carmen*, *Aida*, *Turandot*, and *The Magic Flute* had been presented. But over the following years, less well-known pieces were interspersed – for example, Verdi's *Giovanna d'Arco* was put on between *Don Carlos* and *The Pearl Fishers* (1986–8). The production trio (Augusta Miller, with Robert Glen and Patrick Shelley of the Boys' School) experimented with Carl Zeller's *Der Vogeländler* in 1982, and Peter Heyworth reviewed it in *The Times*:

> A characteristic English mix of amateur enthusiasm with professional stiffening . . . the amateurs had the best of the day, a lusty chorus delivering its numbers with panache and precision.

The importance of the Schools' backstage role was much in evidence when *Carmen*

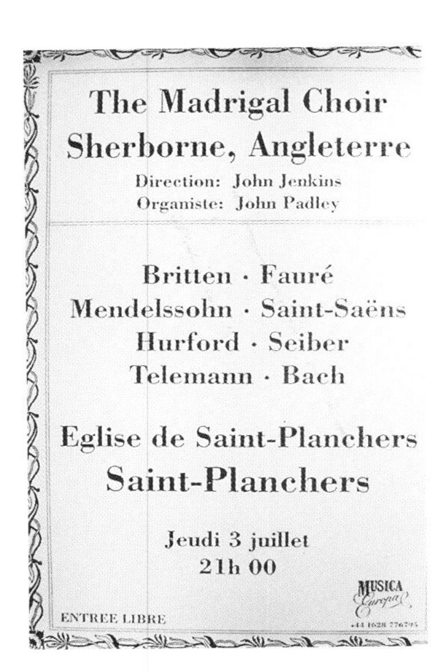
The Madrigal Choir
Sherborne, Angleterre
Direction: John Jenkins
Organiste: John Padley

Britten · Fauré
Mendelssohn · Saint-Saëns
Hurford · Seiber
Telemann · Bach

Eglise de Saint-Planchers
Saint-Planchers

Jeudi 3 juillet
21h 00

ENTREE LIBRE

Part of the 1997 visit to Normandy.

was ambitiously and spectacularly repeated in 1992 – hectic efforts were required as every member of the large chorus had to be fitted with two or three different costumes. The chorus, of course, is the great attraction for the girls and many have written of their impressions of the different productions. One said,

> I'm one of the motley crew that can convey sympathy, respect, hate, fear, anger, religious conviction and joy all within the space of a few minutes – I'm one of that distinct species known as the chorus.

Another girl tells how her emotions were really caught:

> We are all in costume and made up. The whispering in the wings stops as the conductor takes up his position. There is a moment's silence; the notes of the overture begin, hesitantly at first, but soon build up until stirring chords echo and re-echo. The Opera has begun – I take a deep breath . . .

Augusta was right: it is the most civilising experience.

DISTINGUISHED OLD GIRLS

EMMA KIRKBY
(E 1965)

The music critic Andrew O'Connor described Emma in 1996: 'Modest and good-humoured, an unlikely person to spark a musical revolution – that she has done so is indisputable.' Today an internationally acclaimed classical concert soprano – with a voice, in Edward Greenfield's opinion, 'like a lark in a cornfield' – she has revived interest in pre-Romantic vocal music, and particularly in how 'authentic' singing should sound. At School and at Oxford, she was a classicist who simply sang for pleasure; she taught Latin for a while . . . until 1973. Then she began her long association with the Consort of Musicke; a young lutenist, Anthony Rooley, asked her to join a group of Renaissance music voices. Since, she has had spectacular success, making over a hundred recordings: including madrigals of the Italian and English Renaissance, songs of Dowland, Purcell and Greene, cantatas and oratorios of Bach and Handel, opera and concert arias of Vivaldi and Mozart. Emma prefers live concerts, making her London début in 1974 and in the USA four years later; she has had three tours of the Middle East and five of Japan; Australians come to her concerts in large numbers, enjoying them robustly. Recordings and concerts receive glorious tributes: 'a musical Eden on earth' (*Nürnberger Zeitung*); 'great delicacy, superb ornamentation' (*Toronto Star*); and O'Connor on her Vivaldi opera arias, 'an astonishing display of Baroque pathos and vocal fireworks.' For a Canadian reviewer Emma is 'one of the treasures of the music world'.

12

'Admit the Fact, She's Burning to Act' then 'Send in the Clowns'

Girls' thespian ambitions in the first quarter of the School's existence were wholly thwarted by what Miss Stuart later referred to as 'the older evangelicals' disapproval of acting and the banning of dancing on religious grounds'. Beatrice Mulliner brought with her from Cheltenham that tinge of Victorian puritanism which feared theatres and music-halls as cockpits of the Devil. She was strict on this: no acting for the older girls.

The frustrations of the Senior School were evident in the ingenuity used to get round the ban, and it was obvious that Miss Mulliner did not have the wholehearted support of her staff either. Dun Holme led the way. In 1908 the House invited the School and outside visitors to an 'Entertainment'. The curtains were drawn back to display a series of *tableaux vivants* representing scenes from works of well-known poets and dramatists such as Tennyson, Browning and Shakespeare. The audience was invited to identify the 'quotations'. In 1915 Aldhelmsted produced shadow pictures and Aylmar put on a charade, and a year later, staff of the Boys' and Girls' Schools gave a reading of *Macbeth*. Miss Stuart was to be quite scathing about it all: 'The theory seems to have been that it was not wrong to dress up and act a scene if you did not speak, nor to speak a scene if you did not dress up and act.'

By the early 1920s, Peggy Shackelton (T 1927) remembers, 'the system had started to creak.' Ealhstan, inspired by Miss Perry, broke the taboo against acting in 1922 when it produced extracts from *A Midsummer Night's Dream*; the other Houses eagerly followed suit. Then in 1924 Milton's *Comus* was performed: the first School play. It was a spectacular success, raising the large sum of £79 for the recently established Children's Home in Marston Road. This charitable base had clearly undermined Miss Mulliner's views and even she remarked 'we all wondered at the beauty of electric colour'. Elizabeth Souttar (E 1925, later Deaconess and School Governor), wrote a review praising, 'the tireless energy and patience of Miss Perry and Miss Harris-Jones, who brought the acting and music to perfection.' Then, as Peggy Shackleton recalls,

> in 1925 an inexplicable happening: the big, outside world encroached. The V and VI forms were invited to *Julius Caesar* at the Boys' School. Preparations were prodigious – Matron gave minute directions for dress: white confirmation dresses and shawls, plus overcoats and tam o'shanters. But we must wear our thick green games tights ('as

> a precaution against the cold,' Matron curiously added!). The evening was a great success and we all fell in love with Cassius.

But Miss Mulliner was not really persuaded. House and group plays flourished (the Sixth Form produced a fine *Toad of Toad Hall* in 1929) but there were no more School plays in her time.

Cautiously, Miss Stuart dipped her feet in dramatic waters. She encouraged staff plays first. In 1932 *The Purple Mask*, full of villains and comic figures was staged. The *School Magazine* describes how,

> HJ stepped into the character of the crafty Majolin as easily as she stepped into his buckled shoes . . . and Miss Waller stamped about the stage as Fouché, echoing Cicero's ranting oratory which she declaimed in Upper V lessons.

In 1933 a conference with housemistresses developed what were to become two long-standing traditions: a House play for the School at Christmas (*Grumpy* was the first production), which much influenced OGs to return for a reunion at that time of the year; and the Nativity Tableaux, interspersed with carols and lessons, which remained an annual event until Dame Diana retired.

1934 was a signal year. The first School play since *Comus* was performed at Commemoration: *Twelfth Night* – conveniently selected as it was the School Certificate set play. 'It might', said Miss Stuart, tongue-in-cheek, 'have a beneficial effect on the candidates.' The floodgates were opened, for House and School plays have since then been an important strand in the School's history. Not that tying the Commem. play to the apron-strings of examination needs lasted very long. The Headmistress was much irritated to discover in 1937 that, 'the School Certificate examiners have been tactless enough to choose a flagrantly unsuitable play' (it is not recorded what the play was!).

John Masefield's Philip the King, *1939, with Dorothy Dakin as Philip and Anna Griffith as the Infanta.*

The beneficial effect of this though was dramatic freedom; all things became possible from dark tragedy to light comedy, from operetta to hilarious farce; with the addition of music, dancing followed, and junior plays, senior drama and specially written staff performances were often running in tandem. *She Stoops to Conquer* in 1937 combined the acting talents of both sixth formers and staff. Something original was attempted in 1939, with two plays at Commem. based on a Tudor theme. Shaw's *Dark Lady of the Sonnets* had fine performances from Lyla Hamilton (W 1940) who played Queen Elizabeth with a mixture of dignity and impudence, and from Prudence Morgan (T 1939), a strikingly beautiful girl, who much impressed the audience by acting the title role on a bare stage in subdued lighting. This was followed by what became one of the legends of School drama: John Masefield's *Philip the King*. Dorothy Dakin (A 1939, later staff) in the part of the King and Anna Griffith as the Infanta scored a dramatic triumph: they spoke and interpreted the poetry admirably, all set against a fanatical monarch's false hope of an impossible Armada victory. Anna (K 1944, granddaughter of the School's founders) was very young for the part but proved a natural actress, and had another success in 1943 in the difficult role of Shaw's St Joan.

Anna's talents were central to two developments in the 1940s. The 22 Club was formed in 1941 comprising the best 15 actresses with seven 'technicians' for wardrobe, lighting, make-up and suchlike; the aim was to raise the standard of production, and it did just that. The Headmistress was most impressed:

> The Club lifted performances onto another plane: gone were the long waits between scenes and curtain difficulties, and the quality of acting reached heights undreamt of.

By the mid-1940s two cups were to encourage dramatic talent still further. Anna herself presented a trophy for the outstanding performance in each year's School Play, and there were some worthy early winners – Paula Whitehead (W 1947) as Mrs Hardcastle in *She Stoops to Conquer*, and Joy Congdon (AW 1948, later staff) in the title role of Miss Stuart's own piece *St Theresa*. The three Jackson sisters, all equally talented on the stage (Mary, W 1938, Felicity, W 1945 and Elizabeth, W 1946), also presented an acting cup to the House which best dramatised scenes from a famous novel. Thurstan was an early winner with *A Tale of Two Cities*. Dame Diana, herself no mean thespian, followed Miss Stuart's enthusiasm for drama by giving the staff and girls much encouragement. *The Mikado* in 1951 was the first production of the School's second half-century: it proved a source of great enjoyment to parents and guests from the town, who were all beguiled by the gorgeous costumes and the rich variety of songs, with Helen Ashbridge (K 1951) outstanding as the nimble, scurrying, worrying Ko-Ko.

The early 1960s were to see another remarkable flowering of dramatic talent, following the arrival of Jane Cowell, fresh from drama school and with a wonderful facility for getting fine performances from her young charges. 1960 was the première for the girl who was to be Sherborne's most successful professional actress, Maria Aitken (AW 1962). In *The Importance of Being Earnest*, Wilde's highly stylised creation, with epigram, paradox, perversity and pun by the score, Maria played Cecily Cardew. Miss Gwen Beese reviewed the performance:

> At first sight full of ingenuous charm, she soon proves to have all the guile of Eve in getting her own way. Maria was well cast, revealing under her girlishness a formidable intelligence and will of steel.

The play had a splendid cast: Georgina Foss (K 1960) was excellent as Lady Bracknell, and Georgia Taylor-Smith (W 1960) as Gwendolyn had the right degree of hard artificiality. The whole proved light, swift, stylish and very funny, and the Commem. audience enjoyed it hugely. Jane Cowell followed this with versions of both the Lewis Carroll *Alice* books. Jacqueline Rose (DH 1964) was memorable as the ruthless, autocratic Duchess, and Susan McCormick (W 1962) brilliant in the Caterpillar's conversation with Alice. Susan had a busy year as she also took on the demanding role of Shylock in Wingfield's *The Merchant of Venice*. Maria Aitken's masterpiece was still to come. In 1962 she was given the exacting part of Richard II in Gordon Daviot's *Richard of Bordeaux*. Written as it was twelve years after the First World War, Maria found herself the mouthpiece of a passionate denunciation of war and its miseries and waste. Joy Congdon (by now on the Staff) reviewed Maria's achievement:

Richard of Bordeaux *performed at the 1962 Commemoration, with Maria Aitken as Richard (third from left).*

> Amidst his obstinate, war-mongering councillors, Maria's King was excellent. She showed us the intelligent idealist, whose sensitivity made him susceptible to bullying, but who learnt after bitter humiliations, how to outwit his enemies. This was a convincing performance of grace and wit in a remarkably fine production.

The Senior Dramatic Society (the renamed 22 Club) returned to Gilbert and Sullivan in 1965 with *HMS Pinafore*, 'a treat, sheer enjoyment from start to finish', said Miss Beese, an admittedly self-confessed aficionado of G.& S. But no one would have regarded *Pinafore* as anything other than a triumph for Gwen Hanvey's musical control and Joy Congdon's direction. The operetta, clearly a favourite of Dame Diana's, was to be performed again as a fitting tribute to her when she retired in 1975. Meanwhile Joy, who had followed Jane Cowell so successfully in the drama field, had left the staff in 1970, but not before a wonderful final production of Thornton Wilder's *Our Town*. Joanna Tremellen ('Aunty Tremmers' to the girls) directed some admirable performances in the 1970s. Among these was *A Man for All Seasons*, Bolt's tale of Thomas More's battle for conscience; Mary Pryer (E 1975) in the lead dominated the play. And with her final production in 1976 (another interpretation of *Richard of Bordeaux*, with Caroline Gent (W 1977) in the title role), Joanna showed her powers of organisation and imagination to the full.

Changes in drama in the last 25 years have paralleled those in music. In 1979, following the opening of the Stuart Centre for Music and Drama, a decision was made to appoint a full-time drama specialist in the foreseeable future. In the meantime Sherborne School co-operation in Commemoration productions began. Georgina Foss (now on the staff) had pressed for this in 1977. Miss Coulter was wary – 'perhaps too revolutionary?' – but Georgina persisted and a year later paved the way with the support of Robert Glen of the Boys' School. The result was *Under Milk Wood.* Not that matters always went smoothly. Records rarely reveal preproduction difficulties, but Katie Howells (W 1979), herself the 'First Voice', put pen to paper in 1978 on,

> the disastrous dress rehearsal of *Under Milk Wood*: we panicked – several pages of script were skipped; then the tape recording went berserk with the crowing cock sounding like a strangled turkey; and the children burst into an off-tune rendering of 'Johnnie Crack and Flossie Snail' when 'Kiss me on Llareggub Hill' was expected.

But on the night it was superb! By 1982 co-operation was going well: Robert Glen directed and Augusta Miller conducted the music for *The Yeomen of the Guard.* The whole was an excellent production to both eye and ear, with Katherine Power (T 1983) projecting a powerful stage presence as Phoebe. The following year in complete contrast the Commemoration production was Anouilh's *Antigone.* Philippa Scott-Moncrieff (AE 1984) and Michael Wright, playing Antigone and Creon, impressed the audience with their strong, passionate performances.

In the mid-1980s a young Director of Drama was appointed. Lucy Richardson, with confident professional skill, took on that most difficult of plays, Arthur Miller's *The Crucible.* It has always been traumatic and disturbing ever since its first Bristol Old Vic production in 1954; this time the audience came away chastened but full of admiration for many fine individual performances; for instance, Alex Keats (K 1988) as Abigail, the jealous troublemaker, and Yewande Animashawun (DH 1989) as the demon-haunted slave, Tituba.

Rosamund Hall arrived in 1987 and over the next decade brought new dimensions to Drama. Just a few of her major productions include *A Midsummer Night's Dream, Lady Windermere's Fan, Ring Round the Moon, Billy Liar, Pygmalion, A Doll's*

Far left: *The 1988 production of* A Midsummer Night's Dream *for Commemoration.*

Left: *Lady Windermere's Fan, 1990.*

House, Three Sisters and *The Threepenny Opera*; plus for a new generation of girls, *Antigone* and *The Crucible.* For the *'Dream* (1988) and *Lady Windermere's Fan* (1990) she had some very good young actors and actresses to direct: Mary Eames (T 1991) was a delightful Puck, whilst Hippolyta proved a first success for Nina-Maria Potts (AE 1991), who for three years was to follow in the footsteps of Anna Griffith and Maria Aitken. In 1989 she won a place with the National Youth Theatre, and in the next year triumphed as Mrs Erlynne in *Lady Windermere's Fan,* counterpointing beautifully the Lady Windermere of Camilla Bray (AE 1991). By now, Mrs Hall had injected such energy and enterprise into the School's drama that three or four productions a year were seen as normal. Girls were also encouraged to direct: Emma Deverell (E 1995) and Kate Owens (E 1995) produced a delightful Ayckbourn, *Table Manners,* in 1994. More National Youth Theatre places were gained – Georgina Lewis (AE 1994) and Hope Dickson Leach (K 1993), the latter for Stage Design in 1993; and Charlotte Gainey (K 1996) and Helen Renwick (W 1996) for Design and Stage Management respectively. Girls were encouraged to 'get their grades' and the 1990s saw a flood of Grade 8 Merits and Honours from the Guildhall Speech and Drama examinations; in 1994, 180 girls were involved with some kind of dramatic activity. Mrs Hall was especially pleased to award the newly presented Harris Drama Trophy, for consistent and wide involvement in productions, to its first recipient, Charlotte Pyke (W 1995).

Gemma Barnett (T 1994) as Low-Dive Jenny in Rosamund Hall's 1992 production of The Threepenny Opera *– one of Mrs Hall's favourite plays in which she collaborated so well with Martin Walker as Musical Director.*

In Beatrice Mulliner's mind, dancing was the equal of drama: neither was fit for young ladies at Sherborne. But with Miss Stuart, 'instruction in the graces' brought many girls to the dance floor. First, dance was offered as an 'extra' subject, but with the arrival for five years of the formidable but inspiring Mrs Ripman, it was made a full school subject in 1943. She had her own Dance Academy in London, but came down very regularly. Soon competitions were introduced and in the mid-1940s an annual Inter-House Dancing Competition began, with its entertaining mixture of formal and informal dance routines. It became a popular event with the girls, much time being spent on the 'group' dance. Aylmar was an early winner (1949) when special emphasis was put on the tango. Two years later a Reel Club was formed, with very crowded meetings learning to dance both reels and strathspeys. By 1959, when Mrs Ripman returned to adjudicate, the format had become traditional, but the girls were amazed when an exhibition dance included jive. Preparations for all kinds of dance have often had hilarious moments, as with the 'tiny tots polka' when the untutored and gauche reveal their two left feet and regular casualties appear on polished floors. The Group Dances, in Tina Xynias' (AE 1987) words, 'can be predictable, showing the rebellious streak which is ingrained in the depths of Sherborne School for Girls' – whether it be 'a general showing of thighs, shaking to unsuitable music' or 'dressing as Miss Taylor does not allow'. But they can often be spectacular, and many OGs from the 1970s will remember an amazing Chinese Dragon Dance. For 30 years the formality of the occasion was graced by what one girl described as 'the Tartan Wonder', Mr Iain Stuart Robertson, appearing in full regalia.

The Dancing Competition 1992: far left: *a Senior Reel and* (above) *West's Group dance,* Killer Clowns.

'The Staff Entertainment' has a long tradition behind it. The first big one celebrated the Armistice in November 1918: its centrepiece was various staff mimicking the Inter-House Singing Competition, dressed in short white dresses or gymnastic tunics. Lilias Wills (A 1919) remembered, 'the award of the Cup, or rather a highly polished saucepan, to the Housemistresses' choir'. In the 1920s it became a brief tradition for the OGs to 'entertain' the School, usually taking the form of a burlesque. But from the 1930s it fell to the staff on an occasional basis to 'send in the clowns'. It all began accidentally in 1937 when a chickenpox epidemic thinned out the school, and in order to cheer up the survivors Miss Gwendolyn Harris-Jones and Miss Stuart wrote and staged, with the help of a few staff and some prefects, their own operetta – *The Girl Who Stayed at School, or The Spotted Iolanthe.* Three years later the principle was repeated in *Love in a Cottage,* based on the *Snow White* story; it was topical, full of wit and repartee, and major figures of the day – Churchill, Lord Haw-Haw, evacuated schoolgirls and Hitler – were written into the performance.

The staff had many other comic talents revealed in the 'sketches and skits' entertainments over many years. In 1934 they acted out the School History under the title *1899 and All That,* and included memorable lines:

> The first really memorable date is 1899 BCM: Miss Mullidear established herself in Oldbedstead, to be joined by Miss Duffer-Duffer-Duffer, who taught the pupils limbnastics to strengthen their gymns and who became Housemistress of Ail-more, a Good Thing. Poor Miss Perry found her House was All-Stone so she had to sit on a cushion. The next Memorable Date is 1930 when the Royal Scot came on a wave of saints including Leonard.

Miss Stuart herself was often involved in these absurdities, even writing some of them. In the Jubilee Year, 1949, she wrote a whole delightful burlesque on the School – and produced it. By now each generation of girls hoped for (even expected) the staff to prance about the stage making fools of themselves: the sight of three

The 1990 Staff Revue: four housemistresses (Mesdames Franks, Glasby, Scott-Moncrieff and Walker) in the hilarious 'Boom, ooh, Yatatata'.

history mistresses in beards and bibs was the funniest of the 1951 entertainment, until Marjorie Eva appeared: associated only with Bach fugues, she launched with great spirit into 'I taut I taw a Puddytat'. Total secrecy on the part of the staff has always been *de rigueur* – though Bice Crichton-Miller partly let the side down in 1954 by delicate enquiries in Wingfield about borrowing a pair of striped pyjamas. The rule was clear: the more out-of-keeping with the expected behavioural norm, the greater the hilarity. In 1971 an advertised 'nostalgic panorama' had an item:

Temptation Sordid or Virtue Rewarded
with

Gwen Beese	a Lady of Substance
John Hartley	Sir Jasper Breakneck, a Villain
Dawn Guinness	Fanny, a Very Accommodating Lady

with Scene 3: 'A bar in a low-down hostelry in a gold-mining town' !

The most jealously guarded of all was *What the Queen Mother Missed*, the frolic of 5 November 1974 – the day of the Royal visit (see Chapter 13). Diana Gorsky (AW 1976) wrote home:

> Daddyo was brilliant as a dashing suitor to none other than Guinness. The best thing was *The Shambles of Sherborne*, based on the Wombles, with Barry, Hartley, Simpson and Linton as the big ones and four little staff as the others – they had all made little womble masks and wore fur coats – adorable.

My own fond memory of the occasion is feeling frightfully hot in the fur coat, cavorting about the stage as the Hall reverberated with noise.

The 1990 Revue, with staff assembled and browbeaten into shape by Polly English, was perhaps the best parade of comic flair for many decades. The School learned that the teachers do not have homes to go to – they sleep in the Staff Room;

and over the next two hours, said Julia Weston (A 1991), they 'revealed talents of singing, acting, dancing and witty repartee hitherto quite unexpected.' As usual, it was the costume that captivated, such as any of the female staff who appeared in school uniform, even myself in a pink tutu. The *pièce de resistance* was the sight of four housemistresses performing 'Boom, Ooh, Yatatata' – for days afterwards the girls, especially those in Thurstan, and not a few of the staff, talked about the antics of Mrs Lysbeth Franks – 'the funniest thing I've ever seen,' said one girl; 'worth paying another six years' school fees to see the next one.'

Then in the 1996 Revue, the Headmistress wore jeans – clearly a defining moment in the School's history.

DISTINGUISHED OLD GIRLS

MARIA AITKEN
(AW 1962)

For 25 years Maria – daughter of OG Penelope Maffey (Ald 1928) – has been one of the country's leading actresses, indulging from time to time her taste for comedy. Tall and striking ('lanky,' said one critic; 'she of the liquid eyes,' in Halliwell's view), she has graced stage, film and television roles. She read English at Oxford, and had been clearly destined for the theatre since her schooldays, when Jane Cowell ('my superb teacher') offered her the daunting part of Richard II. Her first 'break' came in 1974 at the RSC in Tom Stoppard's *Travesties*, and next year she appeared at the Adelphi in Sondheim's *A Little Night Music*. Two years at the National, 1976–7, brought out her comic talents – *Blithe Spirit* and Ayckbourn's *Bedroom Farce* – with a return to Coward in *Private Lives* at the Duchess in 1980. She adored this play, acting in it again four years later, when she directed it as well. This control clearly appealed: in 1985 she went to the States to direct Sheridan's *The Rivals* at Chicago's Court Theatre. With this experience she was invited by BBC2 to do a late-night 'TV Theatre Workshop' session on Comedy. Her major film success came in 1988, playing John Cleese's 'wife' in *A Fish Called Wanda*. The late 1980s brought non-comic roles – at the RSC in Granville-Barker's political scandal *Waste*, and in 1989 in Coward's early drama, *The Vortex*, at the Garrick. In 1992 she directed *As You Like It* for the Regent's Park Open Air Theatre. Her personal best-loved roles? Florence Lancaster in *The Vortex*, Wendy in *A Fish Called Wanda*, and ('really!' she said) Richard II in *Richard of Bordeaux* at School. Jane Cowell 'undoubtedly set me on my path', although she had 'a disconcerting habit years later of popping up in my dressing room at the National and proclaiming loudly, "I made a silk purse out of a sow's ear!"'

13
'To See Oursels as Others See Us'

Royalty, members of Parliament, celebrities and the BBC have, on occasions, descended on Sherborne School for Girls. Parents, too, arrive in large numbers, particularly for Commemoration, that annual showcase which dates from 1906. Mindful of its good name, School has always prepared for these moments in a proper celebratory manner, and has been rewarded with many touching responses. None more so than that of HM Queen Elizabeth, the Queen Mother, who wrote to Dame Diana concerning 'the excellent arrangements for that wonderfully successful day which I will long remember with feelings of great pleasure.'

'That day' was Tuesday, 5 November 1974, when the Queen Mother honoured the 75th anniversary celebrations. When Dame Diana told the staff of the impending visit, she expressed the hope that the Queen Mother could arrive to find the School 'working normally' – there was a moment's silence during which this most unlikely of scenarios was considered! In the event the formalities were adhered to. An amazingly detailed programme (down to every two minutes at times) was drawn up for the three-hour visit; Dame Diana herself paced out the royal 'tour' to ensure accurate timing. It proved to be a packed schedule involving luncheon in West, music and dancing displays, presentations to governors, staff and girls, the final exchange of gifts, and a 'walk-about' to meet pupils invited from neighbouring schools.

The Queen Mother's visit in 1974: after signing the Visitors' Book.

Timetable agreed, the next problem was security. Henrietta Bulley (DH 1977) wrote in her diary:

> School was normal till 10.50; then we went to our form room to search it thoroughly. All 'fishbags' were taken to House and all suspicious boxes removed. Then CID men arrived to search West for IRA bombs.

What 'Henty' did not know was that the police required every door in West and in the Main School building to be locked or guarded by staff after the searches.

The Queen Mother flew into the Royal Naval Air Station, Yeovilton; a four-car convoy brought her to the School's entrance at 12.30, precisely on time. Protocol was observed: John Hall, the School caretaker, 'broke' her personal standard from the clock tower mast, and cheering crowds of girls greeted her and all the dignitaries (including the Lord Lieutenant of Dorset, the Chief Constable, Sherborne's Mayor and Sir Reginald Verdon-Smith, Chairman of Governors) whilst she was welcomed by Dame Diana, some of the staff and four past and immediate Heads of School – Kerstin Boyd, Jennie Campbell, Mary Pryer and Penny Russell-Smith.

Above left: *watching the Scottish dancing.*

Above: *stopping to talk to Jean Stewart and the girls of East.*

The lunch in West was the first highlight of the visit. The School archive has three records of this: Dame Diana's 'blue book' (of all the letters, plans and photographs of the day) and two very informal pieces by Nancy Downing, Housemistress of West, and by Diana Gorsky (AW 1976), a 'sixth-form waitress'. Preparations proved immaculate. Miss Downing had been told that the Queen Mother did not eat grape-fruit, smoked salmon or beef, and that she preferred martini to sherry. The official menu of Prawns in Paradise, Noisettes of Lamb Papillon, Ratatouille and Duchesse Potatoes, an accompanying claret, followed by profiteroles and coffee had been approved. A dress rehearsal ten days before amused many, when Inge Ferry, wife of one of the music staff, donned a fur coat and hat, and with great composure played the Queen Mother. On the day, the below-stairs cohort of twelve senior girls of West also had what Diana Gorsky called

> a major waitress practice with the tables in E shape. But breakfast in the cloakroom and our lunch of corned beef, coleslaw and apple crumble did not quite match what we were serving.

Miss Downing had other headaches: 31 'royal' guests eating with the Queen Mother and 37 others having a fork luncheon in the girls' sitting room, meant that silver and china had to be garnered from many quarters, mostly staff ('no losses and no breakages' to Nancy's immense relief). All the flower arrangements, with Kaffir lilies as the centrepiece, were only finished at 1.30 a.m., though Nancy also records that she and her helpers had 'several practice mixes of the royal martini' late into the evening. Meanwhile her bedroom had been adapted as the 'royal retiring room' and she remembers:

> Her Majesty's detective asked me to show him the room so that he could leave the royal bag; a very shabby little bag, I thought. I was not amused when he left black footprints on the well-hoovered carpets.

The Queen Mother arrived: everyone noticed her striking outfit of sky-blue matching coat, dress and feathered hat, befitting the glorious day, dry and warmish for November. Within the hour she commented, 'This House has a lovely atmosphere.' Miss Downing was relieved it was all going so smoothly. There was a slight delay over clearing away the prawns though, when a 'waitress', strictly brought up in West to leave nothing on her plate, hesitated as the Queen Mother had clearly left some. Diana Gorsky was pleased: 'I opened the door for Her Majesty, and she whispered to me "Such a nice lunch" and we made up for our own fare with left-over profiteroles and a spot of good claret.'

Two special displays followed. A recital by the Madrigal Society in the Hall was well received, and Her Majesty was presented with a commemorative programme designed by Elizabeth Symes (E 1975). Then the royal party watched some country dancing by 16 girls in the gymnasium. Iain Stuart Robertson, the School's Director of Art, had composed a special medley: a strathspey, 'The Queen Mother's Progress', and a reel, 'Dame Diana's Delight'. Her Majesty was clearly enthusiastic; 'So beautiful and simply charming,' she told the dancers.

In moving about the School, the Queen Mother met scores of girls with their cameras, and many staff, both past and present. Eleven staff who had each served the School for more than 30 years, including 92-year-old Nellie Hughes (1912–57), were specially presented to the royal visitor. Then, having signed the Visitors' Book, Her Majesty departed at 3.40 as her standard was lowered. It had been a memorable occasion whose smooth passage had removed the rigidities of formality, and made it all so enjoyable. Even an official press spokesman, who had been to so many similar events, wrote a special letter: 'The visit was one of the most pleasant Royal occasions I can remember.'

Other royalty have graced the town and School. The Prince of Wales (later Edward VIII) came to play polo at the ground near Pinfold Lane. The School turned out to watch, and Anne Norris (Ald 1926) remarked: 'It was the first time we were allowed to cheer – Miss Mulliner thought it unladylike and bad for our voices.' *The Times* reported the visit and the 'hardly-rivalled cheering of the Girls' School who, dressed in white uniforms, shouted, waved and laughed in the very frenzy of high spirits.' Ruth Filleul (Ald 1924) composed a Dorset dialect ditty:

> . . . but Oi've a-zeed the Prince of Wales
> Wot coom 'ere last July
>
> They zay 'e were asleep, Miss,
> From Yeovil town to 'ere
> Oi reckon 'e were toired, and
> The noddin' zent un queer.
>
> Volks zay 'e were awakened
> By the ringin' o' the bells
> But Oi reckon 'twere the roarin'
> O' the Sherborne School for Gels.

The visit of the King and Queen of Afghanistan, 1928. Miss Mulliner (left) greeting the royal party.

All this in 1923, the year that electric lighting first came to Sherborne.

Five years later King Amanullah and Queen Souriya of Afghanistan came to the School. The day was to be one of pleasant memories, except for the prolonged wait in drizzling March rain, and considerable language difficulties, though as Beatrice Mulliner commented wryly, 'he still managed to extract a two-day holiday for the girls.' Preparations for the visit had included problems with lighting decorations, getting an Afghan flag from London, and long discussions over displaying Persian mottoes, in case in translation they clashed with the King's sweeping social reforms in Afghanistan (Western dress for men and the abolition of the veil for women).

On 6 June 1950, Sherborne town and schools were ablaze with flags. It was the Boys' School 400th anniversary celebrations and their special cricket match was to be graced by King George VI and Queen Elizabeth. The girls, invited to attend, 'moved down Horsecastles in a long, hot, excited green crocodile', and onto the Cricket Field to greet Their Majesties and watch the match.

More recently, HRH Crown Prince Hassan of Jordan and Princess Sarvath have visited the School – he to lecture (see Chapter 8) and both more informally to see their three daughters in Ealhstan (1982–92). Parental security meant special cars and bodyguards – watched with some interest by the girls. The princesses gave no such problems until they left Sherborne for university interviews: any journey by rail meant notifying the police of each county along the route!

In 1931 Winifred Spooner and her colleague Amy Johnson flew in, landing in front of Kenelm to launch the School Fête. Raising money for a swimming pool was the object, the biggest such effort in the history of the School. The pool had been planned for 1915, but war appeals meant diversion of funds and the abandonment of the plan. When the idea was resurrected in the early 1930s, times were still difficult – the World Depression was under way. The cost was to be £2,500 and the Fête was launched hoping to raise £1,000. It was a brilliant success, providing £1,400 net, and the 'flights at 10 shillings' were so popular that many people left disappointed. Winnie had recently had press headlines when she saved her own life, and that of another, by a two-mile swim after her plane ditched in the sea. Her address to the girls on the need for a pool and learning to swim was never more poignant. Amy Johnson too had captured the public imagination with her solo flight to Australia in 1930. Everyone wanted to fly with these two women.

In 1957 David Eccles, Minister of Education, arrived to open the Summer Fair. It raised the handsome sum of £1,600 towards a new Science Block, but when inflation (though not as great as post-1970) is taken into account, it can be seen that he did not have the drawing-power of Spooner and Johnson.

The invasion of the School by the BBC in December 1956 caused a great stir. The Head Girl, Mary Scott (K 1957), gave an account of her part in the live television programme, 'A School for Girls, 1956' :

> Going on the train to London, I could not help feeling just a little important – the BBC required my services at Hammersmith Studios. I was to do a small part of the commentary on a pre-filmed section of the programme. I had to rely almost entirely

Sir David Eccles visiting the Science Laboratory in 1957: Cecil Armitage and Diana Reader Harris on the right.

> on cues: in my own vanity I could hardly wait to hear the sound of my own voice. I went back to School with a great sheaf of papers – the programme, times, cues, plus all the jargon, 'cam dolly', 'Wembley dolly', etc. The invasion prior to the live broadcast consisted of thirty visitors and two enormous green vans, with their network of cables, which went everywhere. School life went on – staff and girls stepping over those cables as if they had always been there. I had an invitation to the 'scanner' to watch the technology of TV unfold. At last we were on air; I worried whether I could smile for one whole minute! It was difficult to realise that at that moment and for thirty short minutes thousands and thousands of people were watching us all over the country. Afterwards I measured its success by comments to me: 'What a lovely school! How lucky you are to have gone there.'

The School's 'birthday' occurred on Wednesday, 27 September 1899, when Beatrice Mulliner said the first prayers and work began at Greenhill. The foundation stone of the present building was laid on 20 May 1902. In view of terms and work schedules – and possibly the weather – the second date or thereabouts was a more sensible point for annual celebrations, when parents and OGs could join with the School. This was to be 'Commemoration', and Hilda Violet Stuart, looking back from Jubilee Year (1949), made the point:

> Because the School was founded with a religious purpose, the central function has always been a service, and not, as in many schools, 'speeches'. There is no tradition in our school of a formal Speech-day.

The first Commemoration was on 20/1 June 1906. It began with the Old Girls' Union business meeting – again the first of its kind – which fixed annual membership at three shillings, while a fund-raising sale of work brought in £50. On the 21st a Service was held in the School Hall and opened with Hymn 45, 'To Him that overcometh' – to be repeated so many times over the coming decades. Canon Westcott addressed the girls on a text from Psalm 144, 'that our daughters may be as the polished corners of the Temple'. He delivered an impassioned plea for 'gracefulness', that characteristic virtue of woman – not, he reminded the congregation, 'of that shrieking sisterhood whose voices may be heard on the switchback railways at Olympia.' The School team won the tennis matches (8:1) against the Old Girls in the afternoon, and a Garden Party was the closing event of Commem. from 7.30 p.m. with tea, coffee, a concert and Chinese lanterns.

Programme cover designed by Kate Seekings (K 1984).

By 1910 Commem. had become a long weekend and six years later the Service was first held in the Abbey. These were still combined OG-parent celebrations. In 1919 they divided – the hotels could no longer cope with the numbers – and slowly 'Parents' Day' became recognised as Commemoration proper. By the 1930s the Old Girls' Reunion had moved to the end of the Christmas term to coincide with the Carol Service, Nativity tableaux and House plays. Such change was inevitable and Miss Mulliner was even now referring to OGs as 'those of antiquity' at the 20th Commem. And, four years before, Nora Wallace (Ald 1915) had written of the impact of the World War, sighing:

> The bustle of the Sale, the crowds of gorgeously-attired parents and old girls – these

Founded in 705 by the great Saxon scholar, teacher and singer St Aldhelm, Sherborne Abbey has been used by the School for its Commemoration Service annually since 1916, and regularly for School Services. It contains some of the finest fan vaulting in England.
Left: The Magi *from the west window of Sherborne Abbey by John Hayward, 1997.*

Sunday afternoon: mixed hockey with the Boys' School in the mid - 1990s. Such sporting ventures were unheard of until very recent times.

> are things of the past. A sobered and diminished party, we said our farewells, and we went back to work and the War.

Only once was Commem. to be held on 27 September in 1920, the School's 21st birthday. It proved a most successful and joyous occasion, though the preparations had been dogged by difficulties – Beatrice Mulliner called it 'a nightmare – solve a syllogism, given no premises!' The miners had called a strike, with a possible transport collapse. The Headmistress raised disquieting questions: 100+ visitors and there might be no return trains, how long could the girls be fed, would coal be rationed? (The miners were to delay their stoppage, but only at the very last minute.)

Of course the colour and high spirits returned. And in 1934 a School play, *Twelfth Night*, was performed – so beginning a long secular tradition at Commemoration, the purpose and seriousness of which has never diminished. Three examples may be cited. First, in 1933 after the news of the tragic death of Winifred Spooner, the Headmistress proposed in her address, 'We want to erect a memorial to her – she is the first great daughter of Sherborne worthy to be honoured.' Out of this came the Spooner Award. Secondly, in 1949 the Sherborne School for Girls' Jubilee Window was installed in the south aisle of the Abbey. Miss Stuart said:

> We thought it a worthy commemoration of our fifty years if we presented the Abbey with this window. £500 has been collected. It will be dedicated in December 1951 by the Lord Bishop of Salisbury.

Not that the enterprise was straightforward: one artist approached disapproved of the subject, the next wanted £600, a third £900. The fourth accepted the commission. Another Jubilee decision was to apply for the School's own coat-of-arms, to be placed on the Tower, the design to quarter the Wingfield and Digby arms with those of the Abbey and the School's own torch.

The style of Commemoration remained much the same for three-quarters of a century. Beatrice Mulliner's 'sale of work' disappeared, but Hilda Violet Stuart's 'drama' remained an annual event; add also concerts, art exhibitions, dancing and gymnastic displays, the Fathers *v.* Daughters cricket or tennis matches, sherry in the Houses and tea in the marquee to the centrepiece of the Service in the Abbey, and this was 'Commemoration' until the arrival of Elizabeth Coulter. Then parental wishes for something more in the mid-1970s were satisfied by her addition of academic exhibitions, demonstrations and lectures.

June Taylor has maintained this spectrum. A lecture on the intricacies of university entry attracts a hundred Lower Sixth parents each year – 'I want to know as much as my daughter in this UCCA-game,' said one parent, making detailed notes; another brought a tape-recorder. The Geography staff have given illustrated talks: 'Looking at landscape' and 'The Dorset coast' among many. Practical demonstrations – e.g. Fibrous Fantasies – by the Home Economics teachers and girls became popular. Mathematical puzzles, an English Literature 'Labyrinth', some spectacular 'hands-on science' have vied with the School's history archives on display and General Studies' oddities like 'Nuts and Bolts and 99 Red Balloons'. Modern

Vivien Leigh outside West in 1946. She came down for Commemoration to be with her daughter Suzanne Holman (AW 1949), and to see the School play, She Stoops to Conquer.

Languages have offered many *divertissements* (including *Asterix, Tintin et leurs amis*) and the popular Russian tea-and-slideshow (*Russkii chai*) along with life styles in Germany, Spain and Italy. Beside the displays of Art are the products of the CDT department, with its striking models, jewellery and metalwork pieces.

Each year Commemoration crowds show how parental interest in the vitality of the School has been maintained. Outwardly formal it remains at heart a comfortable occasion for the School, in Robert Burns's phrase, 'to see oursels as others see us'.

DISTINGUISHED OLD GIRLS

WINIFRED SPOONER
(W 1918)

Winnie Spooner in 1927, beside her De Havilland Moth and with her favourite Alsatian, Dragon.

In January 1933 Winifred died – a victim of pneumonia: she was only 32. Aircraft and flying, either in sporting races or for a professional livelihood, had been central to her life for six years. After leaving school she went to Germany to learn the language, and then travelled around Europe; in 1924 she said, 'I flew back from Cologne to London. The flight takes three hours.' With a fresh perspective on life, she resolved to learn to fly. By 1927 she had her Commercial Pilot's Licence and some engineering qualifications; whilst helping her brother with his stabling business and caring for his 8-year-old daughter (Vivien, later W 1936), she developed one of his fields as an aerodrome. She began an Air-Taxi Service (£4 an hour or one shilling a mile) covering Britain and France, and started to teach flying. Air races in the 1920s attracted huge publicity, and Winnie quickly indulged in the passion. She was the first woman to compete in the King's Cup Air Race, and in 1930 came fourth in the 'Circuit-of-Italy-Race'. In a spectacular 'Round Europe' contest she came fourth overall and first in the light-aircraft class, being awarded the Gold Medal of the German Aero Club and the Lufthansa Prize. For all this success she received the trophy of the International League of Aviators. The newspapers were ecstatic: 'excellent sportsmanship' and 'Miss Spooner has enhanced British prestige'. Her untimely death shocked everyone: Miss Stuart said at the memorial service, 'sans peur, sans reproche'. Within months Winnie's friends set up a Trust Fund, which in 1936 became the Winifred Spooner Memorial Prize for a Sherborne girl of outstanding character – thus preserving the ideals of courage, independence and enterprise. The Prize was £15; by 1995 it was £1,200 (see Chapter 15).

14
Fees, Fêtes and Finances

In the first years of the School the annual fees, tuition and boarding, were between 69 and 91 guineas (depending on a girl's age); in 1997 they were £12,240; over the same period government figures reveal the rate of inflation to be just over a multiple of 50. Dorothea Beale, Headmistress of Cheltenham Ladies' College, addressed a conference in 1865: referring to the medieval educational endowments which had been swept away in the dissolution of religious houses in the sixteenth century, she said that many boys' schools were re-established,

> But the girls' endowments were seized by royal court favourites; our sex to this day has not recovered from this fatal blow.

This quotation and the preceding statistics spotlight attention on both sides of the economic equation: parents seeking value for money in the ever-rising fees; and governors balancing the getting-and-spending – fair fees for fair remuneration of academic and domestic staff and maintenance of the fabric, yet with a proper concern for future capital expenditure.

Lack of endowments meant a considerable act of faith at the start; without the commitment of the Wingfield Digby family, and particularly the initial £1,000 share guarantee (see Chapter 1), there would have been no School. In the first term fees from the pupils brought in a mere £80 13*s.* 0*d.* But the success of the School and its rising numbers meant that fees rapidly became the real base of its financial structure; when Miss Mulliner retired in 1929 she calculated, 'no more than £17,400 has been raised in shares'.

Parents enjoy that most finely focused of economic realities: the end-of-term account. Basic fees reflect a myriad of pressures, but over the century three things have contributed most to the upward movement: general UK inflation, the achievement of equal pay for women and the spiralling construction costs in the post-1970 period – which coincided with the School's own building expansion programme.

The first fees, under £100 p.a., doubled by 1946 – from the vantage point of the 1990s 'merely doubled' would seem appropriate! Even so, many parents faced financial difficulties. In the 1930s' Depression, Audrey Hamilton (T 1936) was typical: 'The School kindly lowered my fees as my father had been made redundant from the Indian Medical Service.' In 1945 appeals were received from recently demobilised officers in straitened circumstances.

By mid-century the fees were £225, to double again in less than 20 years under the pressure of equal pay and inflation. Alarming to parents at the time, no one could forecast the hyperinflation (propelled by housing and oil costs) of the next 25 years. £800 in 1974 doubled in three years and continued inexorably upwards; £2,100 in 1978 became £9,225 in 1991 and passed the £12,000 mark as the School's Centenary approached. To the first two Headmistresses such figures would have been unimaginable. Put into another perspective, Anne Dudley Smith (A 1943) wrote as Treasurer of SOGU in 1987 about the Emolument Fund and its bursary to help OGs' daughters: donations by OGs who left in the 1930s 'were of the significant sum of 2*s.* 6*d.* – whereas an annual donation of 12½p by banker's order today would seem a little strange!'

Added to the basic fees were 'extras'. The School prided itself that most were not compulsory, as the Governors early on adopted the policy of fee-inclusiveness – particularly to subsume textbooks. A letter to Cynthia St Quintin's (A 1926) parents stated: 'About £120 a year covers everything.' But it had not always been that simple. The first prospectuses advertised termly 'extras' in Music (2–4gns.), Art (1–2 gns.), Gymnastics (1 gn.), French and German conversation (10*s.* 6*d.*) and about 2*s.* for exercise books. The optional element became problematic when it transpired that daughters *without* gym and art wrote home feeling 'inferior' or 'excluded'. Most of these 'extras' disappeared over the decades – payment for exercise books, for instance, was discontinued in 1939. Now parents *choose* to take on 'extras', thus avoiding with great relief what one called in the 1970s, 'nasty little shocks on the bill'.

Two family records show what it cost to keep daughters at Sherborne. From 1931 to 1936 Audrey Hamilton's mother carefully listed fees totalling £918, including two concessions in 1932; also noted were total uniform costs – £58. These make an interesting comparison with the situation in the 1990s: Tessa Rowland (DH 1956) sent her daughter Caroline in 1991 when the basic boarding and tuition fees were £3,075 per term; by 1997 she had spent just under £70,000 which

> included two musical instruments, uniform and the considerable increases in pocket money she needs – or thinks she needs – with all that Mulliner freedom!

The national perception of English independent schools is that they are only open to the rich. Investigations by the Independent Schools Information Service (ISIS) conclude, 'It is simply not true to say that such education is the preserve of the wealthy.' The costs were difficult for many, even before the inflationary years. Ann Barrett (W 1945) acknowledges, 'what a sacrifice it was for my parents'. Since 1970 the prudent have taken out insurance policies, and many OGs remember the useful armed forces concessions, help from grandparents, scholarships, bursaries, and even Dame Diana's pertinent advice – 'if you can't afford all the years, try just for the VI form: we do offer something special.' Clearly a deliberate choice has been made about the *value* of this kind of education, beyond such things as better cars and expensive holidays. David Woodhead, Director of ISIS, in 1996 posed the question, 'Why pay?' His answer:

> the best possible all-round education, with such priorities as academic results, size of classes, good discipline and the instillation of qualities sought by employers – self-reliance, responsibility and high-standard oral and written English.

The School has been fortunate in its governors. Cdr. Derek Willis (Bursar from 1975 and Clerk to the Governors since 1987) says:

> Their role is very wide: they are ultimately responsible for everything that happens in School – from policy on education and discipline, appointment of Headmistress, Bursar and Clerk, control of budgets, fees and salaries to staffing levels and maintaining the fabric, grounds and equipment.

On them devolves the complex task of balancing motley financial obligations. Many brought expertise and insight, and not a few served on the Governing Council for decades. At the start it was the Wingfield Digbys and their kith and kin who led the Council. Kenelm's parliamentary work prevented him from accepting the chairmanship, but Charlotte's Irish Huguenot childhood gave her both courage and a set of convictions which she certainly used at Council meetings for 30 years. A contrasting range of personalities supported her in the early years, with loyalty to the School's ideals in common. The first Chairman of the governors was Canon Westcott, remembered for his energy punctuated by periods of dreamy, whimsical humour. Col. Everard Digby, a 'county' dignitary, Canon Lyon the blind Vicar of Sherborne and Sir John Kennaway – a massive patriarchal figure, sometime 'father' of the House of Commons and then Chairman of the Church Missionary Society – all gave much support.

Archdeacon Westcott (c.1911), the first Chairman of the Governors.

As the School expanded fresh experience was needed. The Revd Shields, elected in 1907, ensured the particular religious commitments of the founders were preserved over the next 39 years; and Col. Sir Robert Williams gave valuable financial advice in his 28 years as a governor. He was joined by another with a fiscal background in 1935 – Sir Hubert Medlycott remained for many years, boosting the sparse attendance at Council meetings during the war years. This economic specialism was maintained by the presence from 1955 to 1993 of Ralph Hedderwick (husband and father of OGs, for many years Chairman of Finance), and Michael Barnes from 1974 to 1995. Two recent distinguished governors who became Chairmen were Sir Reginald Verdon-Smith, with wide management experience (Bristol Aeroplane Co. and director of Lloyds Bank), and the present occupier of the Chair, Anthony Pitt-Rivers, one of Dorset's Deputy Lieutenants, who has been on the Council since 1978.

The Council also sought to stiffen its own professional educational commitment: Dr David, Headmaster of Rugby, served for five years in the difficult times after the First World War. He was followed in 1924 by Dr (later Sir) Cyril Norwood – Headmaster of Harrow, later Principal of St John's College, Oxford – who became a senior adviser to the government and produced the famous Norwood Committee Report, so influential to the 1944 Butler Education Act. He remained a governor until 1942, and his three daughters were educated at Sherborne; one of them, Enid

(Ald 1919, later Mrs Canning, founder of Hanford School) was elected to the Council in 1935. Ann Smart, Oxford don, serves on the current body, with the former Headmaster of Bradfield, Anthony Quick; the Harrow connection was revived in the 1990s with the appointment of Nicholas Bomford, himself the father of two OGs.

The presence of OGs on the Council has been a feature since 1930. Cecily Willink (DH 1912), later Lady Starmer, brought great zeal to the School's Darlington underprivileged children's Home (see Chapter 9) in the 1930s before joining the Council; Deaconess Elizabeth Souttar (E 1925), whose background ranged from Lady Margaret Hall, Oxford, to social work on the Isle of Dogs in the 1941 Blitz, became a Governor in 1954 and served until 1978. Today, two more are well into their third decade of service on the Council: Elizabeth Parry-Jones (DH 1947, now Mrs Melvin) and Patricia Brewster (T 1948, now Mrs Grayburn).

Finally, the duty performed by the founders' family has been well-nigh continuous: their son Col. 'Freddie' Wingfield Digby, talented soldier and country landlord, was Chairman from 1924 to 1952 during the grim years of the Depression and the War. His obituary in *The Times* called him 'one of the kindest and most generous of friends – with a ready sense of humour', characteristics he used to great effect in Council meetings. His son, Simon, joined the Council in 1942 and served until 1969, matching his father's length of service.

Without question the commanding family influence has been that of Venetia Griffith. With her death in 1982, aged 90, Dame Diana said, 'the first chapter in

An early pencil sketch of Venetia Wingfield Digby (Day Girl 1908) and her mother, Charlotte.

the story of the School has come to an end'. Kenelm and Charlotte's daughter, it was she who, aged 7, 'played' with Miss Mulliner on her first visit to Sherborne; it was she who became a pupil (Day Girl, 1908), a first-class horse woman, and a life-long friend of Amrit Kaur (see Chapter 1); it was she who joined the Governing Council in 1930, becoming Chairman from 1952 to 1970. And through two great-granddaughters of the founders the link is maintained – Mrs Venetia Peake (also related to Col. Williams) has been a Governor for over 25 years, and was more recently joined by Dr Rosa Beddington (AW 1972) in 1994.

Venetia (Mrs Griffith) c.*1970.*

The Governors' preoccupation with financial matters is revealed in the Minute Books, kept over the century by so few 'clerks' that their service too is best measured in decades rather than years. Edward Bartlett's keen legal acumen was on offer for 46 years as Clerk to the Governors, 1899–1945; he was followed for another 24 years by his nephew Tom, and in the last quarter of the century by Patrick Moule and Derek Willis.

Careful husbandry was always the watchword. From the second decade, aiming to save £5,000 a year in a Reserve Account, a very useful capital sum was built up. Despite land purchases (£323 per acre in 1928) and essential House building and classroom extensions (Aldhelmsted East cost £13,700 in 1938, roughly the same as Kenelm ten years earlier), the Account recorded £100,000 in the late 1930s. Miss Stuart gave much publicity to this financial success, as when she became Headmistress mortgages and bank overdrafts had reached the alarming sum of £30,000; by 1941 this had virtually disappeared.

The steady increase in School numbers had certainly helped towards solvency; and this increase was in itself the result of a growing academic reputation. The Governors were informed in 1935 that the School was oversubscribed: one Governor peered at the long waiting list, saying, 'I think the Headmistress should be a little more rigid in her acceptances'; Miss Stuart riposted that she was working out a 'permitted maximum'. This was entered in the records in 1936 as 310 and reached a year later.

All talk of tidy accounting and ideal numbers vanished in the War years. London schools wrote pleading for evacuation facilities – in 1939 an extra 40 were accommodated. In 1942 six from Wycombe Abbey had to 'sleep-out' in town. The number was already 378, despite leavers to Canada. Fee problems dominated Council business: late payers multiplied tenfold – serving fathers abroad, war-widows in difficult circumstances, and a parent who wrote, 'I am keeping my daughter away as the concentration of children is inadvisable.' Fire precautions cost money – £276 for blast protection in the School. Also, insurance premiums mounted as building valuations increased from £156,000 to £208,000 in 1941.

Meanwhile a major constitutional change had occurred in two stages, 1927 and 1936; it provoked much heated debate and had a twist in the tail. 17,300 shares in the School Company had been sold by the mid-1920s, and a dividend limit of 5 per cent had been fixed as a fair rate of return. It became clear that some share-holders were not overly interested in the School's educational and religious aims,

An Old English Fair
TO BE HELD AT
Sherborne
SCHOOL FOR GIRLS
SHERBORNE, DORSET
ON
JUNE 5th & 6th, 1931
FRIDAY—2 P.M.-7 P.M.
SATURDAY—11.30 A.M.-7.30 P.M.
ADMISSION:
before 5 p.m., 1/-
after 5 p.m., 6d.
children under 14, half price

The 1931 Fête programme. Fêtes (below) *were a regular method of involving OGs and parents in raising funds.*

and wanted a much higher rate, especially as the Revenue Account was over £50,000. There followed a celebrated legal case before Mr Justice Romer in the Chancery Division of the High Court. He listened to those opposing the 5 per cent limit – 'an attempt to deprive shareholders of their just rights in the profits of the Company' – but they numbered only 2,300 in share support. In 1927 Romer declared for the remaining '15,000' on the grounds that the founders 'had never intended the School to be a commercial undertaking'. As a result considerable funds were safeguarded for scholarships and other strictly educational purposes.

By 1935 all the shares were in the possession of well-wishers, so the Governors proposed that the School be rid of its 'company share' status. Within six months the transfer of School monies and property from the old Company to a new Association, based on non-profit making, educational, charitable ideals, had taken place. In May 1936, a signal date in the School's history, the Sherborne Ladies' College Company was finally wound up. But then came a final twist: the change of legal status required payment to the Inland Revenue of 1 per cent – on the value of the School's assets of £126,000 this meant the huge sum of £1,200. The Governors, represented by Edward Bartlett, vigorously contested this, and the tax authorities relented: the documents were stamped with a ten shilling duty!

In the second half of the century the Governors faced financial decisions of entirely new dimensions. Their Minutes admitted that, 'in 1950 it is apparent that considerable leeway needs to be made up due to the War years.' Electrical rewiring of the main School cost £1,520. In 1960 the impact of rising costs was starkly revealed: extensions to Dun Holme were priced at £22,000 – not far short of twice the cost of a whole House in 1930.

Staff salaries were the biggest ongoing problem. Nationally, teachers were not well paid, especially women, who had limited opportunities elsewhere, and around 1900 there was considerable variation in pay. Miss Mulliner told one senior mistress:

> I engage my mistresses for a term on trial; I do not think of offering you more than £75 per annum.

This was higher than in many other schools. Then in 1919 the Government accepted the 'Burnham Report' laying out national scales in state schools. Most girls' public schools followed this as a sensible solution to the salary problem, though the scales were not generous and women were paid far less than men. Mary Elderton (DH 1935) joined the School staff in 1938 as a part-time teacher – 'I was paid 5*s.* an hour'. Gillian Avery in her 1991 authoritative history of girls' schools concluded,

'The middle classes were purchasing a cheap education with sweated labour.'

All this was to change after 1945. The War had created serious teacher shortages, so that Mary Elderton, now Mrs Watkins with two children, remembers, 'I was asked to teach History with a timetable geared round Baby's feeding times!'; such shortages lasted many years. Burnham salary levels increased in 1951, adding £5,000 to the School's costs. Then came equal pay, implemented in seven annual stages in the same decade. Though Dame Diana told the Governors, 'For mistresses of the best type and quality salaries have to be fair and adequate', the School remained tied to Burnham, unlike many boys' independent schools which had their own scales. It was June Taylor who persuaded the Governors that the present Burnham Scale did not offer a long-term salary structure to attract and keep high-calibre staff. So in 1987 the School developed its own scale – Sherborne and Roedean were the first girls' independent schools to do so. (Increases in teachers' salaries had earlier had one unfortunate effect. In 1960 embarrassed Governors learned: 'some senior mistresses are receiving approximately the same salary as the Headmistress'! This was immediately rectified – her salary was increased by £500.)

Inflation in the 1950s also wreaked havoc with pensions – not yet inflation-proofed and at best meagre. The case of Kathleen Moore in the 1930s was typical. After 18 years at Sherborne as Second Mistress from 1899, she had become Headmistress of Queen Anne's School, Caversham; on retiring in 1937 she received an annual pension of only £100, which Sherborne's Governors decided to supplement by a further £50. In 1960 the effect of inflation on an inadequate state pension was highlighted when Dame Diana told the Governors, 'I was appalled at the poverty in which Miss Perry (staff, 1911–40) was living', and a grant was made. Four years later Miss Harris-Jones's (staff, 1911–45) pension of £50 after 34 years' service was raised to £200.

Rewarding domestic staff gave the Governors more headaches. Here again the historical background is of low pay: Mrs Kirkby, with caretaking duties from 1899 to 1920, worked from 7 a.m. to 6 p.m. for 14*s.* 9*d.* a week and no meals. Pensions were almost non-existent so special grants were made to long-serving 'retiring servants': in 1936 a gardener with 23 years' service was given a lump sum of £50. But in the 1960s their recruitment and pay reached crises proportions. In some cases the solution proved simple. General living-in staff were paid 2*s.* 6*d.* an hour – the Boys' School paid 3*s.*; so an increase, plus £690 worth of TV sets in the Houses to compensate for lack of local amusements, eased the situation.

'The unsatisfactory catering arrangements of the House system' was the agenda for an emergency meeting of the Governors in 1962: two Houses (AW and AE) had had to resort to outside caterers because of the scarcity of cooks. 'Central Feeding', which many public schools were considering, had some support – it would help check escalating costs. Yet it was noted: 'The Housemistresses do not like the idea – it would end a valuable community feature of the School.' Enquiries were made; at the next meeting the cost of a central kitchen-dining room was put at £120,000. Venetia Griffith was visibly apprehensive at such an expense, so the matter was shelved for the moment. Then the outside catering was itself found to be 'most unsatisfactory – there was a high food cost and it was cooked badly.' The caterers' contracts were terminated, cooks were given a 15 per cent wage increase, and in 1964 Central Feeding was officially made 'low-priority'.

The most unnerving outlays of the 1980s and 1990s were occasioned by the spectacular rise in the cost of books and buildings and the advent of electronics. Headmistresses, Bursars and Governors all had to plan very carefully to establish affordable 'rolling programmes'. 'Cash-flow' dominated conversations and bank loans had to be carefully negotiated, until in Derek Willis's words, 'everything is properly funded, so you *know* when you'll come out of the wood!' His successor as Bursar for ten years, Cdr. Richard Sargent, certainly echoed this particular sentiment.

This 'wood' appeared very dense at times. Between 1975 and 1979 the £254,000 New Science Block was the biggest expenditure, but major Mulliner House extensions at £150,000 and the Music and Drama Centre at £170,000 had to be fitted in. A superficial eight-year lull followed when no new structures emerged – but in amongst some face-lifts (the Sanatorium and the boiler system were upgraded for over £300,000) was a massive programme of improvements to the Houses, costing over half a million pounds. The mid-1980s too saw GCSE arrive with its attendant costly requirements of new course texts and reference books; at the same time the IT revolution in education brought regular annual outlays. So Reginald Verdon-Smith's £10,000 gift to the Library was a particularly welcome piece of generosity.

The impact of nationwide inflation in building costs was seen at its most dramatic at School between 1987 and 1995. First the price of the Art Studio was finally worked out at £622,500, but that did include the expensive equipment in the Design Technology wing; equally striking and airy were the fine Library reconstructed across the top of the Tower (£275,000) and the Language/Geography rooms all built in 1988. Finally, two spectacular edifices appeared in 1992 and 1995: a 'new' Mulliner saw by far the largest expenditure in the School's history – £2,248,000; and for the Sports Complex across the road from Dun Holme, the Governors managed to keep the cost down – to just under a million!

15
Exeunt Omnes: 'Where Have All the Flowers Gone?'

Memories, recollections: those will-o'-the-wisp sources for historians. What do the OGs remember of their schooldays? Have they diaries or letters to span the intervening years?

> I loved every minute: I would run for my doughnut and hot chocolate on Tuesday mornings even now!
>
> Melanie Wray (AW 1978)

One, Lorna Harman (AW 1936), had an identity crisis:

> I went to a reunion in the 1980s – decided to keep a low profile if I saw Miss Crichton-Miller. Then a voice said, 'Lorna Harman, I remember you – you were a naughty little girl!' 'Was I?' I replied nonchalantly. Turning to face her I found she was no longer the terrifying figure of the past, but a frail old lady with a twinkle in her eye.

Generalisations, verdicts even on the impact of the School on the century's total of 11,800 girls are manifestly impossible. Individuals have their own responses, and 'The School' was never immutable – though for many girls their 'five-year snap-shot' became fixed in the memory for ever. Valerie Richardson (A 1938) recalls that school in *her* day, 'was another world: we had maids actually slopping out our china washbasins in the morning.' During the 100 years the 'view from the bridge' by any UIV was coloured by the joint tyrannies of the 'bell' and prefects; whilst being in the UVI conferred a very different perspective of School life – one Head Girl recalls with little goodwill the chore of taking last Prep. on Saturday morning!

So the phrase 'on the whole' dignified the final paragraph of scores of letters which OGs wrote to me in the 1990s: the clear verdict has been favourable. Arnot Robertson's attitude (see Chapter 6), Rosemary Custance's (A 1936) 'I hated Sherborne' and Minette Marrin's (K 1966) animosity to 'bizarre restraint' were rare pieces of general hostility. Many of course remembered specific aversions: 'compulsory anything' mixed with 'I hated tapioca pudding' and 'the humiliation of being put in the Remove'. But all this is substantially outweighed by approval, even enthusiasm. 'The education was very good; I'm still reaping the benefits,' said Elspeth Nicol (T 1953), and Joan Bonsey (K 1936) highlighted the 'fine balance of learning, sport and recreation'. Hilary Ruston (E 1955) was not alone in remembering 'wonderfully dedicated teachers' ; and Fiona Webster (W 1966) concluded, 'The more I've done since, the more I realise how well taught we were.' Ruth Walwyn (DH 1951) found the School 'a real haven, and liberating', whilst Margaret Woodcock (K 1939) waxed lyrical about 'our halcyon days'. Sheaves of letters told of 'happy years': Margaret Colborne (DH 1925) spoke for them all, 'I'm so very glad I went to Sherborne', and Elsa Christie's (A 1932) particular viewpoint gave me the title for this book:

> I thoroughly enjoyed my years there – such interesting people to teach us. Few girls can have been given so many opportunities to learn, to think, to reason – even to rebel!

The Tall Ships Experience: the Malcolm Miller, *1995.*

My personal view of the Sherborne species: adventurous. 'Anyone looking for a challenge, wanting to push themselves just that little bit further before going on to university or a job?', asked Mary Eames (T 1991) on leaving school to join Project Trust for some social welfare work in Brazil. Today organisations exist to support such longings, but until the 1960s girls were very much on their own. Au pairing or some other job on the Continent using 'languages' attracted many, but the big adventure was rare. The lure of 'round-the-world' – much easier in the 1980s and 1990s with well-planned stops at relations or friends' parents – had one Verne aficionado in 1907, though not in 80 days: Vera Mandeville (Ald 1906) took six months, London eastwards to Australia and home via Canada. Sarah Stallard (E 1964) waited until her mid-twenties before working her way round over a period of 18 months.

Climbing mountains and sailing ships presented very different challenges. In 1922 Margaret Clark (Ald 1915) managed the ascent and descent of the Matterhorn in an exhausting, hazardous 20 hours. Fourteen years later Lydia Wingfield Digby (AW 1931) told of her Christmas on Mt. Kenya: hard work over 30 miles and up to 16,300 ft., the highest point for amateurs, 'with a feeling of freedom and awe'. In 1990 Sara Williams (W 1977) also reached that point on Christmas Day, breathless and with 'no alcohol and only freeze-dried pasta and shortbread biscuits for lunch'. In the mid-1990s Jo Willcock (AW 1996) and Katherine Gaillard (A 1996) spent 12 days aboard the 'Tall Ship' *Malcolm Miller*: with 30 other 16–24-year-olds at the helm and climbing the rigging, they journeyed from Portsmouth to Cardiff via Cherbourg and the Irish coast.

During the War some experiences were suffered rather than sought. Eileen Robinson (W 1929) was in the embassy in Warsaw in 1939 and only just managed to escape; she had to flee again – from France in 1940 missing the Germans by 'the kindness of French *poilus* giving lifts in army lorries'. Elinor Jones (A 1917) endured three years, 1942–5, in Singapore's Internment Camp under Japanese control. She was a doctor, and with 1,200 other women (in a gaol for 300!) suffered from brutality, callousness and incompetence; daily food rations were ½lb. of rice and less than a pint of vegetable soup, and medicines were minimal.

In the post-war years wanderlust was often linked with another kind of 'war' – the attack on poverty in the Third World. Mary Eames's challenge had already taken many forms. Voluntary Service Overseas was founded in the 1960s and

Margaret Powell (DH 1964) was an early volunteer: aged 18 she underwent an intensive orientation course in first-aid, hygiene and teaching before being sent to Bechuanaland (now Botswana). In 1972 Patricia Rogers (AW 1972) toured Canada and worked in Labrador with an International Mission looking after the health of Eskimos and Indians. Her diary records:

> 17 January : Outside it's minus 20°F. Work in a 147-bed hospital – start today doing simple sugar tests.
> 12 February: Working with a technician on an X-ray survey of 350 Eskimos – much difficulty: language, same names! and a few very obstinate.

By the 1980s more girls were thinking of a 'gap-year', encouraged by organisations such as Project Trust, GAP, Operation Raleigh, Latin-Link and Schools Partnership Worldwide. All these have helped Sherborne girls in recent years. Jo Baker (E 1979) went as a nurse on 'Raleigh' to Borneo and the Caribbean – she talked to the Sixth Form, and interest mushroomed. Just to volunteer was not enough: Antonia Campbell (A 1992) and Cheryl Frost (AW 1992) described their 'selection weekend' and prospects:

> After leaping off a bridge into freezing water in mid-November, then skinning and gutting a rabbit, we felt a great sense of achievement; all part of the development of self-confidence and leadership skills. Shock at being chosen! Then we had to raise £2,950 each before going to Chile for some adventure (trekking in the Andes), and a lot of conservation and community work.

Raising such money poses a major challenge in itself. Some comes from parents, but much more from a girl's own efforts – for example, organising a sponsored concert at School. For some girls, winning the Winifred Spooner Award (see Chapter 13) has been a particularly valuable asset. In its early years the money was used for buying books or even a typewriter, but much of it today is used to fund expeditions. Jocelyn Milner (AW 1986) used it for her air fare to Botswana to work with the Kalahari Conservation Society. Venetia Wingfield (A 1993) went to Romania to teach and help combat the appalling conditions in school-orphanages:

> It was an ugly industrial town full of identikit tower blocks and cold, damp apartments. The children were enthusiastic, but the spartan conditions were often dismal with severe discipline and foul food.

In 1996 the Award of £1,200 was divided between Lettice Moore Ede (A 1996) to work in a Tanzanian orphanage, Lulu Edes (DH 1996) to go to India, whilst Juliet Haysom (T 1996) used her share to study ancient art in Greece.

Julia Weston (A 1991) went to work for six months in 1994 in a Tibetan refugee school in northern India. Her stay encompassed many of the facets of volunteer work: exhilarating adventure, hazardous travelling, some hostility mixed with an embarrassment of good treatment, daunting and frustrating teaching problems, enthusiastic learners, and the ever-present bouts of disease among the children. On a personal note Julia says, 'lunch was not for the faint-hearted, and washing clothes was a loathsome task – in a cold river, using stones!'

Dorset student in Alaska

Most young people who go off on Operation Raleigh expeditions expect to take sprays to protect themselves against mosquitoes and other tropical insects, but Dorset graduate Harriet Tory is sleeping with a bear spray under her pillow in Alaska!

Press account of Harriet Tory's (A 1986) 'gap'-year expedition.

'Gap-Year' Survival: Jo Baker (E 1979) was selected (after a 'weekend crossing ropes' – see right*) for Operation Raleigh's 1984 Bahamas Expedition 'to promote the native economy and National Parks facilities'. Coping with boa constrictors* (far right) *and baking bread on the beach* (facing page) *were two of her sidelines.*

Earning an independent living assumed an ever-increasing priority in the minds of girls in the second half of the century, especially from the 1970s when it gradually emerged that a degree was not an *automatic* passport to a job. At School, Mary Watkins (OG Mary Elderton, DH 1935) began developing what she admitted was 'only a cinderella careers advice service', and in 1972 the first small Careers Convention was held when 13 OGs came to talk about their professions. Wendy Laid, taking over the growing service in the late 1970s, spoke of the huge efforts made 'to help the girls make informed choices in the unpredictable scene of the job-market.' These now include computerised tests, work-experience courses ('Shell to Gleneagles'!), job-orientated mock interviews – and talks spanning everything from advertising to merchant banking, tourism to the diplomatic service.

Despite far fewer career openings in the early part of the century, Sherborne had its successes. In 1932 a quippish SOGU survey revealed:

> Transported to a desert island, we could form a well-equipped community: two architects and several gardeners would build a 'new' Sherborne with an inn-keeper, 18 doctors, a great many nurses and a business quarter with an excellent range of shops; also four authors and two barristers, and if the School's 'grandchildren' accompanied their mammas there would be 246 daughters and 266 sons for four headmistresses to fight over plus of course a famous aviator to liaise with the outside world.

A number of OGs have achieved national or international renown and honour in their chosen fields, as previous chapters have shown. Headmistresses have been proud to refer to them as role models for any generation to follow. The public perception of such fulfilment is one of glittering prizes; perhaps this chapter points more to substance than glitter. Scores of others have made their mark; my own

eclectic choice can only give a flavour of such lives.

The world of academe and education attracted many. In 1920 Winifred Dixon (Greenhill, 1903) was appointed Headmistress – Sherborne's first – of The Maynard School, Exeter; Angela Mason (E 1920) became Vice-Principal of the newly formed Westonbirt School in the late 1920s – to be followed there by Margaret Newton (T 1946) as Headmistress for 15 years. Headmistresses were soon scattered around the world. Winifred Cocks (Ald 1910) of Queen Mary College for Girls, Lahore, India, and Marjorie Carter (A 1913) of Ceylon's School for the Deaf and Blind, were both honoured with MBEs. Veronica Owen (W 1942) was Head of Limuru School in Kenya, before returning home to take over Malvern Girls' College for 15 years. More locally Dorothy Dakin (A 1938) became Head of the Red Maids School, Bristol, thought to be the oldest girls' boarding school (1632) in the country; Gillian Morris (E 1954) took on the Headship of a prep. school in Hampshire in 1974 and still thrives; and Enid Norwood (Ald 1919, later Mrs Canning) opened her own girls' prep. school – familiar to generations of OGs as Hanford – with 25 girls in 1947, to be followed by her daughter Sarah (A 1949). Two other Headmistresses (DRH and JMT) need no introduction.

University staff lists have shown a peppering of OGs. Isobel Leslie (Ald 1918) was the first – to Besançon in France; later Evelyn Wilson (W 1932) was secretary to the Royal Commission on Indian Currency before becoming Economics Tutor at St Hilda's, Oxford; and Persis Wingfield (DH 1913) achieved prestige with her appointment as Principal of Edinburgh College of Domestic Science in 1932, and later the OBE. Nina Coltart (E 1945), *not* recognised by the School as a scientist, read languages at Oxford, turned to medicine and became Director of the London Clinic of Psycho-Analysis in 1972. There have been many overseas distinctions:

Elizabeth Juniper (AE 1964) became Clinical Professor of Epidemiology at McMaster in Canada; and Sarah Waterlow (W 1959), now at Princeton, took the professorial chair of Classical Philosophy in 1984 at the University of Texas ('with tenure, a rarity for ex-pats,' she said). Sarah Shorten (A 1961) who died in 1990, was honoured for her years as Professor of Philosophy at the University of Ontario: a gifted scholar, she had a university award named after her, 'recognising her contribution to advancing the status of women in Canadian universities'. Closer to home the many OGs working in British universities are exemplified by Helen Macbeth (W 1956) as Principal Lecturer at Oxford Polytechnic; Nicola Helme (W 1973) who is Fellow and Admissions Tutor of Fitzwilliam College, Cambridge; and Rosa Beddington (AW 1973), Head of the Mammalian Division of the National Institute for Medical Research.

The School has always had a capacity for altruism. Its success is shown in the extensive service to the community, paid or voluntary, that the lives of OGs reveal. In 1926 a survey listed 20 in teaching, 27 in medicine and nursing, ten missionaries, 15 in social work (one as a Poor Law Guardian, another as a probation officer), and 42 in the Girl Guide movement – Phyllis Bond (W 1912) became national head of the Rangers in 1930; only 15 had ventured outside these fields, mainly as secretaries. Half a century later the range of endeavours had widened dramatically, but a social conscience remained strong: work with brain-damaged adolescents and with the rehabilitation of offenders are examples. Hilary Arnott (AW 1962) typifies this attitude. Her early death in 1995 occasioned an obituary in *The Independent*:

> To the very end she chose commitment and truth above ease and comfort. Working at the Institute of Race Relations, she was instrumental in changing its image of a cosy charity advising governments to one serving the needs of black communities.

In the national chronicle of women invading traditional male occupational preserves Sherborne has played its part. Practising female barristers were a very rare breed until the 1930s; Cecilie Bridgewater (W 1924) was one of the earliest to be called to the Bar in 1934. Katharine Kennedy (K 1931), one of the School's brightest intellects, had climbed the Civil Service 'ladder' to be Assistant Principal by 1947; she presented a jaundiced view of some of her work in the austerity period after the War:

> The Ministry of Education has little to do with education – it is mainly concerned with buildings, and much of that what is officially called 'sanitary offices'! I spend a great deal of time circumnavigating controls; it is a very complex game and the rules are frequently changed.

In the 1970s two OGs achieved notable 'firsts'. Susan McCormick (W 1962), the Governor in 1973 of Askham Grange (an open prison in Yorkshire) was at 28 the youngest woman to hold such a position; whilst Hilary Root (A 1962) was 'delighted to be able to take advantage of a famous change in the rules' to became one of the first 13 women members of the London Stock Exchange in 1974. Later, Diana Forman (E 1936) was one of seven ordained in 1986 as Deacons in

Edinburgh, 'the first Anglican Communion in this country to admit women to Holy Orders,' she said. And Clara Jones (DH 1970) became in 1996 Marks & Spencer's first woman executive director on its 18-member Board. M&S has been criticised in the past for its lack of females in management; but Clara says, 'where the right women are available, they're starting to come through.' And children are *not* a hindrance – she has combined a 21-year career with raising two.

Initiative and independence of mind nurtured at School have persuaded a number of OGs to branch out on their own. An early example was Barbara Urquart (W 1919) who ran her own registry office in the early 1930s 'for the servant class':

> My sympathies are equally divided between mistresses and maids – hard to believe that some women treat their servants with downright cruelty, but I also found many a serving-girl needed a good old-fashioned spanking! However the whole tribe of charwomen won my heart.

Sally Bridgman (K 1979) has a travel firm: from one small office it grew by the late 1980s into a chain-operation in the Exeter region with eight offices and two charter aircraft to Iberia; and Helen Bayley (AE 1973) is a director of her own sports sponsorship firm, working for television and government agencies. Pippa Lawrence (AE 1955) became the National Trust's first Staff Conservator, setting up a scheme using 130 volunteers at Knole Park, Kent, to restore seventeenth century textiles – the magnificent cloth-of-gold-and-silver of the King's Bed, 1675, for instance; then she was appointed consultant to the Salisbury family at Hatfield House, before in 1977 getting a Churchill Fellowship to study costume conservation in the USA and France; on her return she went to work at Castle Howard.

No one could accuse Sherborne girls of being afraid to leave their original career paths. Jenny Dann (E 1975) worked for a time as a solicitor, before preparing for missionary work in Pakistan; Luci de Nordwall (E 1980) took her Sussex University degree in Linguistics and Artificial Intelligence – she then opened a flourishing business in oriental frozen foods. Tansy Aked (E 1989) studied theology and philosophy at Durham, and followed this with theatre musical direction, TV cabaret and international fashion work; and Joanna Udal (K 1982) went from her work investigating drug smuggling for the Council of British Shipping to read for a degree in theology, seeking ordination in the Church of England. Another sudden change of direction: Sally Romanes (T 1974) studied Australian constitutional law, and worked in a Melbourne law firm for 18 years to become a senior associate – then switched to be a professional watercolour artist! For changes of direction (in the plural) Vanessa Howe (K 1974) may hold the record:

Pippa Lawrence (AE 1955), at work in the Gabled Room of Knole Park, Kent, in 1976 – repairing a cloth-of-gold curtain from the 'King's Bed'.

> After a geography degree in the middle-class comforts of Bristol I took an M.Phil. in Town Planning at London; I then launched into the grimy world of advertising, jetting about for four years with an American company. Escape – travelled the world – wonderful. Back home: current affairs work for LWT, then off to the NW frontier in Pakistan for Save-the-Children Fund when the Afghan jihad was in full swing. A year later I became an (aged!) Foreign Office trainee on the South African 'desk' during the heady days of de Klerk and Mandela – not happy in the diplomatic fast lane, so back to SCF with duties in Vietnam and Cambodia. Tired of

> offices and aeroplanes: took off sailing, and I ended up in 1995 in the Dordogne running historical-geographical outward-bound style courses in Entre-deux-Mers.

Other atypical Sherborne work: Josephine Gardner (AW 1937) and her husband bought a shipyard at Berwick in 1976, and had four hectic years building ferries and refitting trawlers before recession struck. Yvonne Morel (A 1942) was the first woman student of automobile engineering at Loughborough, raced her own 106-mph MG at Brooklands, and moved on to fuel systems for aero-engines. Thira Hayes (W 1976) left the police to become security manager for Jolly's of Bath in 1988 and Daphne Oram (K 1943) enjoyed much esteem for ORAMICS (graphic sound), which she invented whilst in charge of the BBC's Radiophonic Workshop.

Work in film, TV and the press acted as a magnet for some girls. Phyllis Crocker (A 1932 and Head Girl) had a distinguished career as Continuity Girl on many films – the Ealing comedies, *Lavender Hill Mob* and *Kind Hearts and Coronets*, and later on *Ryan's Daughter* and *Nicholas and Alexandra*; and Christabel Albery (W 1969) worked as production manager for television's *Tinker, Tailor, Soldier, Spy* and *Cleopatra*. Others opted for a more public image: Louisa White (W 1979) became a familiar face on TV as spokeswoman for Camelot when the National Lottery was launched; Jessica Davies (AE 1980) is a regular columnist in the *Mail on Sunday* and on Breakfast TV; and Penny Russell-Smith (AE 1975 and Head Girl) was 'front page' news in 1996 when she became No. 2 to the Queen's Press Secretary.

A profusion of OGs has ventured overseas – a quick count of those in Australia for example in 1991 came to 65. India under the Raj and the Far East attracted many; life there could be amiable enough – Gwen Powell (Ald 1924) spent several years in the 1930s as companion to the 15-year-old Maharani of Balraupur. Others had found political and social conditions difficult. 'India is not a very pleasant spot at the moment!' wrote Muriel Maude (Ald 1912) in the aftermath of the Amritsar Massacres of 1919. Margaret Clark (Ald 1915) devoted many years to rescuing little girls destined for a life of temple prostitution in southern India. In later years work with the less fortunate continued: Elizabeth Dun (AW 1941) was Director of the Save-the-Children Fund in Hong Kong, and found much of her work involved drug-dependency; whilst Hilary Beresford (DH 1972) worked for the Overseas Missionary Fellowship in the 1980s and 1990s dealing with leprosy and with the Aids epidemic in Thailand.

These examples merely touch on the fringes of the 'imperial connection'. In one year, 1934, OGs wrote to the *School Magazine* of Simla in the very hot weather; Zanzibar administration with only two other Europeans; supervising a 600+ compound in India; farming on the slopes of Mount Kenya; an earthquake in Ceylon; manning a Tibetan outpost; teaching children on a Kenyan coffee estate by postal courses from the Parents' Union in Ambleside; collecting East African flowers and sending them to Kew by air; the quiet life on a Ceylon tea plantation; and Margaret Barber (A 1920) launching her own English Motor Car Co. in India, offering car repairs and a wireless agency.

The attraction of Africa was as powerful as India. By the mid-1920s ten OGs were already dotted over the continent, and one, missionary Phyllis Manning (T 1922), had died of disease in Uganda. Another, Evelyn Tracey (Ald 1912) depicted life in a CMS school in Lagos as 'very civilised – electricity, good water and motors abound.' But Pauline Studd (DH 1911), a missionary in the Belgian Congo, told a very different story of

> the horrors of heathendom, the misery, terror and bondage to superstition. We open schools but the little girls – full of chat and yells of laughter – are never allowed to stay long. They love the school life, but unexpectedly down will swoop avaricious parents who have sold their child to some old polygamist.

Contrasts were legion. Mary Douglas (E 1917) spoke of the 'good life' in the 1930s; 'go for a ride, watch a little polo in Omdurman', but she never came to terms with the Sudanese sand: 'eternal sand, a nightmare of sand'. Mary Steel (T 1919) could describe a comfortable life on her tea and fruit plantation in Rhodesia in 1932: '3,000 acres, 5,000 ft. up and a 60-mile view from my verandah.' Yet later, in the same country, Faith Rebbeck (DH 1942) worked for the Mothers' Union in Mashonaland, covering 360 branches in an area the size of the British Isles: 'we carried everything with us, camp-beds, first aid, even washbasins, packing and repacking daily'. Mary Hallam (W 1949) produced a fine piece of political waspishness in 1984:

> My husband and I have farmed this beautiful country for 26 years (tobacco, then maize, cotton and beef), living first in the Capitalist, Fascist, Colonialist country of Rhodesia, and now in the Marxist, Socialist State of Zimbabwe. The second appears to enjoy equal unpopularity with the first.

Sherborne's 'Australians' clearly love the place, but some despair of its climatic vagaries. Phyllis Fagan (DH 1924) experienced years of 'our wool economy, which varies like a yo-yo,' and bemoaned in 1964, 'it's hopelessly dry again.' A great wave of settlers had gone there in the 1920s, but one OG, Phyllis McMillan (DH 1914) complained bitterly about 'the impossibility of getting domestic help willing to work 30 miles from a railway in temperatures of 100°F.'. Even so, many OGs there had enriching lives: Katharine Charlewood (DH 1938) spent years collecting data for the *Atlas of Australian Birds*, whilst Sara Mullins (A 1973) is busy at work in the 1990s with the Royal Flying Doctor Service in remote parts of Western Australia.

Other OGs have worked or settled in places from Sweden to Switzerland, from Ontario to British Columbia, New England to California and south to Argentina. Penelope Turton (W 1929) enjoyed 25 years organic farming in Massachusetts, and Penelope Porter (T 1940) opened The Nearly-New Shop in Vancouver with such success that she also launched Penny-Pincher: Dress-for-Less, and dreamed of a chain across Canada. By contrast Sally Letts (AW 1965) worked as an hydrologist in Oman and the Yemen; and Janet Hetherington (K 1959) had 'the most delightful, idyllic existence' in the Gilbert and Ellice Islands of the Pacific, 'with the temperatures at 80°F. all year, day and night!' But her work as a doctor and the first female Family Planning Officer covered 30 atolls over 2,000,000 square miles: 'difficult,' she said in 1968, 'with many natives of Catholic faith who don't understand that the population will double in 25 years – but we're winning.'

Careers and/or marriage? It used to be a clear case of 'or' – many women teachers had to resign on marriage until after the Second World War. Dame Diana in 1972 put it to the girls that, 'this generation does not see a career as an *alternative* to marriage – a most important change', linked of course to advances in contraception and the formica/freezer revolution. Though Margaret Sturrock (W 1962) achieved the trio of career, marriage *and* children, it did not become commonplace until the 1990s. This was illustrated at the 1995 London Reunion of the UVI of 1975: 29 OGs were there, all but seven having careers, and boasting 51 children. Chatter no doubt included phrases rare or non-existent 50 years earlier: flexi-hours, work-from-home-on-computer, full-time plus live-in nanny.

But 'the family' matters; page after page of OGs' accounts of their lives speaks of fulfilment in the home, 'enjoying a busy life'. From Jean Sorley's (Ald 1911) ditty of the 1930s,

> In spite of the gloom of Glasgow
> I'm very much alive;
> My interests centre round my
> Growing flock of five

to Jill Lees' (A 1967), 'I'm an ordinary housewife with husband, seven horses, 18 cattle and endless livestock!' to Fiona Sinton's (AE 1977) 'three dogs, three cats, three children' (now four of the latter), life is evidently hectic and full.

Not all manage pride in the family with the adroitness of some OGs. Heather Turner (K 1946) has a very special family record:

> I was one of four Domesday Book (1086) descendants invited to the 900th Celebration in London. I can trace my family back through 31 generations to the Conqueror in one line, and back to Alfred the Great, Charlemagne and the kings of Scotland through another.

Finally, there is another pedigree – perhaps 'tribe' would be a better word – which reveals itself in the extended 'family' of OGs. One strand regularly exhibits itself in the *SOGU Magazine* – the list of present Sherborne girls with mothers/grandmothers who were also at the School. This peaked in 1974 with 101 on a school roll of 450. OGs show much *amour propre* in this matter, none more so than Diana Lentaigne (E 1958 and in the mid-1990s Chairman of SOGU). She wrote in 1991,

> I love going back to Ealhstan – nothing much changes! My daughter, Lucinda Prain, enjoys being at Sherborne; and I recently arranged an OGs' lunch-reunion which included an 82-year old – my mother, Susan Taylor (E 1926).

In the mid-1980s the 'family' game became competitive: which had the largest number of School members? The Dickson/Morgan clan first claimed the honour with 12, but the Ferard's current 15 sweeps away its rivals.

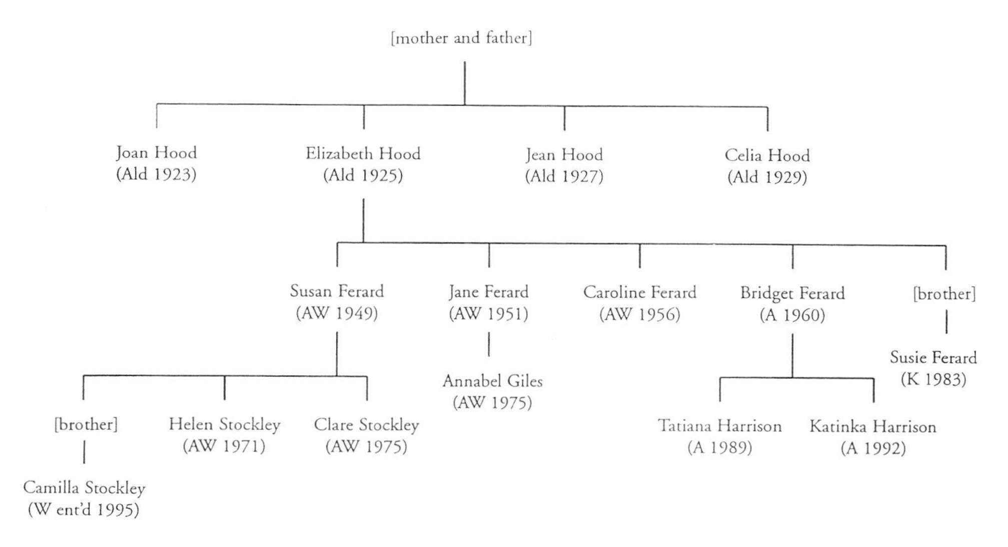

A second strand stretches nation- even world-wide. 'I still play tennis with . . .' can echo from Sydney, Capetown, Vancouver or Berkshire in any decade. The sentiment: 'in touch'; the instruments: the SOGU Committee and the Circle Secretaries; the line of communication: the Record Keeper at School and the *Magazine.* There are some astonishing coincidences. Jane Pople ran into Jennifer Jocelyn (both A 1954) in 1979 in a wine cellar, 100 miles from Budapest; and Jane Armitage (AE 1959) 'discovered Wendy Lendrum was an OG when she played in the Fathers' Cricket Match at our sons' Prep. School!' Cricket brought other OGs together in 1950. Jean Stratton (E 1939) tells the story:

> The village cricket captain challenged me to raise 11 ladies. I turned to the hard-working OGs who abound here in Wessex. Husbands cried, 'over my dead body' and boy-friends became chilly . . . My team complied with the order 'To the Games Field' – engraved on every OG's heart! The men batted first (left handed!); one insolently hit the ball low – he had not reckoned Ealhstan training. A hand (more used to rocking the cradle) held on bravely. Was Sherborne ever better served? They made 140. We let them win . . . but only by 14 runs. For did not Sherborne teach us that tact and charm are more important than winning?

Further afield, in 1979 Patricia Steen met Marylyn Winchester and Katherine Montgomery (all A 1973) in Kenya: 'we ate maize-porridge, cooked bananas and talked endlessly'; a year later Marylyn came to England to be Patricia's bridesmaid.

So what is the satisfaction? Something must keep these OGs together. Marjorie Elphinstone (Ald 1910 and mother of three Congdon OGs) enthused when she returned for the 1949 Jubilee Commemoration:

> A crowd of us turned up . . . once recognised, time was in liquidation, 'then' and 'now' became interchangeable terms. We could dip for a random handful of names and events, and run them through memory's fingers . . . I found myself the fourth in a group with three Headmistresses (Misses Stuart, Moore and Tanner) – they peered at this grandmother, but I'm sure they still saw the be-spectacled shrimp whose untidy

> mind had annoyed them in the past! But the real pleasure was a consciousness of the vitality of the ideal on which our School is built.

Another OG has been more laconic, but no less pointed. Last words to Janet Riddell (W 1938 and Head Girl), now living in South Africa – in 1984 she toured North America and said:

> I met many I hadn't seen since 1940 when they sailed to Canada with my sisters. Their hospitality was tremendous. It's very powerful, this 'Sherborne Bond'.

Index of Names

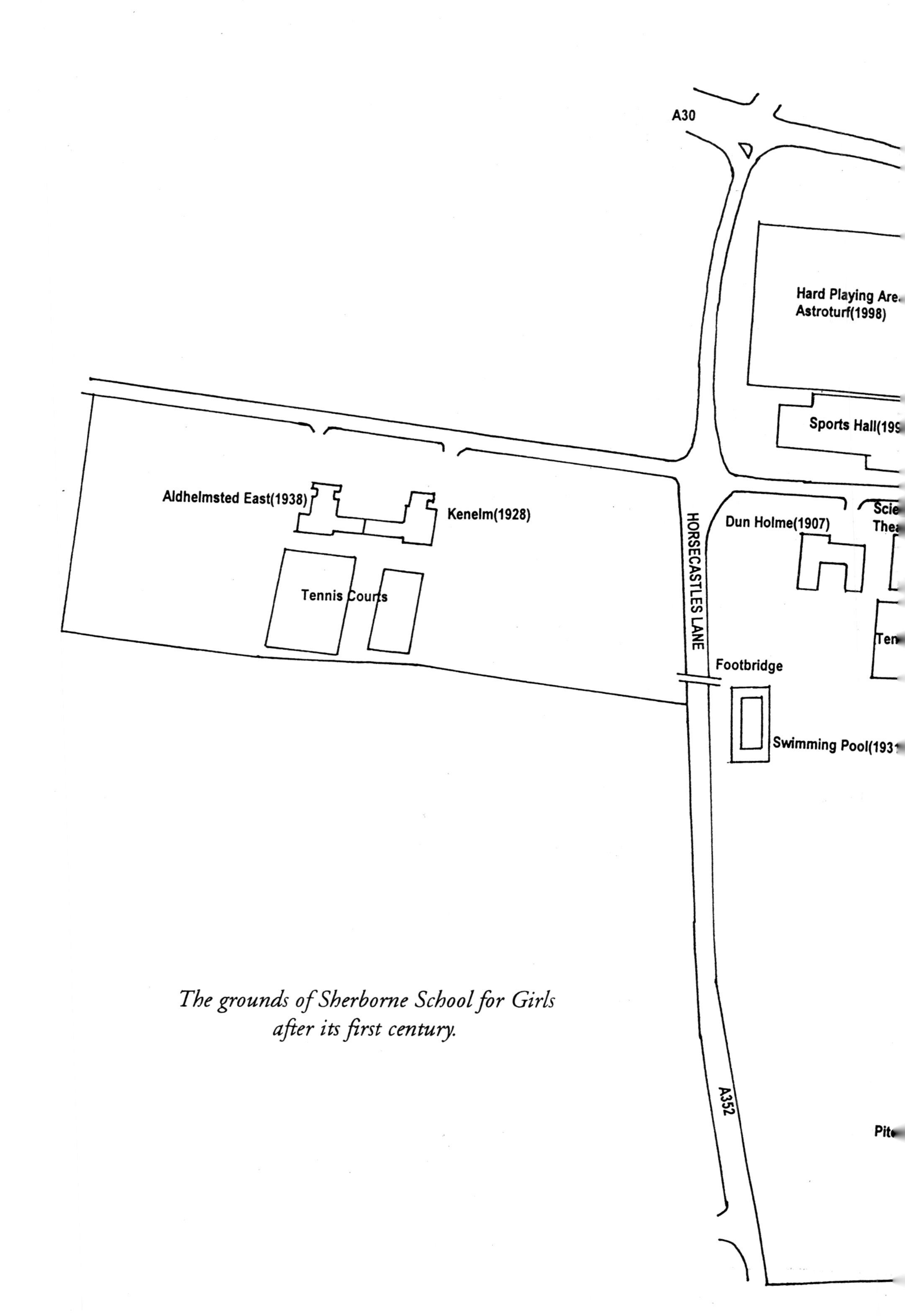

The grounds of Sherborne School for Girls after its first century.